Gaetz • Phadke

The Writer's World
Essays
2009 MLA Update Edition

Third Custom Edition for Truman College

English 100

Truman Content Contributors
Ayana Rhodes Morton, Ana King, Gail Gordon-Allen,
Kimberly Steffen, Lara Ravitch

Taken from:
The Writer's World: Essays, 2009 MLA Update Edition
By Lynne Gaetz and Suneeti Phadke

Cover Art: *Untitled 9,* by George Herman

Taken from:

The Writer's World: Essays, 2009 MLA Update Edition
By Lynne Gaetz and Suneeti Phadke
Copyright © 2009 by Pearson Education, Inc.
Published by Longman
New York, New York 10019

Pearson Learning Solutions, 501 Boylston Street, Suite 900, Boston, MA 02116
A Pearson Education Company
www.pearsoned.com

Printed in the United States of America

3 4 5 6 7 8 9 10 V092 16 15 14 13

000200010271690115

CW/TP

ISBN 10: 1-256-84026-2
ISBN 13: 978-1-256-84026-8

Copyright Acknowledgments

Contents

Taken from: *The Writer's World: Essay, 2009 MLA Update Edition*
by Lynne Gaetz and Suneeti Phadke

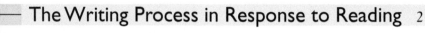

PART I — The Writing Process in Response to Reading 2

Revising and Editing   92

 Two-Source Summary/ Response Essay   115

 Writing About Literature   139

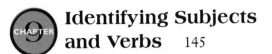 **The Editing Handbook**   143

SECTION I   **Effective Sentences** ▪ *Section Theme* **CONFLICT**

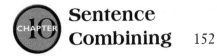 **Identifying Subjects and Verbs**   145

 **Sentence Combining**   152

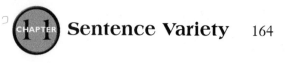

SECTION 2   **Common Sentence Errors**   ▪   *Section Theme* **URBAN DEVELOPMENT**

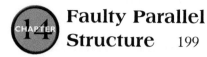

SECTION 3   **Verbs**   ▪   *Section Theme* **INTERNATIONAL TRADE**

SECTION 4   **More Parts of Speech** ▪ *Section Theme* **FORCES OF NATURE**

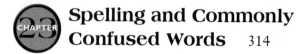

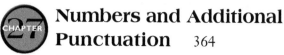

SECTION 7   Editing

 **Editing Practice**   373

— Appendices

The Writing Process in Response to Reading

The writing process is a series of steps that most writers follow to advance from thinking about a topic to preparing the final draft. Generally, you should follow the process step by step. However, sometimes you may find that your steps overlap. For example, you might do some editing before you revise, or you might think about your main idea while you are prewriting. The important thing is to make sure that you have done all the steps of the process before preparing your final draft.

Before you begin the next chapters, review the steps in the writing process.

Academic Writing

CONTENTS

The academic world is much more than memorizing facts for a test or putting together a clever PowerPoint presentation. It is about engaging with ideas, concepts, theories, interpretations, and arguments. Thus, a college history professor will not only ask students to learn the dates of important events and the names of those who were central to making those events happen; the professor is also likely to ask questions about how the events are interconnected, how the personal histories of important people led them to make the decisions that shaped the world, or how our lives in the present have been affected by those events and people of the past. Such thought-provoking questions are most often answered in essays, and a college student who expects to be successful must learn to write academic essays.

Writing in Response to Reading

One of the characteristics that sets academic writing apart from many other types of writing is that it engages with knowledge and ideas that are already part of a wider cultural discussion. This is why the English department at Truman College requires students to write essays in response to something they have read. The Communications Department wants students to become aware of what is happening in the world and what arguments are being made so that they can engage with the discussions.

Let's take a popular culture topic and look at how what starts out as a weak discussion of one's own opinions can become a good academic argument.

Topic: the rapper Eminem and his music

If I were to write a five-paragraph essay that required no previous reading on Eminem, my essay would probably be limited to why I like or dislike his music. An essay like this could be written by an eighth grader whose mom allowed him or her to buy the radio play versions of Eminem's albums. Such an essay does not indicate that the student can think critically or that the student can connect his or her thoughts to the wider body of knowledge which is examined in college classrooms.

How does a college instructor make this a thought-provoking assignment that asks a student to analyze, evaluate, argue, and support? What if the teacher asked students to read the following two articles and write an essay in response to them?

- "Misogyny Set to Music: Eminem's Lyrical Assault on Women" by Femme I. Nist
  - Argues that the music of Eminem promotes violence against and disrespect towards women.
  - Makes the point that such lyrical content is most dangerous because of the audience to whom Eminem most appeals—teenage boys.
- "Modern Metamorphosis: How Slim Shady Became a Responsible Citizen" by Secun D. Chanse
  - Argues that the arc of Eminem's career is one that is inspirational in the best way because his story includes the flaws of a real person.

□ Discusses his public struggles with marriage, with being a good father, with violence, and with drugs and how each of those struggles is detailed in his music.

After a student reads these articles, what can this student write about?

Sample Outline

I. Summary of "Misogyny"
   a. Author's main argument in my own words
      i. Author's reason 1
      ii. Author's reason 2
      iii. Author's reason 3

II. Introduction
   a. Personal anecdote
   b. Thesis statement: Although many of Eminem's songs have been disrespectful to women, his new message about getting off of drugs and surviving, along with his undeniable talent, makes him one of the most important musical figures in this generation.

III. Topic Sentence: Eminem's songs on his past albums have hated on women, but that's not as destructive as "Misogyny" argues.
   a. Eminem songs and lyrics
   b. Quote from "Misogyny"
   c. So over-the-top that clearly exaggerated
      i. Song "Stan" basically says so

IV. Topic Sentence: The new leaf that Eminem has turned over is one that has a lot of social value for kids dealing with the same kind of issues and idolizing celebrity life.
   a. Story of my friend who got caught up with drugs
   b. Issues faced by teenagers
   c. Quote from "Metamorphosis"
   d. Negative celebrity images like Charlie Sheen

V. Topic Sentence: His fame lasted through a lot of controversy, his own personal problems, and two weaker albums mainly because he is a talented writer and rapper.
   a. Quote from "Metamorphosis"
   b. Awards that he has won
   c. My favorite song

VI. Conclusion

This example outlines a possible summary/response essay, the kind of essay which you will be asked to write in this course. This particular outline would produce a college-level essay because of the kinds of thinking it employs and because it discusses ideas that are already being argued. This is one reason why this course does not ask students to write essays about their favorite singing group, their summer vacation, or three problems faced by high school and college students. None of these topics provides the writer with a controlling idea that produces an argument of academic or intellectual value.

The following are two examples of student essays that are written in response to a reading. They are both revised versions essays written in class.

Sample Essay Prompt I

Read the essay "Freedom's Just Another Word" by Anna Quindlen. Write a summary/response that provides a reader with Quindlen's argument and reasoning and that then agrees or disagrees. In your response, specifically consider young people's participation in the political system and whether you believe this to be one of their major responsibilities as Americans.

Sample Student Essay I

Americans Vote?

In "Freedom's Just Another Word," by Anna Quindlen, she argues that Americans do not vote as much as we should and that there should be a requirement to vote, just like the Australians have. Quindlen believes that if America requires people to vote, it would raise the voting percentage because if Americans do not vote, they would be fined fifty dollars. Quindlen also believes that Americans have a low voting percentile, that Americans take voting for granted, and that people who do not vote not only hurt politics but everyone.

Americans do not avoid voting because they take it for granted or abuse the meaning of the word freedom. Americans do not vote because many Americans are half-witted when it comes to the process and benefits of voting. I, myself, would not know where to go to register or to vote. I also do not know about the candidates who are running. Providing Americans with the knowledge of voting would still let them have their freedom, but it would raise the voting percentile. Although I agree with Anna Quindlen that Americans do not vote as much as they should, I disagree that making voting a requirement would solve the problem. Instead, America should educate its people on the process and benefits of voting.

Since Americans do not vote, it harms not only the system of politics but us, as well. Low voting percentiles and turn-outs destroy the government. Some Americans complained about the way the Bush ran our country. They did not like how he sent many troops to Iraq; if they had voted, they would not have to complain about the way he ran the country. Quindlen states, "Only 51 percent of all voting-age Americans bothered to show up in the last presidential election." She also states, "The United States has not had 60 percent of its voting-age citizens turn out since 1968." These percentiles are not good; they are too low. Americans need to straighten up their act and start voting.

Mandatory voting would not solve the problem, though; it would make the problem worse, and it interferes with our right of freedom. Mandatory voting would be more of a problem because people will just go to polls and mark any candidate; they would not care, and they would just do that so they would not get fined. Quindlen states, "We are barely a participatory" democracy. Since we barely participate in anything, making voting mandatory and handing out fines to people who don't vote would only make Americans vote so they wouldn't have to get fined. Is that really the best way to choose the people who will run our cities, our states, and our country? Mandatory voting also interferes with our right to freedom. Having freedom means that we have the right whether to vote or not. Forcing people to do something they do not want to do is not a way to solve the problem or any type of problem for that matter. That is not the type of government we have.

Young adult Americans often do not vote because they do not know the process and benefits of voting. I am 19 years old, and I know that I can vote. The problem with that is I do not know how to register, where to go to do so, who is running for office, and what the candidates will do to make this a better country. Of course, there are ads all over the place, people handing out flyers and putting them in mail boxes, but that doesn't help. The people who are handing out the ads don't help because when they give me an ad, they don't really say anything. They just stand there handing them out. If they do say something, they ask if I am registered to vote, and if I am not, they don't really tell me where to go to register. I think that if some of the ads were posted on Facebook or another social network, then young adults might actually read them and go vote. I, honestly, do not think that I am the only one who does not know the process of voting. Since our voting percentile is so low, there must be many people who are not familiar with voting at all, and if the ads and information on where to go to register for voting were posted on websites that young adults log onto, the voting percentile would go up.

As the strong Americans that we are, it is our job to spread the knowledge about voting. We can spread the knowledge by telling people how and where to register, how to make their vote, and even tell them who is running and what the candidates will do for our country. Instead of having the candidates just make commercials on how they will change the country, they should also go to the high schools and colleges and inform young adults on how they will make changes to our country. We especially need to inform the younger generation on the process and benefits of voting. Like people say, "they younger generation is the future generation." Whatever decision we make will affect the future. If our younger generation is not informed on the voting process and benefits, we may never raise the voting percentile.

Many people may agree with Quindlen and may argue that making voting a requirement is a good thing because Americans will follow that law. That makes some sense because many Americans respect and follow all of the laws that they know about. However, what they do not consider is that maybe mandatory voting shouldn't be mandatory because most Americans only follow laws that they feel are important. For example, many people go over the speed limit, yet there are many signs that tell us what the speed limit is. People don't follow the speed limit signs because they feel as if it's not important. If voting were mandatory, some Americans wouldn't follow it because they feel as if it's not important, and if they don't know what's going on in the voting world, how would they be able to vote?

Voting is important in today's society. Anna Quindlen may be right about America's low voting percentile but wrong about making it a requirement. Americans need to be informed with the process and benefits of voting in order to raise the voting percentile.

Sample Essay Prompt 2

Read "Where Have All the Protests Gone? Online." By Jennifer Earl. Write a summary/response essay that provides a reader with Earl's major points and that then offers your opinion about the power that the internet has to move young people to support or act for a cause.

Sample Student Essay 2

The Power of the Internet

In the article "Where Have All the Protests Gone? Online," by Jennifer Earl, Earl claims that the internet is something that could now be used for people to speak out and protest in a faster and cheaper way. She talks about how instead of people going to the mall for social movements, they are now doing social movements on the internet, and it's just effective. She also states that since teenagers already use the internet to protest for things like having their favorite music artist perform in their neighborhood, when they get older, they might use the internet to protest for more important things like politics.

When I was growing up, I was barely interested in politics, and I still am not. Since I don't watch the news and hardly ever read a newspaper, I'm never aware of what's going on in the world politically unless I hear my mom talk about it or see it on Facebook. I think that if politics were discussed more on websites that I'm always on or if my favorite rappers and singers spoke on politics, I would be more aware of them. I agree with Jennifer Earl and her idea of using the internet to reach out to younger people because that's their main source of everything today.

Getting today's younger people to support a cause or take action might be difficult because we have so many other things grasping our attention. I believe if people used things that younger people like most to reach out to them and get them to take action, it would work. With things like Facebook, reality television shows, and music taking many of the younger people's focus, it's hard to get a younger person interested in other things. If people are on Facebook and, instead of spams about cell phones and iPods being posted on their wall, a spam about helping to feed the needy pops up, it would probably affect them because someone is bringing the issue to their attention, and it might encourage them to do something. And if Lil' Wayne had a concert and in his concert he spoke on the importance of voting, I believe more young people would vote also. It's all about how young people are approached with things. If adults want more young people to be a part of movements, and the adults' ways aren't working, they should come up with better ways. And since right now the internet is a big deal for young people, adults who have a cause should try different things with the internet.

The internet has the power to change minds and inspire people to support a cause. Wael Ghonim has proven this. According to Mohamed ElBaradei in *Time Magazine's* "100 Most Influential People of 2011," Ghonim used social media like Facebook to communicate and speak upon his beliefs, and because he did that, he helped form a call for peaceful revolution in the Egyptian society. Just like Ghonim did it with the internet, anybody else can. The internet is the best thing to use to reach out to people because many people have access to it, and many people use it. Because of the fact that the internet has things that pop up on every website and social network, it's the best way to influence people. Pop ups, for instance, persistently show up on people's computer screens with different sales and information on them. If people used pop ups to inform others about certain movements, and those pop ups constantly show up on a person's computer screen, those pop ups just might get him or her interested in the movement and encourage him or her to get involved. These days, if someone wants to spread a word or influence people, the internet is the best way to do it.

Protest over things that are less important, like games, can transition to protests that deal with issues that affect many. The reason I believe this is because when teenagers protest about things that they believe are more important, like video games and music, they are developing the courage and skills to stand up and speak up for what they believe in. When those teenagers become adults, what's important to them may change, and they might stop having "trivial" protests and then start speaking out about serious issues like having safe sex. The fact that the teenagers have the courage and skills to protest about things means that when they are older, they will have the same skills, and that's a good thing.

Jennifer Earl's idea of using the internet to reach out to younger people was a good idea. If a person wanted to get me to fight for a cause, that would be the best way to get me involved. There are other ways to grasp people's attention and get them involved, and the internet has many options. If a person wants to get someone involved, that person must be creative and has to be able to think of ways to attract whomever he or she wants. If those he or she wants to attract are young people, the internet is the best way.

College Reading

Reading is about making meaning of a text, and one cannot do this well without some prior knowledge to which one can connect the text. That is why your teachers continually encourage you to read more.

Our prior knowledge is organized in various "containers" in our brains, each called a schema. Each schema holds information about specific things or categories of things and continues to grow as we learn more. For instance, as a one-year-old, my schema for the word cat might contain only the black and white, small, furry creature whose tail I tried to catch at my grandmother's house. As I get a little older and have contact with more cats, I learn that they come in many colors, don't necessarily enjoy having their tails pulled, can jump pretty high, scare away mice in storybooks, and make the sound "Meow." Once I get to school, I learn that there are large, scary, dangerous cats called lions, tigers, leopards, and cheetahs. I learn that they live in faraway countries and can be visited in zoos. My schema for cats is filled with interesting information that I then must access when I read something new about them.

In a college classroom, I might read the following sentence:

> At first glance, Felix, the family cat, bears little resemblance to the magnificent and threatening big cats of the Kalahari Desert in Africa, but upon closer observance, one can see that the evolutionary process has not weeded out the instinctual hunter in our domesticated felines.

This sentence could come from a zoology textbook or a biology textbook that is introducing Darwin's theory of evolution. Prior knowledge helps me to comprehend new information that I then add to my schema and later use to help me to comprehend something even newer. While I may not understand the concept of evolution yet, my schema for cats helps me to make meaning out of the comparison made in the sentence, which will, in turn, help me to visualize the concepts of species relationships, evolutionary change over time, and environmental adaptation.

College reading involves exactly this kind of learning from the things that one reads. It is more than memorizing facts but involves making connections, allowing information to build on other information, forming one's own opinions about what one has read, and analyzing what one has read to determine the hows and whys. This means that students should approach college reading with these purposes in mind, understanding that your reading cannot be passive because you must use what you have read. In the context of college composition courses at Truman, you must use what you read as the basis for response papers, as the building blocks of argument papers, and as subjects for in-depth analysis.

Reading to Respond

What you have learned about reading throughout your life and education is important. Decoding symbols, learning to pronounce words, using context clues to understand unfamiliar words, accessing information you may already know about the topic in order to make meaning of what you read are all very important in any given reading situation. In this course, the primary purpose for much of the reading that you will be asked to do is to write an essay in response to it. This means that there will be specific things that you must look for when you read.

Annotating Texts

Reading for academic purposes should be an interactive experience. You should write in your textbooks and highlight important information in your handouts. Doing so helps you to make sense of what you read, to retain information, and to keep track of your ideas about what you read. This is called **annotating a text**. Much of the information included in the following steps for annotating a text come from a later section in *The Writer's World* by Gaetz and Phadke, but we will include it here because annotating should be your first activity each time you read for class.

When you annotate...

- Look in the introductory and concluding paragraphs. Underline sentences that sum up the main idea. Using your own words, rewrite the main idea in the margin.
- Underline or highlight supporting ideas. You might even want to number the arguments or ideas. This will allow you to understand the essay's development.
- Circle words that you do not understand. Use context clues to help you to understand what the words mean. Use a dictionary to define any words whose meaning you cannot guess.
- Write questions in the margin if you do not understand the author's meaning.
- Write notes beside passages that are interesting or that relate to your own experiences.
- Jot down any ideas that you might want to explore in more detail in your writing.

TRUMAN ASSIGNMENT 1   Read "Superman and Me," by Sherman Alexie. Use the above steps to annotate the reading.

"Superman and Me," by Sherman Alexie

I learned to read with a Superman comic book. Simple enough, I suppose. I cannot recall which particular Superman comic book I read, nor can I remember which villain he fought in that issue. I cannot remember the plot, nor the means by which I obtained the comic book. What I can remember is this: I was 3 years old, a Spokane Indian boy living with his family on the Spokane Indian Reservation in eastern Washington state. We were poor by most standards, but one of my parents usually managed to find some minimum-wage job or another, which made us middle-class by reservation standards. I had a brother and three sisters. We lived on a combination of irregular paychecks, hope, fear and government surplus food.

My father, who is one of the few Indians who went to Catholic school on purpose, was an avid reader of westerns, spy thrillers, murder mysteries, gangster epics, basketball player biographies and anything else he could find. He bought his books by the pound at Dutch's Pawn Shop, Goodwill, Salvation Army and Value Village. When he had extra money, he bought new novels at supermarkets, convenience stores and hospital gift shops. Our house was filled with books. They were stacked in crazy piles in the bathroom, bedrooms and living room. In a fit of unemployment-inspired creative energy, my father built a set of bookshelves and soon filled them with a random assortment of books about the Kennedy assassination, Watergate, the Vietnam War and the entire 23-book series of the Apache westerns. My father loved books, and since I loved my father with an aching devotion, I decided to love books as well.

I can remember picking up my father's books before I could read. The words themselves were mostly foreign, but I still remember the exact moment when I first understood, with a sudden clarity, the purpose of a paragraph. I didn't have the vocabulary to say "paragraph," but I realized that a paragraph was a fence that held words. The words inside a paragraph worked together for a common purpose. They had some specific reason for being inside the same fence. This knowledge delighted me. I began to think of everything in terms of paragraphs. Our reservation was a small paragraph within the United States. My family's house was a paragraph, distinct from the other paragraphs of the LeBrets to the north, the Fords to our south and the Tribal School to the west. Inside our house, each family member existed as a separate paragraph but still had genetics and common experiences to link us. Now, using this logic, I can see my changed family as an essay of seven paragraphs: mother, father, older brother, the deceased sister, my younger twin sisters and our adopted little brother.

At the same time I was seeing the world in paragraphs, I also picked up that Superman comic book. Each panel, complete with picture, dialogue and narrative was a three-dimensional paragraph. In one panel, Superman breaks through a door. His suit is red, blue and yellow. The brown door shatters into many pieces. I look at the narrative above the picture. I cannot read the words, but I assume it tells me that "Superman is breaking down the door." Aloud, I pretend to read the words and say, "Superman is breaking down the door." Words, dialogue, also float out of Superman's mouth. Because he is breaking down the door, I assume he says, "I am breaking down the door." Once again, I pretend to read the words and say aloud, "I am breaking down the door" In this way, I learned to read.

This might be an interesting story all by itself. A little Indian boy teaches himself to read at an early age and advances quickly. He reads "Grapes of Wrath" in kindergarten when other children are struggling through "Dick and Jane." If he'd been anything but an Indian boy living on the reservation, he might have been called a prodigy. But he is an Indian boy living on the reservation and is simply an oddity. He grows into a man who often speaks of his childhood in the third-person, as if it will somehow dull the pain and make him sound more modest about his talents.

A smart Indian is a dangerous person, widely feared and ridiculed by Indians and non-Indians alike. I fought with my classmates on a daily basis. They wanted me to stay quiet when the non-Indian teacher asked for answers, for volunteers, for help. We were Indian children who were expected to be stupid. Most lived up to those expectations inside the classroom but subverted them on the outside. They struggled with basic reading in school but could remember how to sing a few dozen powwow songs. They were monosyllabic in front of their non-Indian teachers but could tell complicated stories and jokes at the dinner table. They submissively ducked their heads when confronted by a non-Indian adult but would slug it out with the Indian bully who was 10 years older. As Indian children, we were expected to fail in the non-Indian world. Those who failed were ceremonially accepted by other Indians and appropriately pitied by non-Indians.

I refused to fail. I was smart. I was arrogant. I was lucky. I read books late into the night, until I could barely keep my eyes open. I read books at recess, then during lunch, and in the few minutes left after I had finished my classroom assignments. I read books in the car when my family traveled to powwows or basketball games. In shopping malls, I ran to the bookstores and read bits and pieces of as many books as I could. I read the books my father brought home from the pawnshops and secondhand. I read the books I borrowed from the library. I read the backs of cereal boxes. I read the newspaper. I read the bulletins posted on the walls of the school, the clinic, the tribal offices, the post office. I read junk mail. I read auto-repair manuals. I read magazines. I read anything that had words and paragraphs. I read with equal parts joy and desperation. I loved those books, but I also knew that love had only one purpose. I was trying to save my life.

Despite all the books I read, I am still surprised I became a writer. I was going to be a pediatrician. These days, I write novels, short stories, and poems. I visit schools and teach creative writing to Indian kids. In all my years in the reservation school system, I was never taught how to write poetry, short stories or novels. I was certainly never taught that Indians wrote poetry, short stories and novels. Writing was something beyond Indians. I cannot recall a single time that a guest teacher visited the reservation. There must have been visiting teachers. Who were they? Where are they now? Do they exist? I visit the schools as often as possible. The Indian kids crowd the classroom. Many are writing their own poems, short stories and novels. They have read my books. They have read many other books. They look at me with bright eyes and arrogant wonder. They are trying to save their lives. Then there are the sullen and already defeated Indian kids who sit in the back rows and ignore me with theatrical precision. The pages of their notebooks are empty. They carry neither pencil nor pen. They stare out the window. They refuse and resist. "Books," I say to them. "Books," I say. I throw my weight against their locked doors. The door holds. I am smart. I am arrogant. I am lucky. I am trying to save our lives.

McQuade, Donald, Ed. *The Writer's Presence: A Pool of Readings, Fifth Edition.*
Boston: Bedford/St. Martin's, 2006. 73–76.

The Basic Categories

There are two major categories of writings to which students respond in our composition courses: objective writings and subjective writings.

- **objective writings** = pieces of writing that deal with reporting facts and not with a writer's opinions about these facts. The most common example of this type of writing used in our courses is a newspaper article.
    - **When a student must comprehend and, later, summarize objective writings, he or she should ask the six journalism questions: Who? What? When? Where? Why? and How?**
- **subjective writings** = pieces of writing that deal with expressing the author's opinion or perspective. Narratives, newspaper editorials, and argumentative essays are examples of this type of writing.
    - Comprehending such writings is a little trickier because the reader must hone in on the topic, decipher the main idea of a piece, and determine which supporting details are major and which are minor.
    - **Topic = the general subject of a piece of writing**
    - **Main idea = the most important thing the writer has to say about the topic. This will be an opinion, not a fact.**
    - **Supporting details = information about the topic that helps prove the writer's point**
        - **Major details = what directly relate to the main idea**
        - **Minor details = explain major details and indirectly relate to the main idea**

What to Look For

Main ideas can be clearly stated, where a reader can find a sentence or two that makes the author's argument; or main ideas can be **implied**, where the reader must use his or her ability to make inferences to figure out what the author's argument is based on clues within the reading. With an implied main idea, the essay is like a puzzle. The reader must look at several pieces together to see the big picture. In subjective arguments, major details answer who, what, when, where, and how, but WHY is often the most crucial question. Its answers are the most important details. Students should also look for answers to the question "What else?" as an author's main idea usually has smaller arguments that help to build support.

TRUMAN ASSIGNMENT 2   The essay "Superman and Me," by Sherman Alexie, is an example of a subjective essay where the main idea is implied. You must look at the essay in its entirety to figure out what that idea is. Reread the essay and answer the following questions:

a. What is the topic?
b. What is the most important point that Alexie makes about the topic?
c. Why does he believe this?
d. Answer the who, what, when, where, and how questions most central to supporting Alexie's main point.

Reading Strategies

The reading strategies discussed in this chapter can help you develop your writing skills. They can also help you become a more active reader. You will learn about previewing, finding the main and supporting ideas, understanding difficult words, and recognizing irony. When you read, you expand your vocabulary and learn how other writers develop topics. You also learn to recognize and use different writing patterns. Finally, reading helps you find ideas for your own essays.

You don't have to burn books to destroy a culture. Just get people to stop reading them.

RAY BRADBURY,
AUTHOR

Previewing

Previewing is like glancing through a magazine in a bookstore; it gives you a chance to see what the writer is offering. When you **preview**, look quickly for the following visual clues so that you can determine the selection's key ideas:

- Titles or subheadings (if any)
- The first and last sentence of the introduction
- The first sentence of each paragraph
- The concluding sentences
- Any photos, graphs, or charts

Finding the Main Idea

After you finish previewing, read the selection carefully. Search for the **main idea**, which is the central point that the writer is trying to make. In an essay, the main idea usually appears somewhere in the first few paragraphs in the form of a thesis statement. However, some professional writers build up to the main idea and state it only in the middle or at the end of the essay. Additionally, some professional writers do not state the main idea directly.

> ## *Hint*   Making a Statement of the Main Idea
>
> If the reading does not contain a clear thesis statement, you can determine the main idea by asking yourself *who, what, when, where, why,* and *how* questions. Then, using the answers to those questions, make a statement that sums up the main point of the reading.

Making Inferences

If a professional writer does not state the main idea directly, you must look for clues that will help you to **infer** or figure out what the writer means to say. For example, the next paragraph does not have a topic sentence. However, you can infer the main idea. Underline key words that can lead you to a better understanding of the passage.

> Algie Crivens III was 18 and fresh out of high school in 1991 when he was sentenced to twenty years in prison for a murder he did not commit. He spent the next eight-and-a-half years consumed with educating himself while his appeals crawled through the courts. Crivens is nothing if not energetic; he tends to speak in paragraphs, not sentences. While in prison, he channeled this energy into earning an associate's degree in social science and a bachelor's in sociology. He also took courses in paralegal studies and culinary arts. His fellow prisoners used to ask how he could spend so much time reading. But, to him, reading was a way to escape the boredom of prison life.
>
> —From "Righting a Wrong" by Liliana Ibara

PRACTICE I   Ask yourself the following questions.

1. What is the subject of this text?

   _____

2. What points can you infer that the writer is making? _____

   _____

   _____

Finding the Supporting Ideas

Different writers use different types of supporting ideas. They may give steps for a process, use examples to illustrate a point, give reasons for an argument, and so on. Try to identify the author's supporting ideas.

Highlighting and Making Annotations

After you read a long text, you may forget some of the author's ideas. To help you remember and quickly find the important points, you can highlight key ideas and make annotations. An **annotation** is a comment, question, or reaction that you write in the margins of a passage.

Each time you read a passage, follow these steps:

- Look in the introductory and concluding paragraphs. Underline sentences that sum up the main idea. Using your own words, rewrite the main idea in the margin.
- Underline or highlight supporting ideas. You might even want to number the arguments or ideas. This will allow you to understand the essay's development.
- Circle words that you do not understand.
- Write questions in the margin if you do not understand the author's meaning.
- Write notes beside passages that are interesting or that relate to your own experiences.
- Jot down any ideas that might make interesting writing topics.

Here is an example of a highlighted and annotated passage from an essay titled "Sprawl Fallout" by Patricia L. Kirk.

What is a euphemism? ➤   1   For suburbanites who spend hours in traffic each day commuting to
General background   city jobs, the concept of urban sprawl is more than a (euphemism) batted
for the introduction ➤   around by city planners. Many commuters know the psychological tolls of
Main point suggests   their long, slow journeys—irritation, anxiety, less time at home—but the
urban sprawl is not   negative impacts might be broader than most realize.
good.   ➤   2   Urban sprawl—a phenomenon that results in people living far from
Definition of sprawl ➤   their workplaces—has been linked to asthma, obesity, and just plain foul
Shows the effects of   moods. In one study, people with long commutes reported more headaches,
sprawl   ➤   stomach problems, and fatigue than people with shorter drives. Irritability
Traffic jams drive me   from long commutes was also shown to transfer to job performance,
crazy.   ➤   resulting in lower productivity.

Understanding Difficult Words

When you come across an unfamiliar word in a passage, do not stop reading to look up its definition in the dictionary. First, try using context clues to figure out the term's meaning on your own. If you still do not understand the word, circle it to remind you to look up its meaning in the dictionary when you have finished reading through the passage. You can keep a list of new vocabulary in the "Vocabulary Log" at the end of this book on page 391.

Using Context Clues

Context clues are hints in the selection that help to define a word. To find a word's meaning, try the following:

- **Look at the word.** Is it a noun, a verb, or an adjective? Knowing how the word functions in the sentence can help you guess its meaning.
- **Look at surrounding words.** Look at the entire sentence and try to find a relation between the difficult word and those that surround it. There may be a **synonym** (a word that means the same thing) or an **antonym** (a word that means the opposite), or other terms in the sentence that help define the word.
- **Look at surrounding sentences.** Sometimes you can guess the meaning of a difficult word by looking at the sentences, paragraphs, and punctuation marks surrounding it. When you use your logic, the meaning becomes clear.

In most cases, you can guess the meaning of a new word by combining your own knowledge of the topic with the information conveyed in the words and phrases surrounding the difficult word.

PRACTICE 2   Can you define the words *strewn, emanate,* or *haven?* Perhaps you are not quite sure. Looking at the words in context makes it much easier to guess the definitions of the words.

> When I arrived in my hometown, I was baffled by the changes in my old neighborhood. Garbage was **strewn** across front lawns, paint peeled on the graying wooden homes, and roofs sagged. The auto body shop on the corner **emanated** horrible fumes of turpentine and paint, forcing me to cover my nose when I passed it. I wondered what had happened to my former safe **haven**.

Now write your own definition of the words as they are used in the context.

strewn _____   emanated _____   haven _____

Hint   Cognates

Cognates (also known as word twins) are English words that may look and sound like words in another language. For example, the English word *responsible* is similar to the Spanish word *responsable*, although the words are spelled differently.

If English is not your first language, and you read an English word that looks similar to a word in your language, check how the word is being used in context. It may or may not mean the same thing in English as it means in your language. For example, in English, *sensible* means "to show good sense," but in Spanish, *sensible* means "emotional." In German, *bekommen* sounds like "become" but it really means "to get," and the German word *gift* means "poison" in English. If you are not sure of a word's meaning, you can always consult a dictionary.

Using a Dictionary

If you cannot understand the meaning of an unfamiliar word even after using context clues, then look up the word in a dictionary. A dictionary is useful if you use it correctly. Review the following tips for proper dictionary usage:

- **Look at the dictionary's front matter.** The preface contains explanations about the various symbols and abbreviations. Find out what your dictionary has to offer.
- **Read all of the definitions listed for the word.** Look for the meaning that best fits the context of your sentence.
- **Look up root words, if necessary.** For example, if you do not understand the word *unambiguous*, remove the prefix and look up *ambiguous*.

Here is an example of how dictionaries set up their definitions:

Word-Break Divisions

Your dictionary may indicate places for dividing words with heavy black dots.

Stress Symbol (') and Pronunciation

Some dictionaries provide the phonetic pronunciation of words. The stress symbol lets you know which syllable has the highest or loudest sound.

Parts of Speech

The *n* means that *formation* is a noun. If you do not understand the "parts of speech" symbol, look in the front or the back of your dictionary for a list of symbols and their meanings.

for•ma'•tion / fŏr′māshən/ *n* 1, the process of shaping. 2, that which is shaped. 3, formal structure or arrangement, esp. of troops.

From *The New American Webster Handy College*, A Signet Book, 2000.

Determining Connotation and Denotation

A **denotation** is the literal meaning for a word that may be found in the dictionary. For example, the dictionary definition of *mother* is "a female parent." A **connotation** is the implied or associated meaning. It can be a cultural value judgment. For instance, the word *mother* may trigger feelings of comfort, security, anger, or resentment in a listener, depending on that person's experience with mothers.

Authors can influence readers by carefully choosing words that have specific denotations. For example, review the next two descriptions. Which one has a more negative connotation?

Terry left his family.   Andrew abandoned his family.

PRACTICE 3   Read the next passages and underline any words or phrases that have strong connotations. Discuss how the words support a personal bias.

1. Furthermore, in too many states, welfare keeps flowing while the kids are in jail, or middle-class parents continue to claim children

as tax deductions even as the state pays for their upkeep in detention facilities. We must demand that parents reimburse the state for housing their failures.

from "Enough Is Enough" by Judy Sheindlin

2. There is no question about whom Ms. Politkovskaya held responsible in years of unflinching reporting from Chechnya: the Russian Army and Mr. Putin himself. When he finally got around to acknowledging her death yesterday, it was in a cold-blooded statement that the authorities "will take every step to investigate objectively the tragic death of the journalist Politkovskaya."

from "Another Killing in Moscow" (*The New York Times* editorial)

3. Rohe could have chosen to give a substantive speech detailing why she believes "pre-emptive war is dangerous and wrong"—or as she so categorically put it, how she "knows" that it is. Instead she took the easy way out by insulting the speaker and throwing out some leftist chestnuts about the still missing Osama bin Laden and weapons of mass destruction. But the former would have required her to grapple with ideas; she chose to take potshots.

from "The Real Meaning of Courage" by Linda Chavez

Recognizing Irony

Irony is a technique that some writers use to make a point. When an author is being ironic, he or she says one thing but really means the opposite. When the author uses an ironic tone, he or she does not intend the reader to interpret the words literally. Sarcasm is a type of verbal irony.

> **EXAMPLE:** The charred burger lay in a grease-soaked bun. "That looks wonderful," he muttered.

PRACTICE 4   Read the next selection from an essay called "The Greatest Player" by Gary Lautens. Then answer the questions.

Occasionally, I run into sports figures at cocktail parties, on the street, or on their way to the bank. "Nice game the other night," I said to an old hockey-player pal.

"Think so?" he replied.

"You've come a long way since I knew you as a junior."

"How's that?"

"Well, you high-stick better for one thing—and I think the way you clutch sweaters is really superb. You may be the best in the league." He blushed modestly. "For a time," I confessed, "I never thought you'd get the hang of it."

"It wasn't easy," he confided. "It took practice and encouragement. You know something like spearing doesn't come naturally. It has to be developed."

"I'm not inclined to flattery but, in my book, you've got it made. You're a dirty player," I continued. . . . "There isn't a player in the league who knows as many obscene gestures."

How is the selection ironic? What does the author really mean?

_____

_____

From Reading to Writing

After you finish reading a selection, you could try these strategies to make sure that you have understood it.

Summarize the reading. When you summarize, you use your own words to write a condensed version of the reading. You leave out all information except for the main points.

Outline the reading. An outline is a visual plan of the reading that looks like an essay plan. First, you write the main idea of the essay, and then write down the most important idea from each paragraph. You could make further indentations, and under each idea, include a detail or example.

Analyze the reading. When you read, look critically at the writer's arguments and evaluate them, point by point. Also analyze how the writer builds the argument and ask yourself questions such as _Do I agree? Are the author's arguments convincing?_ Then, when you write your analysis, you can break down the author's explanations and either refute or agree with them, using your own experiences and examples to support your view.

Another Useful Strategy

One more very useful strategy is discuss a reading with others. Students should talk with their fellow students and with their teachers about the articles, books, essays, and short stories that they read. This can help students who are aural or verbal learners to figure out what they think. This can also help any student to practice putting an author's ideas into the student's own words. Finally, in this way, students are able to get feedback about their own understanding and gain insight through others' understanding of the assigned readings.

Writing Summaries

CONTENTS

In any type of writing, authors must consider their audience. Two major questions they must ask themselves are as follows: What knowledge of the topic are readers likely to already have? What information will readers need the author to provide? This is why academic essays include summaries. A summary tells what a piece of writing was about, but it tells it IN YOUR OWN WORDS, not the writer's words. Writers want the readers to have a clear idea of what in the world they are writing about.

- In a Summary/Response Essay, there are two usual positions for summaries. The first is a separate summary paragraph at the beginning of an essay before the introduction paragraph.

Example of Separate Summary and Introduction

In David Brooks's article "People Like Us," Brooks argues that while Americans generally support diversity in public, we segregate our private lives. According to Brooks, we separate ourselves for many reasons, such as race, culture, politics, education, religion, and income. He says that we do this because we want to be comfortable, and the people who make us the most comfortable are the people we identify with, the people like us. This, Brooks says, is not a bad thing but is a human thing. He believes that a commitment to learning about and accepting difference in the workplace and in our schools is a good goal. But the people we eat pizza with or go to the mall with or marry are our choice, and Brooks says that we should be able to be comfortable whether that choice reflects diversity or not.

When I first started high school, like in a lot of high schools across America, the black kids sat together in the lunch room. This phenomenon was so widespread that a sociologist wrote a book called *Why Are All The Black Kids Sitting Together in the Cafeteria?* The interesting thing was that my high school was really diverse. There were Koreans and Latinos, athletes and members of the chess club, gifted students and regular students. And while we talked, laughed, and learned together in class, when we got to the cafeteria and had a choice, we all grouped off into our cliques. As I moved into my sophomore, junior, and senior years, those cliques became less about race and more about who got along. I agree with David Brooks that Americans tend to group themselves off, but what he does not discuss is the fact that, more and more, the definition of "people like us" is getting more complicated and more diverse. This is a good thing because if we get stuck in the America that David Brooks describes, we will miss out on the benefits that come from a global society.

- The second is an introduction paragraph that combines a student's attention-getter, lead-in, summary, and thesis statement.

Example of Combined Summary and Introduction

Chicago is one of the most diverse cities in America and is also one of the most segregated. There are neighborhoods that represent Polish people, neighborhoods that represent Latinos, neighborhoods full of orthodox Jews, and neighborhoods filled with African-Americans, but it is hard to find one neighborhood where a decent number of all of these groups live side by side. In David Brooks's article "People Like Us," Brooks argues that while Americans generally support diversity in public, we segregate our private lives. According to Brooks, we separate ourselves because we want to be comfortable, and the people who make us the most comfortable are the people we identify with, the people like us. This, Brooks says, is not a bad thing but is a human thing. He believes that a commitment to learning about and accepting difference in the workplace and in our schools is a good goal, but he says that we should be able to be comfortable with the choices we make about our home lives whether those choices reflect diversity or not. I agree with Brooks that it is human nature to want to be around people who look like us, and as long as we don't discriminate, this can be a good thing because it builds pride in our culture and makes life less stressful.

If your instructor has a preference, follow his or her directions. Otherwise, you should practice both types of summaries to discover which best fits your assignments and your writing style.

Do's and Don'ts for Writing Summaries

Dos

- Approximate Length:
    - In a separate summary paragraph, aim for 5 sentences. Try not to go beyond 7 sentences,
    - If you combine your summary with your introduction paragraph, then the summary section should be about 3–5 sentences.
- Write using the present tense.
- 1st sentence of the summary section—include the author's first and last name, the title of the piece and the main idea of the piece.
    - Example: In Alice Walker's *The Color Purple*, the main character struggles to find her own self-worth.
- Information—include the major points (claims) made by the author in a logical order.
- Refer to the author—tag the information with a reference to the author. **Use only the author's last name after the first sentence of the summary.**
    - Example: She writes that . . . Walker believes . . . According to Walker, . . . etc.

Don'ts

- Details—Do not include details that are not necessary to stating the major points.
    - WRONG: Meyers writes that 80% of freshman college students continue to use comma-splices, sentence fragments, and run-on sentences.

- ▫ RIGHT: Meyers writes that many college freshmen continue to make sentence boundary errors, such as comma-splices, in their writing.
- Quotes—DON'T use more than one quote.
  - ▫ You can't write something in your own words if you are using the writer's words, so quotes should be used sparingly.
  - ▫ Quotes included in a summary should come in a "quotation sandwich."
    - Introduction of the quote—actual quote—explanation, in your words, of what the quote means.
    - Example: Terrell writes that "a schedule with too many difficult classes in one semester is one of the most accurate predictors of student attrition." What she means is that students who try to take English, math, biology, and history all in the same semester are likely to be the students who withdraw from school and never come back.
- Opinion—Do not include your opinion in the summary. Wait for the response.
  - ▫ WRONG: Stephen King's short story "Stand by Me" is an <u>amazing</u> conglomeration of the buddy genre and the <u>always interesting</u> coming-of-age tales.
  - ▫ RIGHT: Stephen King's short story "Stand by Me" is a conglomeration of the buddy genre and coming-of-age tales.

TRUMAN ASSIGNMENT 3   Write a stand-alone summary paragraph for "Superman and Me." Use the information from the answers to the questions in assignment 2 in your summary. Follow the Do's and Don'ts for writing summaries.

Writing a Response

CONTENTS

The most important part of academic writing is that a student share his or her opinion and explain why he or she believes or feels as he or she does. This is why teachers often assign summary/response essays. It is important for students to engage with what they read, figure out what they think and why, and then prove to their audience that what they have expressed is rational.

When students first enter writing classes, they often have a variety of feelings about their ability to write well. "I am a good writer. I write whatever comes to my head," say some. Others qualify their writing ability with the requirement that the subject about which they are writing be "interesting." Still others enter English courses terrified, proclaiming to their teachers that they just cannot write. All of these claims are faulty. Here are some reasons why:

> Good writing of any kind is a process with multiple steps. Anyone can learn these steps, even students who have not had much success with writing in the past. Within this process, it is the good writer's job to employ his or her own creative and critical thoughts in order to craft a clear, engaging, well-thought-out essay. And if the topic is perceived as "boring," it is the writer's responsibility to find a way to make his or her essay interesting for readers.

Overview of The Writing Process for Summary/Response Essays

1. Reading and Interpreting the Assignment

2. Exploring

3. Planning

4. Drafting

5. Revising and Editing

Reading and Interpreting the Assignment

Very few professors will leave students to come up with their own topics for writing without providing any guidance. They provide a prompt, which may take the form of a single question on an essay test or be included in a more detailed assignment sheet. Thus, the first step in the academic writing process involves reading and interpreting the prompt.

Understand Your Assignment

As soon as you are given an assignment, make sure that you understand your task. Answer the following questions about the assignment.

- How many words or pages does the assignment require?
- What is the due date for the assignment?
- Are there any special qualities my writing should include? For example, should my writing be double-spaced? Should I include a list of works cited?

After you have considered your assignment, consider the following four key steps in the exploring stage of the writing process.

> *How much has to be explored and discarded before reaching the naked flesh of feeling.*
>
> CLAUDE DEBUSSY,
> *French composer*

EXPLORING

STEP 1	⮞	**Think about your topic.** Determine what you will write about.
STEP 2	⮞	**Think about your audience.** Consider your intended readers and what interests them.
STEP 3	⮞	**Think about your purpose.** Ask yourself why you want to write.
STEP 4	⮞	**Try exploring strategies.** Experiment with different ways to generate ideas.

Topic

Sometimes your topic has been assigned and is already very specific. At other times, it may be very general. For example, if your assigned topic is "food," narrow it down so that you can focus on something specific about food. You might write about the dangers of diets or how to cook a certain type of cuisine. You might describe the symbolism of food in a literary work or try to explain the chemical makeup of a specific food. When you are given a general topic, find an angle that interests you and make it more specific.

To find a focus for your topic, ask yourself the following questions.

- What about the topic interests me? Will it interest other readers?
- Do I have special knowledge about the topic?
- Does anything about the topic arouse my emotions?

Audience

Your **audience** is your intended reader. In your personal, academic, and professional life, you will often write for a specific audience; therefore, you can keep your readers interested by adapting your tone and vocabulary to suit them.

Tone is your general attitude or feeling toward a topic. You might write in a tone that is humorous, sarcastic, serious, friendly, or casual. For example, imagine you are preparing an invitation to an event. To determine the design, phrasing, and format, you need to know some important information about your recipients. What are their ages and lifestyles? Are they mostly males or females?

Would they prefer printed invitations or e-mail invitations? Questions like these can help you connect with your audience.

Knowing your readers is especially important when preparing academic or workplace documents. When you consider your audience, ask yourself the following questions:

- Who will read my assignment—an instructor, other students, or people outside the college?
- Do the readers have a lot of knowledge about my topic?
- How will I need to adjust my vocabulary, writing style, or tone to appeal to my readers?

In academic writing, your audience is generally your instructor or other students, unless your instructor specifically asks you to write for another audience such as the general public, your employer, or a family member.

> ## Hint   Instructor as the Audience
>
> Your instructor represents a general audience. Such an audience of educated readers will expect you to reveal what you have learned or what you have understood about the topic. Your ideas should be presented in a clear and organized manner. Do not leave out information because you assume that your instructor is an expert in the field. Also, you should write in standard English. In other words, try to use correct grammar, sentence structure, and vocabulary.

PRACTICE I   As you read the following messages, consider the differences in both the tone and the vocabulary the writer uses. Then answer the questions that follow.

A

yo, :)

im in ur english class on 2sday. how ru? can u help with my essay? >:o b4 i write, i need 2 know what the topic is? what is # of words? plz check my plan cuz i don't no if i'm on the rite track... :'(is it ok? btw, will c u in class.

gtg Andrea :)

B

Dear Professor Gonzales,

I am in your Tuesday morning English class. I have started working on my essay and have prepared an essay plan, but I am not sure if my thesis statement is appropriate and focused enough. Could you please look at my plan and let me know if I am on the right track? Also, could you please remind me of the length of the assignment?
Thank you,

Reginald Harper

1. Why is the language inappropriate in the first instant message?

   _____

   _____

2. What judgments might the instructor make about the two students based on the messages?

   _____

   _____

   _____

   _____

Purpose

Your **purpose** is your reason for writing. Keeping your purpose in mind will help you focus your writing.

When you consider your purpose, ask yourself the following questions.

- Is my goal to **entertain**? Do I want to tell a story?
- Is my goal to **persuade**? Do I want to convince readers that my point of view is the correct one?
- Is my goal to **inform**? Do I want to explain something or give information about a topic?

It is possible to write for a combination of reasons. In fact, most essays have more than one purpose. For example, an essay describing a personal experience with fraud could also inform readers about protecting themselves from identity theft, or an essay describing how the heart pumps blood could simultaneously persuade readers to reconsider smoking.

> **Hint** **General and Specific Purpose**
>
> Your **general purpose** is to entertain, to inform, or to persuade. Your **specific purpose** is your more precise reason for writing. For example, imagine that you have to write about an election. You can have the following general and specific purposes.
>
> General purpose: to inform
> Specific purpose: to compare platforms of two different candidates

PRACTICE 2   The following selections are all about food; however, each excerpt has a different purpose, has been written for a different audience, and has been taken from a different source. Read each selection carefully. Then underline any language clues (words or phrases) that help you identify its source, audience, and purpose. Finally, answer the questions that follow each selection.

EXAMPLE:

slang   ➤

slang   ➤

slang, informal tone   ➤

I just made my very first dessert. It looks <u>awesome</u>. I hope it tastes <u>alright</u>. I almost <u>freaked out</u> when I realized I forgot to turn the oven on. My instructor is <u>super</u>, and he's <u>got a great sense of humor</u> with me and the other students. Next, I am going to try to make a more complicated dessert.

What is the most likely source of this paragraph?

a. Web site article   (b. personal letter)   c. textbook   d. memoir

What is its primary purpose?____*to inform*_____

Who is the audience?____*friend or family member*_____

_____

1. I went out with my old friends Nuzhat Ahmad and Ayla, as the three of us often did, in a comradeship of girlhood. We went driving to Bagh-e-Jinnah, formerly known as Lawrence Gardens, located opposite the Governor's House along the Mall in Lahore. We were trying to locate the best *gol guppa* vendor in town and stopped by to test the new stand in Lawrence Gardens. Gol guppas are a strange food: I have never located an equivalent to them or their culinary situation. They are an outdoor food, a passing whim, and no one would dream of recreating their frivolity inside his or her own kitchen. A gol guppa is a small hollow oval of the lightest pastry that is dipped into a fiery liquid sauce made of tamarind and cayenne and lemon and cold water. It is evidently a food invented as a joke, in a moment of good humor.

What is the most likely source of this paragraph?

a. Web site article   b. personal letter   c. textbook   d. memoir

What is its primary purpose?_____

Who is the audience?_____

_____

2. Eat regularly. Eating is one of life's great pleasures, and it is important to take time to stop, relax, and enjoy mealtimes and snacks. Scheduling eating times also ensures that meals are not

missed, resulting in missed nutrients that are often not compensated for by subsequent meals. This is especially important for school-age children, adolescents, and elderly people.

What is the most likely source of this paragraph?
a. Web site article   b. personal letter   c. textbook   d. memoir

What is its primary purpose?_____

Who is the audience?_____

_____

3.   About 5,000 years ago, another revolution in technology was taking place in the Middle East, one that would end up changing the entire world. This was the discovery of agriculture, large-scale cultivation using plows harnessed to animals or more powerful energy sources. So important was the invention of the animal-drawn plow, along with other breakthroughs of the period—including irrigation, the wheel, writing, numbers, and the use of various metals—that this moment in history is often called "the dawn of civilization."

What is the most likely source of this paragraph?
a. Web site article   b. personal letter   c. textbook   d. memoir

What is its purpose?_____

Who is the audience?_____

_____

Purpose of Academic Writing

One important note is that in academic writing, the overall purpose is not necessarily to entertain, persuade, or inform. The major purpose of academic writing is to argue—that is, to present one's position and support it well enough that one's readers consider it valid. Higher education deals with ideas and with the processes of inquiry, research, and creativity that allow those ideas to be presented, exchanged, analyzed, and evaluated. The point of academic essays is not necessarily to persuade readers to believe the same way as the author but to help readers to understand that the author's particular way of looking at an idea, issue, problem, or solution is reasonable.

A prompt is the primary question that a student's essay should answer. There are several kinds of prompts. Some prompts for summary/response essays will be fairly general, asking the student to respond to the overall content of a piece of reading; some prompts will be more specific, asking a student to focus on a particular idea, concept, or occurrence in that particular reading. Some prompts provide background information, suggest other questions for a student to consider in developing the essay, or require that a student answer other questions within the body of the essay. Finally, some prompts come in a detailed assignment sheet that provides a topic, and audience, format and length requirements, and other details.

Whatever format a prompt comes in, students must read it to find out what he or she is required to answer, what possibilities for writing there are, and how the professor wants the finished product.

TRUMAN ASSIGNMENT 4 Read the following assignment sheet for your first essay. Underline the primary question which your essay is supposed to answer. Put stars next to any other questions provided to help you think. Draw a box around any formatting or length requirements.

Essay Assignment: Summary/Response on The Power of Reading

<u>Topic</u>: Can reading and education save lives?
<u>Audience</u>: Your teachers

<u>The Set-Up</u>: The teachers of the Chicago Public School system want to hear from students so that they can improve the way that they educate students. This is part of the nationwide reform effort and a portion of Illinois's application for funding from the federal Race to the Top program, the successor to the reform efforts of No Child Left Behind. Teachers have decided that they have given students plenty of advice over the years, but they do not know how much the students actually believe what they tell them. They have decided to have a contest for high school graduates, whether recent or not.

The topic of the essay is whether it is true that reading and education are as important as teachers say. You use either Sherman Alexie's "Superman and Me" (p. 35) or Malcolm X's "Coming to an Awareness of Language" (p. 12) as the primary source for your essay. You consider yourself to be an expert on what students' real lives are like, and you want teachers to get real insight into how reading plays into those lives.

<u>The Assignment</u>: You must summarize either Alexie's essay or Malcolm X's essay and then write a response in which you can agree with the authors' premise about how being a good reader and having a good education (even if one is self-educated) can affect people's lives, disagree with it, or you can do both. Use a mix of your

experience, your observations and general knowledge, and the authors' writing to support your argument.

Length: 2–4 pages
Font: Double-spaced, 12 pt., Times New Roman

How Assignments and Prompts Shape Reading

One very important point about prompts and assignment sheets is that they should not only shape your writing but your reading as well. They give you a particular purpose for reading, which is necessary to understand if you are to be successful in a reading activity.

We read differently for different purposes. For instance, in a college-level Introduction to Religion course, students would read sacred texts not as adherents to or believers in these texts but as scholars studying the history, cultural relevance, historical impact, and current understanding of these texts. When those same students go to temple, mosque, synagogue, or church as members of a religion, they read the same sacred texts in order to find out how to apply the teachings to their own lives.

An assignment sheet or prompt gives a student clues about how to approach reading a certain text. It gives the student specific information to look for and helps to orient that student as both reader and writer. This may mean that the student's annotation and underlining strategies are more focused, dealing primarily with what relates to the prompt and with how a student connects with that information.

OPTIONAL TRUMAN ASSIGNMENT   Your assignment sheet gives you the option of focusing your response essay on "Coming to an Awareness of Language" by Malcolm X. In order to make your choice, you must first read Malcolm X's essay. Read "Coming to an Awareness of Language" and annotate it, keeping in mind what the assignment sheet asks you to write.

"Coming to an Awareness of Language" by Malcolm X

Muhammad had only required my mind's saying to me, "That's right!" or "I never thought of that."

But bending my knees to pray—that act—well, that took me a week.

You know what my life had been. Picking a lock to rob someone's house was the only way my knees had ever been bent before.

I had to force myself to bend my knees. And waves of shame and embarrassment would force me back up.

For evil to bend its knees, admitting its guilt, to implore the forgiveness of God, is the hardest thing in the world. It's easy for me to see and to say that now. But then, when I was the personification of evil, I was going through it. Again, again, I would force myself back down into the praying-to-Allah posture. When finally I was able to make myself stay down—I didn't know what to say to Allah.

For the next years, I was the nearest thing to a hermit in the Norfolk Prison Colony. I never have been more busy in my life. I still marvel at how swiftly my previous life's thinking pattern slid away from me, like snow off a roof. It is as though someone else I knew of had lived by hustling and crime. I would be startled to catch myself thinking in a remote way of my earlier self as another person.

The things I felt, I was pitifully unable to express in the onepage letter that went every day to Mr. Elijah Muhammad. And I wrote at least one more daily letter, replying to one of my brothers and sisters. Every letter I received from them added something to my knowledge of the teachings of Mr. Muhammad. I would sit for long periods and study his photographs.

I've never been one for inaction. Everything I've ever felt strongly about, I've done something about. I guess that's why, unable to do anything else, I soon began writing to people I had known in the hustling world, such as Sammy the Pimp, John Hughes, the gambling-house owner, the thief Jumpsteady, and several dope peddlers. I wrote them all about Allah and Islam and Mr. Elijah Muhammad. I had no idea where most of them lived. I addressed their letters in care of the Harlem or Roxbury bars and clubs where I'd known them.

I never got a single reply. The average hustler and criminal was too uneducated to write a letter. I have known many slick, sharp-looking hustlers, who would have you think they had an interest in Wall Street; privately, they would get someone else to read a letter if they received one. Besides, neither would I have replied to anyone writing me something as wild as "the white man is the devil."

What certainly went on the Harlem and Roxbury wires was that Detroit Red was going crazy in stir, or else he was trying some hype to shake up the warden's office.

During the years that I stayed in the Norfolk Prison Colony, never did any official directly say anything to me about those letters, although, of course, they all passed through the prison censorship. I'm sure, however, they monitored what I wrote to add to the files which every state and federal prison keeps on the conversion of Negro inmates by the teachings of Mr. Elijah Muhammad. But at that time, I felt that the real reason was that the white man knew that he was the devil.

Later on, I even wrote to the Mayor of Boston, to the Governor of Massachusetts, and to Harry S Truman. They never answered; they probably never even saw my letters. I handscratched to them how the white man's society was responsible for the black man's condition in this wilderness of North America.

It was because of my letters that I happened to stumble upon starting to acquire some kind of a homemade education.

I became increasingly frustrated at not being able to express what I wanted to convey in letters that I wrote, especially those to Mr. Elijah Muhammad. In the street, I had been the most articulate hustler out there—I had commanded attention when I said something. But now, trying to write simple English, I not only wasn't articulate, I wasn't even functional. How would I sound writing in slang, the way I would say it, something such as "Look, daddy, let me pull your coat about a cat, Elijah Muhammad—"

Many who today hear me somewhere in person, or on television, or those who read something I've said, will think I went to school far beyond the eighth grade. This impression is due entirely to my prison studies.

It had really begun back in the Charlestown Prison, when Bimbi first made me feel envy of his stock of knowledge. Bimbi had always taken charge of any conversation he was in, and I had tried to emulate him. But every book I picked up had few sentences which didn't contain anywhere from one to nearly all of the words that might as well have been in Chinese. When I just skipped those words, of course, I really ended up with little idea of what the book said. So I had come to the Norfolk Prison Colony still going through only book-reading motions. Pretty soon, I would have quit even these motions, unless I had received the motivation that I did.

I saw that the best thing I could do was get hold of a dictionary—to study, to learn some words. I was lucky enough to reason also that I should try to improve my penmanship. It was sad. I couldn't even write in a straight line. It was both ideas together that moved me to request a dictionary along with some tablets and pencils from the Norfolk Prison Colony school.

I spent two days just riffling uncertainly through the dictionary's pages. I'd never realized so many words existed! I didn't know which words I needed to learn. Finally, just to start some kind of action, I began copying.

In my slow, painstaking, ragged handwriting, I copied into my tablet everything printed on that first page, down to the punctuation marks.

I believe it took me a day. Then, aloud, I read back, to myself, everything I'd written on the tablet. Over and over, aloud, to myself, I read my own handwriting.

I woke up the next morning, thinking about those words—immensely proud to realize that not only had I written so much at one time, but I'd written words that I never knew were in the world. Moreover, with a little effort, I also could remember what many of these words meant. I reviewed the words whose meanings I didn't remember. Funny thing, from the dictionary first page right now, that "aardvark" springs to my mind. The dictionary had a picture of it, a long-tailed, long-eared, burrowing African mammal, which lives off termites caught by sticking out its tongue as an anteater does for ants.

I was so fascinated that I went on—I copied the dictionary's next page. And the same experience came when I studied that. With every succeeding page, I also learned of people and places and events from history. Actually the dictionary is like a miniature encyclopedia. Finally the dictionary's A section had filled a whole tablet—and I went on into the B's. That was the way I started copying what eventually became the entire dictionary. It went a lot faster after so much practice helped me to pick up handwriting speed. Between what I wrote in my tablet, and writing letters, during the rest of my time in prison I would guess I wrote a million words.

I suppose it was inevitable that as my word-base broadened, I could for the first time pick up a book and read and now begin to understand what the book was saying. Anyone who has read a great deal can imagine the new world that opened. Let me tell you something: from then until I left that prison, in every free moment I had, if I was not reading in the library, I was reading on my bunk. You couldn't have gotten me out of books with a wedge. Between Mr. Muhammad's teachings, my correspondence, my visitors—usually Ella and Reginald—and my reading of books, months passed without my even thinking about being imprisoned. In fact, up to then, I never had been so truly free in my life.

Exploring

Once students know what they are being asked to do, they must take some time to discover both what they think and why they think it. One of the most basic building blocks of argument is called an **enthymeme** [en-th*uh*-meem]. It is a brief argument that includes a claim and the reason for that claim.

Claim + <u>Reason</u> = Enthymeme

Ex. Listening to news radio in the morning is not a good idea because <u>there is often bad news, which leaves the listener in a bad mood.</u>

Such enthymemes are a central part of what a student should explore in his or her prewriting. The following information on "Exploring Strategies" come from Gaetz and Phaedke and are good ways for students to decide what they want to write.

Exploring Strategies

After you determine your topic, audience, and purpose, try some **exploring strategies**—also known as **prewriting strategies**—to help get your ideas flowing. Four common strategies are *freewriting*, *brainstorming*, *questioning*, and *clustering*. It is not necessary to do all of the strategies explained in this chapter. Find the strategy that works best for you.

You can do both general and focused prewriting. If you have writer's block, and do not know what to write about, use **general prewriting** to come up with possible writing topics. Then, after you have chosen a topic, use **focused prewriting** to find an angle of the topic that is interesting and that could be developed in your essay.

Hint   **When to Use Exploring Strategies**

You can use the exploring strategies at any stage of the writing process:

- To find a topic
- To narrow a broad topic
- To generate ideas about your topic
- To generate supporting details

Narrow Your Topic

An essay has one main idea. If your topic is too broad, you might find it difficult to write a focused essay about it. For example, imagine that you are given the topic "mistakes." If the topic is not narrowed, it will lead to a meandering and unfocused essay. To narrow the topic, think about types of errors, examples of errors, or people who make errors. A more focused topic could be "mistakes newlyweds make" or "mistakes first-year college students make." Find one angle of the topic that you know a lot about and that you personally find interesting. If you have a lot to say, and you think the topic is compelling, chances are that your reader will also like your topic.

Review the following examples of general and narrowed topics.

Topic	Narrowed Topic
jobs	preparing for a job interview
music	protest songs from the past and present

To help narrow and develop you topic, you can use the following exploring strategies.

Freewriting

Freewriting gives you the freedom to write without stopping for a set period of time. The goal of this exercise is to record the first thoughts that come to mind. If you run out of ideas, don't stop writing. Simply fill in the pause with phrases like "blah blah blah" or "What else can I write?" As you write, do not be concerned with word choice, grammar, or spelling. If you use a computer, let your ideas flow and do not worry about typing mistakes. You could try typing without looking at the screen.

Alicia's Freewriting

College student Alicia Parera thought about mistakes college students make. During her freewriting, she wrote down everything that came to mind.

> Mistakes students make? Not doing the homework. Not asking for help when they need it? I sometimes feel shy to speak up when I don't understand something. What else? Some college students leave college early. Why do they leave? Tim. He only stayed for one semester. I don't think he was ready for college life. He treated college like high school and always came late. Goofed off. Cut class. What else? What about Amanda who had that family crisis? She had to leave when her mother was sick. Of course, finances. It's tough. Sometimes I go crazy trying to keep up with my job, friends, schoolwork . . . it's really hard.

Brainstorming

Brainstorming is like freewriting, except that you create a list of ideas, and you can take the time to stop and think when you create your list. As you think about the topic, write down words or phrases that come to mind. Do not worry about grammar or spelling; the point is to generate ideas.

Alicia's Brainstorming

Topic: Mistakes that college students make

- party too much
- not doing homework

- feeling too shy to speak with instructors when they have problems
- getting too stressed
- choosing the wrong career path
- don't know what they want to do
- feeling intimidated in class

Questioning

Another way to generate ideas about a topic is to ask yourself a series of questions and write responses to them. The questions can help you define and narrow your topic. One common way to do this is to ask yourself *who, what, when, where, why,* and *how* questions.

Alicia's Questioning

Who makes the most mistakes?	— first-year students because they aren't always prepared for college life
Why do some students miss classes?	— feel like there are no consequences, don't feel interested in their program
When do most students drop out?	— administrators say that November is the most common month that students drop out
How should colleges encourage students who are at risk of dropping out?	— give more financial aid — offer career counseling
Where can students get help?	— guidance counselors, instructors, friends, family, professionals doing student's dream job
Why is it an important topic?	— new students can learn about pitfalls to avoid, administrators can develop strategies for helping students

Clustering

Clustering is like drawing a word map; ideas are arranged in a visual image. To begin, write your topic in the middle of the page and draw a box or a circle around it. That idea will lead to another, so write the second idea and draw a line connecting it to your topic. Keep writing, circling, and connecting ideas until you have groups or "clusters" of them on your page.

Alicia's Clustering

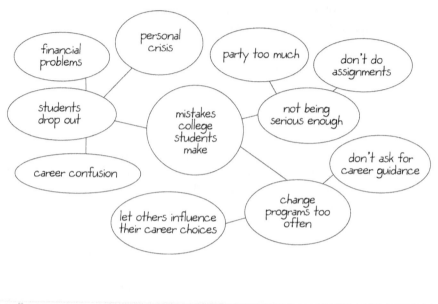

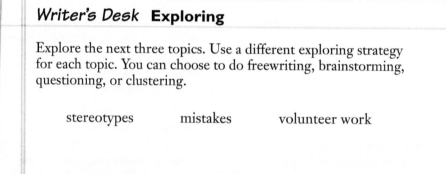

Writer's Desk **Exploring**

Explore the next three topics. Use a different exploring strategy for each topic. You can choose to do freewriting, brainstorming, questioning, or clustering.

stereotypes   mistakes   volunteer work

TRUMAN ASSIGNMENT 5   Choose one of the prewriting strategies discussed by Gaetz and Phadke. Then, use it to explore your responses to the prompt on the "Power of Reading" assignment sheet. Use either Alexie or Malcolm X's essay as a starting point. Go back and read what you have come up with, and highlight the portions that look the most promising as the focus of an essay or as a point that should be included in your essay. Be aware that you are not simply repeating what either author has written. You have prior knowledge and experience that help you to understand what they have written and also to agree or disagree with it.

Planning

CHAPTER 4

CONTENTS

Planning one's essay involves deciding on a main argument and figuring out what reasons and what pieces of supporting evidence are necessary to convince one's audience that the argument is thoughtful, well-reasoned, and worth consideration.

Key Steps in Developing the Main Idea

In Chapter 1, you learned how to consider your reading audience and your purposes for writing. You also practiced using exploring strategies to formulate ideas. In this chapter, you will focus on developing a main idea that can be expanded into a complete essay. There are two key steps in this process.

DEVELOPING THE MAIN IDEA

STEP 1   ➤   **Write a thesis statement.** Write a statement that expresses the main idea of the piece of writing.

STEP 2   ➤   **Develop the supporting ideas.** Find facts, examples, or anecdotes that best support your main idea.

Writing a Thesis Statement

The **thesis** is your main idea that you want to express. A clear thesis statement presents the topic of the essay, and it includes a **controlling idea** that expresses the writer's opinion, attitude, or feeling about the topic. The controlling idea can appear at the beginning or end of the thesis statement.

       topic   controlling idea

Art courses should be compulsory in all high schools.

              controlling idea   topic

School districts should stop funding **art courses.**

PRACTICE 1   Circle the topic and underline the controlling idea in each thesis statement.

EXAMPLE: (Insomnia) is caused by several factors.

1. Three strategies can help you become a better public speaker.

2. Moving to a new country was a traumatic experience for me.

3. There should not be racial profiling at borders.

4. School uniforms should be compulsory in public schools.

5. There are several reasons for Australia's compulsory voting system.

6. Phishing is a dangerous Internet scam.

7. My office is an obstacle course.

8. There are three types of annoying office workers.

Writing an Effective Thesis Statement

When you develop your thesis statement, ask yourself the following questions to help you avoid thesis statement errors.

1. **Is my thesis a complete statement?**
   Ensure that your thesis does not express an incomplete idea or more than one idea. A thesis statement should reveal one complete thought.

Incomplete:	Allergies: so annoying.
	(This is not a complete statement.)
More than one idea:	There are many types of allergens, and allergies affect people in different ways.
	(This statement contains two distinct ideas. Each idea could become an essay.)
Thesis statement:	Doctors suggest several steps people can take to relieve symptoms related to pet allergies.

2. **Does my thesis statement have a controlling idea?**
   Rather than announcing the topic, your thesis statement should make a point about the topic. It should have a controlling idea that expresses your attitude or feeling about the topic. Avoid phrases such as *My topic is* or *I will write about*.

Announces:	I will write about computers.
	(This sentence says nothing relevant about the topic. The reader does not know what the point of the essay is.)
Thesis statement:	When Microsoft develops a new operating system, there are political, financial, and environmental consequences.

3. **Can I support my thesis statement in an essay?**
   Your thesis statement should express an idea that you can support in an essay. If it is too narrow, you will find yourself with nothing to say. If it is too broad, you will have an endless composition.

Too broad:	There are many childless couples in our world.
	(This topic needs a more specific and narrow focus.)
Too narrow:	The average age of first-time mothers is approximately twenty-six years old.
	(It would be difficult to write an entire essay about this fact.)
Thesis statement:	Many couples are choosing to remain childless for several reasons.

4. **Does my thesis statement make a valid and interesting point?**
   Your thesis statement should make a valid point. It should not be a vaguely worded statement or an obvious and uninteresting comment.

Vague:	Censorship is a big problem.
	(For whom is it a big problem?)
Obvious:	The Internet is important.
	(So what? Everyone knows this.)
Invalid:	The Internet controls our lives.
	(This statement is difficult to believe or prove.)
Thesis statement:	The Internet has become a powerful presence in our personal, social, and working lives.

PRACTICE 2   Examine each statement.

- Write **TS** if it is an effective thesis statement.
- Write **I** if it is an incomplete idea.
- Write **M** if it contains more than one complete idea.
- Write **A** if it is an announcement.

EXAMPLE: This essay is about spousal abuse.   _A_

1. The high price of oil.   _____

2. My college has a great sports stadium, but it needs to give more help to female athletes.   _____

3. Nursing is extremely demanding.   _____

4. In this paper, I will discuss global warming.   _____

5. My subject is the torture of war prisoners.   _____

6. There are many excellent commercials on television, but some are too violent.   _____

7. The loss of a job can actually have positive effects on a person's life.   _____

8. The problem of negative election advertisements.   _____

PRACTICE 3   Examine each statement.

- Write **TS** if it is a complete thesis statement.
- Write **V** if it is too vague.
- Write **O** if it is too obvious.

EXAMPLE: Americans are more nationalistic.   _____V_____

1. New York has a large population.   _____

2. We had a major problem.   _____

3. Some adult children have legitimate reasons for moving back into their parents' homes.   _____

4. The roads are very crowded during holiday periods.   _____

5. There are several ways to do this.   _____

6. Children in our culture are changing.   _____

PRACTICE 4   Examine each pair of sentences.

- Write **B** if the sentence is too broad.
- Write **TS** if the sentence is an effective thesis statement.

EXAMPLE: __B__ Plants can help people.

__TS__ Learning to care for plants gave me unexpected pleasure.

1. _____ Music is important around the world.

   _____ Some simple steps can help you successfully promote your music.

2. _____ My neighborhood is being transformed by youth gangs.

   _____ Violence is a big problem everywhere.

3. _____ My life has been filled with mistakes.

   _____ My jealousy, insecurity, and anger ruined my first relationship.

4. _____ The car accident transformed my life.

   _____ Everybody's life has dramatic moments.

5. _____ Good e-mail manners are important in the business world.

   _____ Good manners are important.

PRACTICE 5   Examine each pair of sentences.

- Write **N** if the sentence is too narrow.
- Write **TS** if the sentence is an effective thesis statement.

EXAMPLE: _N_   I grow coriander in my garden.

   _TS_   Learning to care for plants gave me unexpected pleasure.

1. _____ My poodle's name is Short Stop.

   _____ Owning a pet taught me how to be more responsible.

2. _____ Our roads are very icy.

   _____ Driving in the winter requires particular skills.

3. _____ Carjacking rates have increased by 20 percent in our city.

   _____ You can avoid being a carjacking victim by taking the next steps.

4. _____ I hurt myself in various ways during my three days on the beach.

   _____ There are many sharp pieces of shell on the local beach.

5. _____ Identical twins who are raised together have distinct personalities.

   _____ My twin sisters have similar birthmarks on their necks.

Revising Your Thesis Statement

A thesis statement is like the foundation that holds up a house. If the thesis statement is weak, it is difficult to construct a solid and compelling essay. Most writers must revise their thesis statements to make them strong, interesting, and supportable.

When you plan your thesis, ask yourself if you can support it with at least three ideas. If not, you have to modify your thesis statement. To enliven a dead-end statement, ensure that your thesis can answer the *why, what,* or *how* questions. Sometimes, just by adding a few words, a dead-end statement becomes a supportable thesis.

Poor thesis: Many students drop out of college.

   (How could you develop this into an essay? It is a dead-end statement.)

Better thesis: Students drop out of college **for several reasons**.

   (You could support this thesis with at least three ideas. This thesis statement answers the question "Why?")

Hint   **Writing a Guided Thesis Statement**

Give enough details to make your thesis statement interesting. Your instructor may want you to guide the reader through your main points. To do this, mention your main and supporting ideas in your thesis statement. In other words, your thesis statement provides a map for the readers to follow.

Weak: My first job taught me many things.

Better: My first job taught me about the importance of responsibility, organization, and teamwork.

PRACTICE 6   The next thesis statements are weak. First, identify the problem with the statement (write *vague*, *incomplete*, and so on) and ask yourself questions to determine how you might be able to revise it. Then revise each statement to make it more forceful and focused.

EXAMPLE: Spousal abuse is a big problem.

Comments: _Obvious. Vague. For whom is it a problem? How is it a_
problem?

Revision: _Our state government should provide better support for_
victims of spousal abuse.

1. I will explain how the family is falling apart.
   Comments: _____
   Revision: _____

2. I made a difficult decision.
   Comments: _____
   Revision: _____

3. The media is essential in our lives.
   Comments: _____
   Revision: _____

4. I am an environmentalist.
   Comments: _____
   Revision: _____

5. Fashions are too impractical.
   Comments: _____
   _____
   Revision: _____

Overview: Writing a Thesis Statement

To create a forceful thesis statement, you should follow the next steps.

Step 1

Find your topic. You can use exploring strategies to get ideas.

General topic: Traditions

Brainstorming:
- Commercialization of holidays
- My family traditions
- Important ceremonies
- Why do we celebrate?
- Benefits of traditions
- Initiation ceremonies

Step 2

Narrow your topic. Decide what point you want to make.

Narrowed topic: Initiation ceremonies

Point I want to make: Initiation ceremonies can help people make the transition from childhood to adulthood.

Step 3

Develop a thesis statement that you can support with specific evidence. You may need to revise your statement several times.

Initial thesis statement: Initiation ceremonies serve a valuable function.

Revised thesis statement: Meaningful initiation ceremonies benefit individuals, families, and communities.

Writer's Desk **Write Thesis Statements**

Write a thesis statement for each of the next topics. If you explored these topics in Chapter 1, you can use those ideas to help you write your thesis statement. If you have not explored these topics yet, then spend a few minutes exploring them. Brainstorm some ideas for each topic to help you define and narrow them. Then develop a thesis statement that makes a point and is not too broad or too narrow.

stereotypes about beauty   mistakes in relationships   value of volunteer work

EXAMPLE Topic: Mistakes students make   Narrowed topic: *reasons students drop out*

Thesis statement: Students may drop out of college because they are unprepared, have financial problems, or experience an emotional crisis.

1. _____

   _____

2. _____

   _____

3. _____

   _____

Thesis Statements for Summary/Response Essays

Prompts that deal with objective readings will often ask questions about what the student thinks of a particular occurrence or situation reported on in a newspaper article. For example, one professor, as a response to a newspaper article about the Supreme Court's decision to let a church group protest near the funerals of American soldiers, asked her students to write whether the decision was a good one or not.

Thesis statements responding to such a prompt would answer the question and explain why.

- This answer can be fairly simple: I think __A__ because of __B__, __C__, and __D__.
  - Example: I think the Supreme Court's decision to allow the protests to continue was a bad one because it disrespects the families of soldiers, encourages intolerance, and makes our country look silly to the world.

- This answer can also be complex: I think __A__ because of __B__; however, __C__ is true because of __D__.
  - Example: The Supreme Court's decision to allow the protests to continue was a good decision for the country because it upholds the First Amendment; however, it was a bad decision for basic human decency because the death of someone who defended his or her country will forever be connected with negativity.

Prompts that deal with subjective readings often ask whether students agree or disagree with the author about something specific. For example, one teacher asked students to read Anna Quindlen's essay "Freedom's Just Another Word" and to write a summary/response essay that offered their opinions on whether the United States should make voting mandatory.

Thesis statements which respond to subjective readings can agree, disagree, or do both.

- I agree with __A__ about __B__ because of __C__, __D__, and __E__.
  - Example: I agree with Quindlen that citizens should be required by law to vote because what government does affects all of us and because people are unlikely to take this responsibility seriously if there is no punishment.

- I disagree with __A__ about __B__ because of __C__, __D__, and __E__.
  - Example: I disagree with Quindlen that voting should be mandatory because the U.S. is a free country, because people who are not forced to vote will probably make better decisions, and because it is just not easy for everyone to vote.

- A is correct about B, but I disagree with him/her about C and D because of E and F.

OR

- Although I do not believe B and C, A is right about E because of F and G.

OR

- While I agree with A that B, I disagree that C because of D and E.
  - <u>Example:</u> While I agree with Quindlen that voting is an important responsibility for anyone living in a democracy, I disagree that everyone should be required to vote because too many of the uninformed will make irresponsible choices for the rest of us.

One Step Further...

There is one last "trick" with thesis statements that respond to subjective readings. A student can agree with what an author argues but disagree with the way that he or she argues it.

Example: While I agree with Quindlen's solution to the problem of low voter turnout because few people volunteer to do something inconvenient even when it is important, I believe that she bullies her readers instead of convincing them, and this hurts her argument.

Developing the Supporting Ideas

The next step in essay writing is to plan your supporting ideas. Support is not simply a restatement of the thesis. The body paragraphs must develop and prove the validity of the thesis statement.

Each body paragraph has a **topic sentence** that expresses the main idea of the paragraph. Like a thesis statement, a topic sentence must have a controlling idea. Details and examples support the topic sentence. In the following illustration, you can see how the ideas flow in an essay. Topic sentences support the thesis statement, and details bolster the topic sentences. Every idea in the essay is unified and helps to strengthen the essay's thesis.

Thesis Statement

Topic Sentence 1

Topic Sentence 3

Topic Sentence 2

PRACTICE 7   Write a thesis statement for each group of supporting ideas. Ensure that your thesis statement is clear, makes a point, and is not too broad or too narrow.

EXAMPLE: Thesis: *When you buy a car, make an informed decision.*

   a. Ask family members what type of car they would prefer.

   b. Research on the Internet or in car guides to find information about specific models that interest you.

   c. Keeping your budget in mind, compare new and used cars.

1. Thesis: _____

_____

   a. First, internalize and believe in your sales pitch.

   b. Speak softly, and do not scare the customer with a commanding voice or aggressive mannerisms.

   c. Finally, involve the customer in your sales presentation.

2. Thesis: _____

_____

   a. When boys are in all-male classrooms, teachers can modify their activities to keep the boys' attention.

   b. All-female classrooms permit the female students to focus on the material and show their intelligence.

   c. Unlike co-education classrooms, same-gender classrooms are easier for teachers to control.

3. Thesis: _____

_____

   a. Most people under twenty-five years of age simply mimic how their parents or friends vote.

   b. To make an informed choice during an election, people need to have life experiences, which include paying rent and bills.

   c. Twenty-five-year-olds are also less likely to be manipulated by a politician because they have a stronger sense of what they want.

PRACTICE 8   Read the full essay in this practice and then do the following.

1. Determine the topic of each body paragraph. Then write a topic sentence for each body paragraph. Your topic sentence should have a controlling idea and express the main point of the paragraph.
2. Ask yourself what this essay is about. Then compose a thesis statement that sums up the main point of the essay. You might look in the concluding paragraph to get some ideas.

(Introduction) When I was a child, we had a daily routine. My parents both worked, but they got home at about 5 p.m. They spent about half an hour unwinding over a cup of coffee. Then they worked together to cook the meal, and by 6:30 they called us children to dinner. We ate and talked together. The same thing cannot be said about many families today.

Thesis Statement: _____

_____

_____

(Body 1) Topic Sentence:_____

_____

_____

Overtime was not so common in the past, but today many employers expect their workers to spend an extra hour or two in the workplace, so employees don't get home until 7 or 8 p.m. Also, children's lives are filled with more activities than they were in past decades. For example, my daughter takes dance class at 7 p.m., and my son gets together with friends for band practice every evening. They dash through the door at different times, throw a frozen pizza in the microwave, and eat alone.

(Body 2) Topic Sentence:_____

_____

The little box certainly is entertaining, but people won't talk about their daily experiences when the television is on. According to the Census Bureau, a growing number of families have placed televisions in the kitchen. "It keeps the sofas and carpets much cleaner if everybody just watches TV in the kitchen," says Sylvie Labelle, a mother of four. Thirteen-year-old Jeremy Labelle mentions, outside his mother's hearing, that he doesn't really talk to anybody in the family. Daily communication, which is an important staple for healthy family life, is disappearing and being replaced by a television set.

(Body 3) Topic Sentence:_____

_____

_____

Even a seven-year-old child can heat up his own dinner. Most parents don't want to cook from scratch after a long workday. Our grocery stores and specialty markets understand this need and provide families with a wide variety of frozen meals. Brigitte Lofgren says that the microwave oven is the most useful appliance in her house: "We all heat up our own meals. Nobody has to cook." When family members heat up their own meals, one after another, it is less likely that they will bother to eat together.

(Conclusion) Most families recognize that they are losing communication time. They watch in frustration as the family dinner disappears. They assure themselves that because of hectic lifestyles, they have no choice but to stagger eating times. Televisions on the kitchen counter provide something to focus on during meals. And the quality of prepackaged and frozen meals is improving, so who really needs to cook? Yet it is tragic that the family meal, a simple and effective way to keep family members linked together, is no longer a priority in many people's lives.

Generating Supporting Ideas

When you develop supporting ideas, ensure that they all focus on the central point that you are making in the thesis statement. To generate ideas for body paragraphs, you could use the exploring strategies (brainstorming, freewriting, clustering, or questioning) that you learned in Chapter 1.

Review the process that student Alicia Parera went through. First, she created a list to support her thesis statement. Then she reread her supporting ideas and removed ideas that she did not want to develop in her essay. She also grouped together related ideas.

Initial Ideas

Draft thesis statement: Students drop out of college for many reasons.

Supporting ideas:

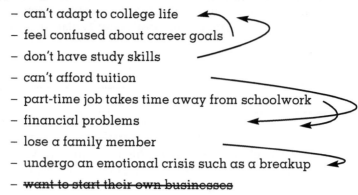

- can't adapt to college life
- feel confused about career goals
- don't have study skills
- can't afford tuition
- part-time job takes time away from schoolwork
- financial problems
- lose a family member
- undergo an emotional crisis such as a breakup
- ~~want to start their own businesses~~

After critically examining her supporting ideas, Alicia chose three that could become body paragraphs. She evaluated each set of linked ideas and summarized the connection between them. These sentence summaries then became her topic sentences. Alicia also reworked her thesis statement.

Revised Thesis and Supporting Points

Thesis Statement: Students may drop out of college because they are unprepared, have financial problems, or experience an emotional crisis.

Topic Sentence: Many students are unable to adapt to college life.

Topic Sentence: Some students face overwhelming financial burdens.

Topic Sentence: Furthermore, they may undergo an emotional crisis.

 **Look Critically at Your Supporting Ideas**

After you have made a list of supporting ideas, look at it carefully and ask yourself the next questions.

- **Which ideas could I develop into complete paragraphs?** Look for connections between supporting ideas. Group together ideas that have a common thread. Then create a topic sentence for each group of related ideas. In Alicia's example, three of her ideas became topic sentences.

- **Does each idea support my thesis?** Choose ideas that directly support the thesis statement and drop any ideas that might go off topic. In Alicia's example, the last idea, "Want to start their own businesses" didn't support her thesis, so she crossed it out.

PRACTICE 9   Brainstorm three supporting ideas for the next thesis statements. Find ideas that do not overlap, and ensure that your ideas support the thesis. (You can brainstorm a list of ideas on a separate sheet of paper, and then add the three best ideas here.)

EXAMPLE: Driving in the city is very stressful.

  – pedestrians and cyclists are careless

  – poor street planning has led to larger traffic jams

  – other drivers act in dangerous and erratic ways

1. Losing a job can have some positive consequences.

   _____

   _____

   _____

2. There are several concrete steps that you can take to help preserve the environment.

   _____

   _____

   _____

3. When young people move away from home, they quickly learn the next lessons.

   _____

   _____

   _____

Writer's Desk Generate Supporting Ideas

Brainstorm supporting ideas for two or three of your thesis statements from the previous Writer's Desk. Look critically at your lists of supporting ideas. Ask yourself which supporting ideas you could expand into body paragraphs, and then drop any unrelated ideas.

The Writer's Room **Topics to Develop**

Writing Activity 1

Choose one of the Writer's Room topics from Chapter 1 and write a thesis statement. Using an exploring strategy, develop supporting ideas for your thesis.

Writing Activity 2

Narrow one of the following topics. Then develop a thesis statement and some supporting ideas.

General Topics

1. good hygiene
2. annoying rules
3. delaying childbirth
4. traditions
5. allergies

College and Work-Related Topics

6. pressures students face
7. credit cards
8. creative teaching
9. improving services
10. benefits of extracurricular activities

THESIS STATEMENT AND TOPIC SENTENCES

When you write a thesis statement, ask yourself these questions.

Is my thesis a complete sentence?

Does it contain a narrowed topic and a controlling idea?

Is my main point clear and interesting?

Can the thesis be supported with several body paragraphs?

(Ensure that the topic is not too narrow, or you will hit a dead end with it. Also ensure that the topic is not too broad. Your essay requires a clear focus.)

Can I think of details, examples, and other ideas to support the thesis?

Is my thesis forceful and direct, and not too vague or obvious?

Does my thesis make a valid point?

Do I have good supporting ideas?

Does each topic sentence have a controlling idea and support the thesis statement?

More on Topic Sentences

Topic sentences in a summary/response essay should set up the argument for each body paragraph.

- A topic sentence should **NOT** be:
  - a question
  - a quote
  - a fact unless the paragraph is purely informative
  - a claim that is unrelated to the rest of your paragraph.

What Counts as Supporting Evidence

One of the most important points to remember about academic writing is that writers must do their best to prove the claims that they make, so what counts as proof?

- examples from students' personal experience
- examples from students' observations
- facts and statistics from previous reading and other sources
- logical reasoning
- paraphrased material from the original author
- quotes from the original reading or from some other source

Whenever students provide evidence of a claim, they must then explain how such evidence connects to the point that they are trying to make.

- Example: Voting is just not that important to people. According to Quindlen, less than half of Americans voted in the presidential election of 2004. These numbers did improve in the presidential election of 2008, but, when I watched the news in November of last year, they said that voter turnout in 2010 for Congress was far lower than two years before. With such low numbers, it is clear that average people find that work, school, and new episodes of *Jersey Shore* are much more significant to their lives than going to the polls.

A Word About Quotes in the Response

As in the summary, quotes should be included as quotation sandwiches. Quotation sandwiches introduce a quote and explain its relevance to your argument. It is confusing and interrupts the flow of paragraph when an author includes a quote without surrounding it without this important information.

Slice of Bread 1: introduction of the quote, Meat: quote, Slice of Bread 2: explanation of how the quote supports your topic sentence or the smaller claim that you are making

Example: While many praise the peaceful nature of Ghandi's and King's movements, their bravery was in their commitment to opposing their governments and
being on the wrong side of the law. Thoreau argues that when faced with the
choice of resisting the government or following one's own conscience, "it is not
desirable to cultivate a respect for the law, so much as the right. The only obligation which I have a right to assume is to do at any time what I think is right."
Following their own morality in this way landed Ghandi and King, as well as
Thoreau in his time, in jail and, later, earned them a place in the history books.

Supporting Paragraph Patterns of Organization

Information within body paragraphs often follows specific patterns that we call
rhetorical modes. Rhetoric is the art of communicating to an audience, and a mode
is a way of doing this. Here are some of the major rhetorical modes that we read
and use in writing:

- **Definition** is used to clarify a complex concept, a difficult word, or what you
  mean when you use a particular word or phrase.
    - Example: If someone grows up in a neighborhood like the one
      that I grew up in, being a good reader is often a matter of life and
      death. I don't mean that a thug will put a gun to a kid's head and
      tell him or her to read a page or die. What I do mean is that those
      of us who read well often do well in school and can, therefore,
      escape the neighborhood where our friends too often are either
      the kids who are killed or the kids who are doing the killing.

- **Classification** places a word, concept, or action into a particular category.
    - Example: Being motivated, persevering, and ignoring peer pres-
      sure are all actions that helped Alexie to succeed. They are what
      good readers need in order to turn what they can do with their
      minds into success. These are not talents or abilities that children
      are born with. These are the kinds of things that we can all learn
      and practice and get good at doing.

- **Comparison/contrast** points out the similarities and differences between
  things in order to make a point.
    - Example: Being tough can get a person the same amount of
      respect as does being smart, but the two kinds of respect don't last
      for the same amount of time. Tough guys get respect that is
      inspired by fear, and as soon as those who are fearful stop being
      afraid—even if just one person stands up to him—a tough guy can
      lose the respect of his peers. Smart guys, on the other hand, are
      respected because they inspire people, because people admire
      them, or because what they know helps others in some way.

Often, no matter what changes in their peers' lives, the smart guys will always garner some respect from them.

- **Argument** makes a claim and then supports it using evidence.
  - Example: Good readers get better jobs than do people who don't read. For example, a doctor is one of the highest careers that we have. A person who wants to become a doctor has to go to school for at least eight years with college and medical school. There are a lot of classes and a lot of books, and those books are tough ones, dealing with subjects like biology, chemistry, anatomy, and medical ethics. A person who only reads comic books or the Cliff's Notes of novels assigned in school is unlikely to become a doctor because he or she can't read the hard stuff.

- **Proposal** suggests a solution to a problem or an action that people should take.
  - Example: If someone does not consider himself or herself to be a good reader now, he or she does not have to accept that situation. Such a person should go to the nearest public library, sign up for a library card, and ask the librarian where the books are on subjects that interest him or her. The person can start with young adult novels that have been turned into movies, like *Hunger Games* or *Harry Potter*, or he or she can start with a biography of a famous person that he or she admires, like Bill Clinton or Condoleeza Rice.

Key Steps in Developing the Essay Plan

In the previous chapters, you learned how to use exploring strategies to formulate ideas and narrow topics. You also learned to develop main ideas for essays. In this chapter, you will focus on the third stage of the essay writing process: developing the essay plan. There are two key steps in this process.

DEVELOPING THE ESSAY PLAN

STEP 1 → **Organize your supporting ideas.** Choose an appropriate method of organization.

STEP 2 → **Write an essay plan.** Place your main and supporting ideas in an essay plan.

> *Good plans shape good decisions.*
> LESTER R. BIDDLE, Management Consultant

Organizing Supporting Ideas

Once you have a list of main ideas that will make up the body paragraphs in an essay, you will need to organize those ideas in a logical manner using time, space, or emphatic order.

Time Order

To organize an essay using **time order (chronological order),** arrange the details according to the sequence in which they have occurred. Time order can be effective for narrating a story, explaining how to do something, or describing an event.

first   then   after that

When you write essays using time order, you can use the following transitional expressions to help your readers understand when certain events happened.

after that	first	last	next
eventually	in the beginning	meanwhile	suddenly
finally	later	months after	then

PRACTICE I   The supporting ideas for the following thesis statement are organized using time order.

THESIS STATEMENT: My one and only ferry ride was a disaster.

1. To begin with, the only available seat was in a horrible location near the back of the boat.
2. Next, the rain began, and the passengers on deck rushed inside.
3. After that, the ferry began to rock, and some passengers became ill.

One paragraph from the essay also uses time order. Underline any words or phrases that help show time order.

> Next, the rain began, and the passengers on deck rushed inside. Suddenly, a sprinkle became a downpour. I was in the middle of the crowd, and water was running in rivulets down my face and down the back of my collar. Then, those behind me got impatient and began to shove. The doorway was narrow, and many people were jostling for position. I was pushed to the right and left. Meanwhile, I was soaked, tired, and cranky. The crowd squeezed me more and more. Finally, I was pushed through the door; I stumbled and tried not to fall. The inner seating room was so crowded that I had to stand in the aisle holding on to the back of one of the seats.

Emphatic Order

To organize the supporting details of an essay using **emphatic order**, arrange them in a logical sequence. For example, you can arrange details from least to most important, from general to specific, from least appealing to most appealing, and so on.

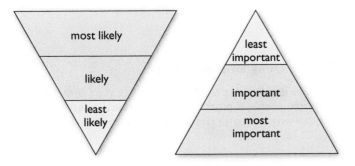

Here are some transitional expressions that help readers understand which ideas you want to emphasize the most or the least in the body paragraphs of an essay.

above all	first	moreover	principally
clearly	in particular	most importantly	the least important
especially	last	of course	the most important

PRACTICE 2   The supporting ideas for the following thesis statement are organized using emphatic order.

THESIS STATEMENT: In our city, some types of public transportation are more dependable and pleasant than others.

1. First, subways can be uncomfortable and even frightening.

2. Bus trips can have certain drawbacks.

3. The most pleasant and reliable way to travel seems to be the suburban train.

One paragraph from the essay also uses emphatic order. Underline any words or phrases that help show emphatic order.

> First, subways can be uncomfortable and even frightening. Above all, subway riders must deal with crowds. In front of the tracks, there is very little seating room, so people line the walls. Of course, the lighting is usually terrible, so ordinary people look sad and even sinister under the fluorescent tubes.

Feeling uncomfortable and unattractive, they avoid eye contact. Moreover, for those who feel claustrophobic, being in a subway can feel like being in a grave. There is no sunlight, no sky, and no outdoors for the entire duration of the journey. Passengers can only stare at the sullen faces of the other travelers. Clearly, the entire subway experience can be unpleasant and disturbing.

Hint **Using Emphatic Order**

When you organize details using emphatic order, use your own values and opinions to determine what is most or least important, upsetting, remarkable, and so on. Another writer may organize the same ideas in a different way.

Space Order

Organizing ideas using **space order** helps the reader to visualize what you are describing in a specific space. For example, you can describe someone or something from top to bottom or bottom to top, from left to right or right to left, or from far to near or near to far.

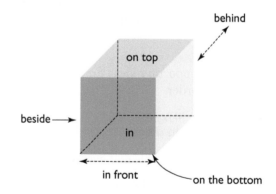

Help readers find their way through your essay by using the following transitional expressions.

above	beneath	nearby	on top
behind	closer in	on the bottom	toward
below	farther out	on the left	under

PRACTICE 3 The supporting ideas for the following thesis statement are organized using space order.

THESIS STATEMENT: With very little money, local students helped turn a tiny old house into a vibrant youth center.

1. Working outdoors, two students cleared the yard.

2. Focusing on the exterior surfaces of the building, a second team of students painted and made minor repairs.

3. Inside the house, some students turned the living room into a recreation and meeting place.

One paragraph from the essay also uses space order. Underline any words or phrases that indicate space order.

> Inside the house, some students turned the living room into a recreation and meeting place. First, they washed and then painted the walls. At the far end of the room, next to the fireplace, there was an old bar with an orange counter and frayed yellow bar stools. The students stripped and varnished the counter of the bar and cleaned the sink. They turned the space into an art corner. Local teenagers who like to paint and sculpt now have a nice workspace. In the center of the room, there was an area rope rug that had seen better days. They removed the rug and replaced it with woven straw matting. Beside the rug was a stained and smelly pink and green sofa. The students discarded the sofa. Rather than purchase a new one, which would have cost hundreds of dollars, they used the center's funds to buy large blue cushions at a discount department store. When the renovations were finished, the room looked like a new and fresh space.

Hint **Combining Time, Space, or Emphatic Order**

You will likely use more than one type of organizational method in an essay. For example, in a time order essay about a journey, one paragraph might be devoted to a particular place that you visited, and in that paragraph, you might use space order to describe the scene.

PRACTICE 4 Read each list of supporting ideas, and number the items in a logical order. Then write time, space, or emphatic to indicate the organization method.

EXAMPLE: Thesis Statement: Painting a basic picture can be a rewarding experience.

__1__ Choose a location that you find particularly peaceful.

__3__ Add colors to your sketch that best represent the mood you are feeling.

__2__ Settle in and make a preliminary sketch of the place.

Order: ___*time*___

1. Thesis Statement: Overexposure to the sun can have terrible consequences.

_____ The skin cells lose elasticity and wrinkles set in earlier.

_____ Some people develop cancers that can lead to premature death.

_____ Brown spots can develop on parts of the face.

Order: _____

2. Thesis Statement: We encountered many problems during our trip from Mexico City to Guadalajara.

_____ We arrived late at night and had a lot of trouble finding our friend's house.

_____ We didn't have enough money for the first tollbooth, so we took the side roads.

_____ On a small road halfway there, an accident completely blocked our route.

Order: _____

3. Thesis Statement: For an important interview, dress conservatively.

_____ Employers may notice every detail, so pay attention to your footwear.

_____ If possible, invest in a good haircut a few days before the interview.

_____ Wear a suit jacket and matching pants or a skirt.

Order: _____

4. Thesis Statement: Harold Roos should win the citizen's award for three reasons.

_____ Every Sunday, Mr. Roos does volunteer work at the hospital.

_____ Last September, Mr. Roos saved Eduardo Borsellino's life when he pulled the young man out of a submerged car.

_____ Mr. Roos employs many local citizens in his downtown clothing store.

Order: _____

Developing an Essay Plan

A contractor would never build a house without making a drawing or plan of it first. In the same way, an **essay plan** or an **outline** can help you to organize your thesis statement and supporting ideas before writing your first draft. Planning your essay actually saves you time because you have already figured out your supporting ideas and how to organize them so your readers can easily follow them. To create an essay plan, follow the next steps.

- Looking at the list of ideas that you created while prewriting, identify the ones that most effectively support your thesis statement.
- Next, write topic sentences that express the main supporting ideas.
- Finally, add details under each topic sentence.

A formal essay plan uses Roman numerals and letters to identify main and supporting ideas. A formal plan also contains complete sentences. The basic structure looks like this:

Thesis statement: _____

   I. _____

      A. _____

      B. _____

  II. _____

      A. _____

      B. _____

Concluding Idea: _____

In the planning stage, you do not have to develop your introduction and conclusion. It is sufficient to simply write your thesis statement and an idea for your conclusion. Later, when you write your essay, you can develop the introduction and conclusion.

Alicia's Essay Plan

Alicia Parera wrote topic sentences and supporting examples and organized her ideas into a plan. Notice that she begins with her thesis statement, and she indents her supporting ideas.

> **THESIS STATEMENT:** Students may drop out of college because they have financial problems, experience an emotional crisis, or are unprepared for college life.
>
>   I. Some students face overwhelming financial burdens.
>
>   A. They may have a part-time job to pay for such things as tuition and rent.

B. Moreover, a part-time job leaves no time for studying and homework.

C. Also, transportation may be expensive and beyond a student's means.

II. Furthermore, some students are faced with life-changing events and must leave college to cope.

A. A pregnancy and childbirth consume energy and attention.

B. Also, a serious illness or death in the family can cause a student to miss classes, and it becomes too difficult to catch up.

C. Of course, a broken relationship can cause a student to feel emotionally fragile and unable to concentrate.

III. They may be unprepared for college life.

A. They might have poor study skills.

B. Furthermore, some students cannot respect schedules.

C. The increased freedom in college causes some students to skip too many classes.

D. Additionally, many students feel confused about career goals and decide to leave college.

PRACTICE 5   Read the thesis statement and the list of supporting ideas and details. First, highlight three supporting ideas (topic sentences) and number them 1, 2, and 3. Then, using numbers such as *1a, 1b, 1c, 2a, 2b, 2c,* etc., organize the details that could follow each topic sentence. On a separate piece of paper, place the ideas in an essay plan.

THESIS STATEMENT: _Men have disadvantages at home and in the workplace._

- High-tower construction work, which is mainly done by males, is very risky.
- In family court, men do not get custody of children as often as women do.
- According to journalist Ian McArthur, most boys are told to "take it like a man" so they learn to rein in their emotions.
- More men do work that puts their lives at risk than women do.
- Sheila Siskel, a lawyer, acknowledges that many judges still consider the woman as the child's primary caregiver.
- Men are more likely to repair roofs, scale electrical poles, and operate heavy machinery.
- Greg Chu says, "It is unsatisfying and heartbreaking when I am reduced to visiting my own children twice a month!"
- Over ninety percent of workplace deaths happen to men, according to the U.S. Department of Labor Web site.
- Some men are ridiculed when they show emotion.

▶

- Manuel Figuera, a graphic designer, says, "Some believe a crying man is an emotional weakling or a wimp."
- Men's groups, including Divorced Dads, protest the attitudes of the courts toward fathers in their fight for parental rights.
- Movies such as *Saving Private Ryan* reinforce the stereotype that men must be stoic and control their emotions.

PRACTICE 6   On a separate sheet of paper, create an essay plan for the next thesis statement.

THESIS STATEMENT: Women have disadvantages at home and in the workplace.

PRACTICE 7   Read the following essay plan. Brainstorm and develop three supporting ideas for each topic sentence.

THESIS STATEMENT: Common fairy tales follow a certain model.

Topic Sentence: Fairy tales never mention a real date or place.

Supporting ideas:

_____

_____

_____

_____

_____

Topic Sentence: The main character must overcome great obstacles to achieve his or her goal.

Supporting ideas:

_____

_____

_____

_____

_____

Topic Sentence: The main character accomplishes his or her goals with the help of magic or some other unnatural phenomena.

Supporting ideas:

_____

_____

_____

_____

_____

PRACTICE 8   Read the following essay plan. Brainstorm and develop three supporting ideas for each topic sentence.

THESIS STATEMENT: I learned valuable lessons during my years in grammar school and high school.

Topic Sentence: First, I learned how to get along with others.

Supporting ideas:

_____

_____

_____

_____

_____

Topic Sentence: I learned to organize my time.

Supporting ideas:

_____

_____

_____

_____

_____

Topic Sentence: Most importantly, I learned about respect, compassion, and gratitude.

Supporting ideas:

_____

_____

_____

_____

_____

_____

A Note About Organization

In planning for summary/response and other types of essays, students will benefit most from organizing their essays using emphatic order. Most of us have arguments that have varying degrees of strength or importance. Writers must decide whether they want to capture their readers early with their strongest reasoning or whether they want to build up to their strongest argument so that the reader goes away with that point at the forefront of his or her thinking. This choice often depends on the topic of the essay, the audience for it, the strength of the arguments, and the writer's effectiveness in using the organizational structure. And sometimes it comes down to style. This writer likes to build her argument because she likes the idea of delivering a knockout punch after she has softened her readers up by throwing argumentative jabs earlier in the essay.

Essay Plan Template

You may use this template to plan your essay. Make sure your essay contains the folowing elements:

I. Introductory paragraph that:
    A. Introduces the topic and tries to interest or "hook" your reader
    B. Explains the issue—familiarizes your reader with the background information he/she needs to know to fully understand the issue (NOTE: This may include a summary or summaries of the reading sources to which you are responding, and this information may appear in the same paragraph as points A-C, or it may be in a separate introductory paragraph.)
    C. States your thesis/claim

II. Body of the essay
  A. Reason one and support
  B. Reason two and support
  C. Reason three and support
  D. Reason four and support

Note: One of your body paragraphs may include a fair and complete summary of an opposing viewpoint and your refutation or concession to the opposing view. You can also anticipate a counterargument for the specific point you are making in each body paragraph.

III. Concluding Paragraph that:
  A. Brings essay to a closure
  B. Restates thesis and sums up key support
  C. Leaves a strong last impression
  D. Often calls for action or relates topic to a larger context of issues

TRUMAN ASSIGNMENT 6   Use the essay plan template provided in the text or by your teacher to make an outline for your "Power of Reading" summary/response essay.

Drafting

Key Steps in Developing the First Draft

In previous chapters, you learned how to develop a thesis statement, support it with ideas, and create an essay plan. To develop a first draft, follow the next five steps.

> *Detail makes the difference between boring and perfect writing. It's the difference between a pencil sketch and a lush oil painting. As a writer, words are your paint. Use all the colors.*
>
> RHYS ALEXANDER,
> *Author*

DEVELOPING THE FIRST DRAFT

STEP 1	**Write an introduction.** Try to attract the reader's attention in the first paragraph of your essay.
STEP 2	**Write complete body paragraphs.** Expand each supporting idea with specific details.
STEP 3	**Write a conclusion.** Bring your essay to a satisfactory close.
STEP 4	**Title your essay.** Sum up your essay topic in a few words.
STEP 5	**Write the first draft.** Tie the introduction, body paragraphs, and conclusion into a cohesive essay.

Writing an Introduction

The **introductory paragraph** introduces the subject of your essay and contains the thesis statement. A strong introduction will capture the reader's attention and make him or her want to read on. Introductions may have a lead-in, and they can be developed in several different ways.

The Lead-In

The point of writing an essay is to have people read it and to entertain, inform, or persuade them. So, try to grab your readers' attention in the first sentence. There are three common lead-ins that you can try:

- a quotation
- a surprising or provocative statement
- a question

Introduction Styles

You can develop the introduction in several ways. Experiment with any of the following introduction styles.

- **Give general or historical background information** that gradually leads to your thesis. For example, in an essay about movie violence, you might begin by discussing some classic films.
- **Tell an interesting anecdote** or a story that leads to your thesis statement. For example, you might begin your essay about film violence by describing how aggressive your younger brother and his friends became after they watched the movie *Fight Club*.

- **Describe something in vivid detail,** and then state your thesis. For example, you might begin your essay about movie violence by describing a particularly gory film scene.
- **Define a term,** and then state your thesis. For example, in an essay about ways to avoid marital conflicts, you can begin by defining a happy marriage.
- **Present a contrasting position,** which is an idea that is the opposite of the one you will later develop, and then offer your thesis. Your readers will not expect you to present one side and then to argue for the other side. For example, in an essay about abortion, you might begin by presenting the arguments of those who would not agree with your particular point of view on the debate.
- **Pose several questions,** and end with a thesis statement. The purpose may be to engage your readers by inviting them to think about the topic. You might also ask questions that you will answer in your essay. For instance, in an essay about lotteries, you might ask: *Have you ever bought a lottery ticket? Why do so many people play lotteries?*

The next example presents the structure of a typical introduction.

Have good manners disappeared? In past centuries, a gentleman would spread his cloak over a muddy road so that his lady wouldn't dirty her feet. Twenty years ago, an elderly man or woman would never have to stand in a bus because other passengers would offer up their seats. Times have certainly changed. Today, many people lack consideration for others. **Parents and schools should teach children basic good manners.**

◄ Lead-in

◄ Historical background information

◄ Thesis statement

PRACTICE I Read the following introductions. Underline each thesis statement and determine what introduction style the writer used.

1. I got out of bed as usual. I shaved, showered and put on a clean shirt. Trotting out to the kitchen where my wife, Nadine, was standing, I looked at her and asked, "Now what?" The day before, I had accepted a generous buyout offer at Verizon Corp., effectively ending my thirty-year career there as a midlevel manager. I was fifty-one. With the papers in front of me, I listened patiently as my financial adviser cautioned me that some people in my position are not mentally prepared to retire, but I never dreamed that his advice would apply to me. I was wrong. Retirement left a void in my life that I filled in some odd ways.

   Peter Borghesi, "I Was Out of a Job and an Identity," *Newsweek*

   a. Underline the thesis statement.

   b. What is the introduction style? Indicate the best answer.

   _____ general background   _____ anecdote

   _____ definition   _____ questions

2. Adolescent males are dangerous. They join gangs, and they are responsible for most of the crime in our society. They drive too fast, causing accidents on our highways. They all experiment with drugs, and they annoy others with their loud music. But is such a portrayal of our nation's young men really fair? In fact, most stereotypes about adolescent males are incorrect and misleading.

    Abeer Hamad, student

    a. Underline the thesis statement.

    b. What type of lead-in did the writer use?

        _____ quotation   _____ question   _____ surprising
                                                                statement

    c. What is the introduction style? Indicate the best answer.

        _____ historical background   _____ anecdote

        _____ definition   _____ contrasting position

3. Where did you buy that blouse? I heard the question every time I wore it. It was a truly lovely designer model that had been marked down to $40. It was pale blue with swirling tiny flower buds running down each front panel. The little buttons were topped with imitation pearls. Unfortunately, the middle button kept coming undone. People at a certain angle to my left could peek in and view the lace eyelets on my brassiere. When I wore the blouse, my head kept bobbing down, looking to see if I was exposing myself. Over the years, I have had several humorous and embarrassing wardrobe and makeup malfunctions.

    Catalina Ortega, student

    a. Underline the thesis statement.

    b. What type of lead-in was used?

        _____ quotation   _____ question   _____ surprising
                                                                statement

    c. What is the introduction style? Indicate the best answer.

        _____ general background   _____ anecdote

        _____ definition   _____ description

4. Nationalism is the sometimes angry belief in the independence of one's people. It often includes resentment or even hatred of alien rulers or threatening foreigners: "No foreigners will push us

around!" It is the strongest and most emotional of the world's ideologies. Most of the world's people—including Americans— are nationalistic.

Michael G. Roskin and Nicholas O. Berry, *The New World of International Relations*

a. Underline the thesis statement.

b. What is the introduction style? Indicate the best answer.

_____ historical background   _____ anecdote

_____ definition   _____ contrasting position

5. "Men only." A century ago, the campuses of colleges and universities across the United States might as well have hung out that sign. Almost all of the students and faculty were male. There were a small number of women's colleges, but many more schools— including some of the best-known American universities, such as Yale, Harvard, and Princeton—barred women outright. Since then, women have won greater social equality. By 1980, the number of women enrolled at American colleges finally matched the number of men. In a surprising turn of events, women now outnumber men on college campuses for several reasons.

Adapted from John J. Macionis,
"The Twenty-First-Century Campus: Where Are the Men?" *Sociology*

a. Underline the thesis statement.

b. What type of lead-in was used?

_____ quotation   _____ question   _____ surprising
                                                    statement

c. What is the introduction style? Indicate the best answer.

_____ historical background   _____ anecdote

_____ definition   _____ questions

6. Why do some hip-hop artists embed jewels and gold in their teeth? Are the grills meant to impress others, or do the grills fit some deep need on the part of the artists to show that they matter? Is the hip-hop artist who shows off his "bling" any different than the accountant who buys a BMW to show that she has succeeded, or the corporate executive who marries a beautiful trophy wife?

> Showing off one's wealth is not new. In fact, throughout history, people have found extravagant ways to flaunt their wealth.
>
> Jamal Evans, student

a. Underline the thesis statement.

b. What is the introduction style? Indicate the best answer.

_____ general background   _____ anecdote

_____ definition   _____ questions

PRACTICE 2   Write interesting lead-ins (opening sentences) for the next topics. Use the type of lead-in that is indicated in parentheses.

EXAMPLE: Bicycle helmet laws   (question)

How many cyclists have needlessly died this year from head injuries?

1. dangerous dogs   (a surprising or controversial statement)

_____

_____

2. ridiculous fashions   (a question)

_____

_____

3. the junk food nation   (a surprising fact or idea)

_____

_____

PRACTICE 3   Choose _one_ of the next thesis statements. Then write three introductions using three different introduction styles. Use the same thesis statement in each introduction.

It's important to know more than one language.

Famous musicians generally make poor (or good) role models.

Computers have made our lives more complicated.

You can choose any three of the following introduction styles:

- Anecdote
- Description
- Definition
- Contrasting position
- Series of questions
- General or historical background

To sum up—Introductions allow the writer to do the following:

- Connect to the reader.
- Get the reader's attention.
- Present any important information that the reader needs to know.
- Lead the reader to the writer's thesis.

EXTRA PRACTICE   Match the introduction styles listed on pages 24 and 25 of Gaetz to its corresponding example.

EXAMPLE 1:

A good education is more than remembering the year of the Norman invasion of England or that the capital of Azerbaijan is Baku. It goes beyond stoichiometry, differential equations, and book reports. Such knowledge is good only for playing Trivial Pursuit or *Jeopardy!* if it is not coupled with creative, critical thinking and a desire to develop and answer one's own questions about life. Those who wish to reform America's educational system should redefine what it means to be educated. They should find a way to measure not retention of facts or memorization of the mathematical order of operations but students' ability to analyze, evaluate, research and problem solve.

Introduction style: _____

EXAMPLE 2:

When I arrived at college and was placed in an Honors calculus class with a lab at 8:00 a.m. Monday through Friday, I was only happy about it because if I received a grade of B or better, I would never again have to see the inside of a math classroom. For years, I never thought about math again beyond calculating my budget or the amount that I should leave for a tip. Then, as a substitute teacher, I landed in a junior high school math classroom for a week with no plans from the teacher, who had gone out-of-town unexpectedly. I remembered nothing specific about the math they were learning, but my education taught me how to think through the situation, gather my resources, and put together a plan that would help 13 year-olds learn pre-algebra for a week. It is this ability to think on one's feet, to analyze a problem, to sort through solutions, and to adapt when necessary that is the crux of any good education; unfortunately, Americans are losing this notion because multiple choice tests are easier to measure.

Introduction style: _____

EXAMPLE 3:

The question used to be "Why can't Johnny read?" But today, the better question is "Why doesn't Johnny read?" Our educational system tests the Johnnys and Janes of America to be sure that they can read well enough to pass a test of minimum comprehension or, more accurately, to be sure that they have minimum competency in multiple choice test-taking skills. But what good is this if students never read? Many students don't even read what's assigned to them, let alone read a book for pleasure or a newspaper for information beyond the sports or the advertisements for sales. Are we serving our students well by teaching them the definitions of words without teaching them to use those words in their writing and speech? Do we want them to know what global wanning is or the preamble to the U.S. Constitution simply to repeat it back on a test and then put it out of their minds? The truth is that until we teach our students how to think, to develop a desire for expanding their own knowledge, to come up with creative ways to solve problems, and to analyze and evaluate the information that they encounter in the world, our efforts in the classroom are simply exercises in futility.

Introduction style: _____

EXAMPLE 4:

In the last decade, not only have Americans' perceptions of the value of education changed, but there has been a constant redefining of what a good education actually is. President George W. Bush's No Child Left Behind education policy was an effort to equalize public education so that children in rural and inner city schools could get educations that were comparable to their suburban counterparts. The sentiment was a good one, but the policy did not work. While there were many problems with it, one of the most essential faults of the program was the idea that a good education should be measured by how well students performed on standardized tests. President Obama's Race to the Top program also errs in its reliance on standardized testing as the measure of success. What Americans must do if they are to succeed in helping all students to become well-educated is to refocus their measures of education to the ways that students learn to question, analyze, evaluate, argue and support themselves; the focus should be on changing the way that students think through life.

Introduction style: _____

EXAMPLE 5:

There is a classroom of 40 students all in various poses of test-taking distress. A few gnaw intermittently on the erasers of their number two pencils. One boy winces each time he fills in a bubble and then proceeds to erase every fifth answer and try again. Several students are bent over their desks like hunch backs, their once innocent faces warped into twisted frowns of concentration. The test's proctor, who is normally vivacious and familiar in her role as teacher, must limit her encouragement only to the cold words printed on her script. She interrupts the students, who all simultaneously look up, to tell them that their time has run out on this section of the test and that they must put their pencils down. This scene replays itself for hours, and after the children have gone home to their parents and their video games, all anyone has learned is that the Educational Testing Service employs sadists. Such tests should not be the measure of whether students have learned; rather, students' ability to think critically, to analyze and evaluate, to solve problems in the real world using knowledge and creativity does much more to demonstrate a student's educational attainment.

Introduction style: _____

EXAMPLE 6:

A student who graduates from elementary school should know his or her multiplication tables. He or she should be able to spell and repeat the definitions of vocabulary words appropriate for a sixth-grade level. Such a student should have completed a science project, read *Where the Red Fern Grows*, and know the presidential numbers of George Washington and Abraham Lincoln. Most importantly, the student should have passed every end-of-grade test and performed satisfactorily on the 3rd and 5th grade state proficiency tests. It does not matter whether the student has ever had an original thought, or whether his or her mission is simply to do as little as possible to get a good grade, or whether he or she gets uncomfortable when presented with more than one way to perform a task. The problem is that these lapses are exactly the things that do matter. Well-educated students should be able to collect data, analyze, comprehend, evaluate, and apply what they've learned to thinking through problems, whether in essays or on projects or in the real world, and these should be the measures that count.

Introduction style: _____

TRUMAN ASSIGNMENT 7   Choose one of the introduction styles and use it to create your own introduction paragraph to your "Power of Reading" summary/response essay. You can write a separate introduction or include your summary in the middle of your introduction paragraph, depending on what your teacher requires. Remember to include your thesis statement at the end of the paragraph.

Writing Complete Body Paragraphs

In your essay plan, you developed supporting ideas for your topic. When you prepare the first draft, you must flesh out those ideas. As you write each body paragraph, ensure that it is complete. Do not offer vague generalizations, and do not simply repeat your ideas. Provide evidence for each topic sentence by inserting specific details. You might include examples, facts, statistics, anecdotes, or quotations.

Examples are people, places, things, or events that illustrate your point. To support the view that some local buildings are eyesores, the writer could give the following examples.

> The car dealership on Labelle Boulevard is run-down.
>
> The gray block apartment buildings that line Main Street are monotonous.
>
> The Allen Drive mini-mall has tacky signs and cracked store windows.

Facts are objective details that can be verified by others. **Statistics** are facts that are expressed in percentages. (Make sure that your statistics are from reliable sources.) To support the view that transportation costs are too high for students, the following facts and statistics could be given as evidence.

> A one-way bus ticket now costs $3.50 for students.
>
> The monthly subway pass just increased to $260 for students.
>
> In a college survey of four hundred students, 70 percent expressed concern about the recent rate increases in public transportation.

Anecdotes are true experiences that you or someone else went through. An anecdote expresses what happened. **Quotations** are somebody's exact words, and they are set off in quotation marks. To support the view that lack of sleep can have dangerous consequences, the following anecdote and quotation could be included as evidence.

> When Allen Turner finished his nightshift, he got into his car and headed home. On Forest Drive, he started to nod off. Luckily, a truck driver in another lane noticed that Turner's car was weaving and honked. Turner said, "My eyes snapped open and I saw a wall growing larger in front of me. I slammed on my brakes just before smashing into it."

Essay with Sample Body Paragraphs

Read the next body paragraphs. Notice how they are fleshed out with specific evidence.

Thesis Statement:

> For personal and financial reasons, a growing number of adult children are choosing to live with their parents.

Body Paragraphs

The cost of education and housing is very high, so it is more economical to live at home. First, rents have increased dramatically since the 1990s. In *The Daily Journal,* Anna Reinhold states that ◄ fact rents tripled in the past ten years. During the same period, student wages have not risen as much as the rents. In fact, the minimum wage is still $6.15 an hour. Also, college fees are increasing each ◄ fact year. Tuition and fees at four-year public colleges rose $344, or 6.3 ◄ statistic percent this year, to an average of $5,836, according to the College Board's annual "Trends in College Pricing" report.

Many young people want to build a nest egg before moving out of the family home. When they remain at home, they can save income from part-time jobs. "I've saved $14,000 by staying in my ◄ quotation parents' place," says Kyle Nehme, a twenty-four-year-old student at the University of Texas. Such students do not need to worry about student loans. According to financial analyst Raul Gomez, "Students ◄ quotation who stay in the family home reap significant financial benefits."

Students who remain in their parents' home have a much more relaxed and comfortable lifestyle. Often, the parents do the shopping and housework. For example, Liz Allen, a twenty-six- ◄ anecdote year-old marketing student, moved back in with her parents last May. She discovered how much more convenient it was when someone else did the vacuuming, laundry, and cooking. Moreover, such students feel more secure and safe in the cocoon of home. In a *Daily Journal* survey of ninety adults who live at home, 64 percent ◄ statistic cited "comfort" as their major reason.

Hint   **Using Research to Support Your Point**

Your instructor might ask you to back up your ideas with research. You can look in several resources, including books, magazines, and the Internet, for relevant quotations, statistics, and factual evidence. For more information about doing research, see Chapter 16, The Research Essay.

PRACTICE 4 Make the next body paragraphs more complete by adding specific examples. You can include the following:

- examples
- anecdotes from your own life or from the lives of others
- quotations (for this exercise, you can make up punchy quotations)
- facts, statistics, or descriptions of events that you have read about or seen

Do not add general statements. Ensure that the details you add are very specific.

THESIS STATEMENT: Prospective pet owners should become informed before buying an animal.

Body Paragraph 1 First, when families choose a dog, they should consider the inconvenience and possible dangers. Some breeds of dogs can become extremely aggressive. _____

_____

_____

_____

_____ Moreover, dog owners must accept that dogs require a lot of time and attention. _____

_____

_____

_____ Furthermore, it is very expensive to own a dog. _____

_____

Body Paragraph 2 Some new pet owners decide to buy exotic pets. However, such pets come with very specific problems and require particular environments.

_____

_____ Also, some exotic pets seem interesting when they are young, but they can become distinctly annoying or dangerous when they reach maturity.

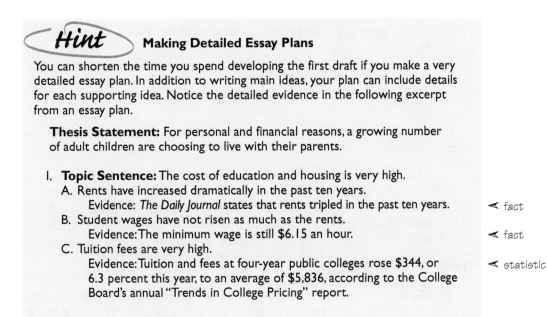

> ### Hint ⟩ **Making Detailed Essay Plans**
>
> You can shorten the time you spend developing the first draft if you make a very detailed essay plan. In addition to writing main ideas, your plan can include details for each supporting idea. Notice the detailed evidence in the following excerpt from an essay plan.
>
> **Thesis Statement:** For personal and financial reasons, a growing number of adult children are choosing to live with their parents.
>
> I. **Topic Sentence:** The cost of education and housing is very high.
>   A. Rents have increased dramatically in the past ten years.
>   Evidence: *The Daily Journal* states that rents tripled in the past ten years.   ◄ fact
>   B. Student wages have not risen as much as the rents.
>   Evidence: The minimum wage is still $6.15 an hour.   ◄ fact
>   C. Tuition fees are very high.
>   Evidence: Tuition and fees at four-year public colleges rose $344, or   ◄ statistic
>   6.3 percent this year, to an average of $5,836, according to the College
>   Board's annual "Trends in College Pricing" report.

Writer's Desk Make Complete Body Paragraphs

In Chapter 3, you prepared an essay plan. Now write complete body paragraphs for your essay. Ensure that each body paragraph contains specific details.

Writing a Conclusion

The **concluding paragraph** gives you one last chance to impress the reader and to make your point clear. A good conclusion makes the essay seem complete. One common and effective way to conclude a composition is to summarize the main ideas. The essay then comes full circle, and you remind the reader of your strongest points.

To make your conclusion more interesting and original, you could also close with a prediction, a suggestion, a quotation, or a call to action.

Hint   **Linking the Conclusion to the Introduction**

One effective way to conclude an essay is to continue an idea that was introduced in the introduction.

- If you began an anecdote in the introduction, you can finish it in the conclusion.
- If you posed some questions in the introduction, you can answer them in the conclusion.
- If you highlighted a problem in the introduction, you might suggest a solution in the conclusion.

Look at the concluding paragraph to an essay about etiquette in our technological age.

> Do not hide behind technology as your excuse for displaying rude or annoying behavior. You can turn off your cell phone when you are with someone you care about. If someone is writing an e-mail, do not read over his or her shoulder. Also, never send nor accept chain e-mails that promise wealth, happiness, or cures for cancer.

The last sentence in the essay could be one of the following.

Prediction: If you follow the basic rules of etiquette, you will ensure that your friends and colleagues maintain their respect for you.

Suggestion: The next time someone forwards you a nasty chain letter asking you to send it to at least ten people or else, return it to the sender ten times.

Quotation: As the French author Colette once said, "It is wise to apply the oils of refined politeness to the mechanism of friendship."

Call to Action: To help the next generation learn good manners, offer to teach a class to local high school students about etiquette in the technological age.

PRACTICE 5   Read the following conclusions and answer the questions.

A.   Laws designed to spook such scammers may be on the way, in the same way legislators tried to wipe out spam a few years ago. California Governor Arnold Schwarzenegger has approved legislation specifically outlawing such scams, giving prosecutors another tool to pursue the fraudulent. But it's still too early to measure whether such laws will be effective at curbing phishing attacks. Until then, consumers should continue to click carefully and be cautious about how and where they hand over personal information.

Mike Musgrove, "Phishing," *The Washington Post*

1. What method does the author use to end the conclusion? _____

B.   Just as a peacock spreads its tail feathers to attract the opposite sex, human beings flaunt their wealth to impress their mates and to establish their power over others. The grills on the teeth of hip-hop artists are simply modern versions of the Taj Mahal, the pyramids, or the elaborate castles of kings and queens. As Mel Brooks said in *The Producers*, "When you've got it, baby, flaunt it."

Jamal Evans, student

2. What method does the author use to end the conclusion? _____

C.   In this new millennium, let's put the concept of IQ to rest, once and for all. Stop giving IQ tests. Stop all the studies on IQ and birth order, IQ and nutrition, or IQ and Mozart. Let's find newer, more fluid, and more fair ways to debate and enable human potential. Let's use our heads for a change.

Dorothy Nixon, "Let's Stop Being Stupid About IQ"

3. What method does the author use to end the conclusion? _____

> *Hint*   **Avoiding Conclusion Problems**
>
> In your conclusion, do not contradict your main point, and do not introduce new or irrelevant information. Also, avoid ending your essay with a rhetorical question, which is a question that cannot be answered, such as "When will humans stop having wars?"

Writer's Desk **Write a Conclusion**

Write a conclusion for the essay you've been preparing in the previous Writer's Desk exercises.

Choosing an Essay Title

Think of a title *after* you have written your essay because you will have a more complete impression of your essay's main point. The most effective titles are brief, depict the topic and purpose of the essay, and attract the reader's attention.

Grammar Hint   **Capitalizing Titles**

Place your title at the top center of your page. Capitalize the first word of your title, and capitalize the main words except for prepositions (*in, at, for, to,* etc.) and articles (*a, an, the*). Leave about an inch of space between the title and the introductory paragraph.

Descriptive Titles

Descriptive titles are the most common titles in academic essays. They depict the topic of the essay clearly and concisely. Sometimes, the writer takes key words from the thesis statement and uses them in the title. Here are two examples of descriptive titles.

> Etiquette in the Technological Age
>
> Avoiding Mistakes in the First Year of College

Titles Related to the Writing Pattern

You can also relate your title directly to the writing pattern of your essay. Here are examples of titles for different writing patterns.

Illustration:	Problems with Internet Dating
Narration:	My Worst Nightmare
Description:	The Anniversary Party
Process:	How to Handle a Workplace Bully
Definition:	The Meaning of Tolerance
Classification:	Three Types of Fathers
Comparison and Contrast:	Fads Versus Timeless Fashions
Cause and Effect:	The Reasons People Pollute
Argument:	Why Writing Matters

> ## Hint   Avoiding Title Pitfalls
>
> When you write your title, watch out for problems.
>
> - Do not view your title as a substitute for a thesis statement.
> - Do not write a really long title because it can confuse readers.
> - Do not put quotation marks around the title of your essay.

PRACTICE 6   Read the next introductions and underline the thesis statements. Then write titles for each essay.

1. Some people fear mistakes more than others fear snakes. Perfectionism refers to self-defeating thoughts and behaviors aimed at reaching excessively high unrealistic goals. Unfortunately, nobody is perfect. In fact, there are many problems associated with the desire to be perfect.

   Title: _____

2. Gang life, once associated with large urban centers in the United States, has become a common part of adolescent experience in towns and rural areas. Many of the gang members have no strong role models at home, and their gang affiliation makes them feel like part of a powerful group. To combat the problems associated with youth gangs, adolescents need to be given more responsibilities in our society.

   Title: _____

3. "A person who is not initiated is still a child," says Malidoma Somé. Somé is from the Dagara Tribe in West Africa, and he underwent a six-week initiation ceremony. Left alone in the bush with no food or clothing, he developed a profound appreciation of nature and of magic. When he returned to his village, everyone welcomed him and other initiates with food and dancing. Somé had passed from childhood into adulthood and was expected to assume adult responsibilities. The ceremony helped Somé and the other initiates feel like valued participants in village life. Our culture should have formal initiation ceremonies for adolescents.

   Title: _____

PRACTICE 7   Read the next body paragraphs of a short essay. First, highlight the topic sentence in each body paragraph. Then, on a separate sheet of paper, develop a title, a compelling introduction, and a conclusion.

Add a title

Add an introduction

Body 1   First, family communication suffers when a television is present. The TV is turned on from morning to night. Families install televisions in the kitchen, living room, and bedrooms. Thus, in locations where families traditionally congregated to talk, they now sit mutely—sometimes next to each other—staring at the screen. Instead of reading a bedtime story together, families deposit children in front of the television to watch a bedtime video. Fourteen-year-old Annie Wong says, "When I get home from school, I head straight for my bedroom. I watch my shows in my room, and my brother watches the TV in the living room. I never have to talk to him."

Body 2   Too often, when people do communicate, their discussions revolve around television shows. It is common to hear people quoting Dr. Phil or Oprah, and water cooler conversations often revolve around the latest hot series. Thirty-year-old William and his friend Jay love nothing more than to reminisce about their favorite programs. When *Lost* was at its peak, they discussed each episode in detail. They also love theme songs. "I know the songs for about fifteen television shows," William says, as he proceeds to do the *Fresh Prince of Bel-Air* rap. Jay admits that his conversations with William rarely stray beyond the lightness of the television world.

Body 3   Most importantly, the health of children has changed since the introduction of television. Before televisions existed, children played outdoors and spent most of their free time doing physical activities. Today, most children pass hours sitting or lying down as they stare at the television screen. According to Anna Franklin, a researcher at the Mayo Clinic, such inactivity is contributing to the obesity epidemic in our nation. Ben Tyler, a 10-year-old from Fort Lauderdale, admits that he watches between six and eight hours of television each day. "I can watch whatever I want," he says proudly. But Ben is also overweight and suffers from asthma.

Add a conclusion

Writing the First Draft

After creating an introduction and conclusion, and after arranging the supporting ideas in a logical order, you are ready to write your first draft. The first
draft includes your introduction, several body paragraphs, and your concluding
paragraph.

The Effort Lecture

In English courses, students may be asked to write several drafts of an essay. This
does not mean that the students should do a poor job by not trying their best on
the first draft. Those students who put in their best efforts from the beginning of
the writing process through to the end will benefit most in the course because
(a) the teacher and student will be able to identify what the student actually has
trouble with and will be able to come up with targeted ways to improve, (b) the
teacher will not feel like his or her time is being wasted by a student who does not
care, and (c) the teacher won't decide that a student's writing and reading skills are
not sufficient for him or her to have placed into the 100 level English class or to
have passed the previous course.

TRUMAN ASSIGNMENT 8   Complete the first draft of your
"Power of Reading" summary/response essay.

CHAPTER 6

Revising and Editing

Key Steps in Revising and Editing

Revising and editing is the final step in the writing process. When you **revise**, you modify your writing to make it stronger and more convincing. To revise, read your first draft critically, and look for faulty logic, poor organization, or poor sentence style. Then reorganize and rewrite it, making any necessary changes. When you **edit**, you proofread your final draft for errors in grammar, spelling, punctuation, and mechanics.

There are five key steps to follow during the revising and editing stage.

REVISING AND EDITING

STEP 1	**Revise for unity.** Ensure that all parts of your work relate to the main idea.
STEP 2	**Revise for adequate support.** Determine that your details effectively support the main idea.
STEP 3	**Revise for coherence.** Verify that your ideas flow smoothly and logically.
STEP 4	**Revise for style.** Ensure that your sentences are varied and interesting.
STEP 5	**Edit for technical errors.** Proofread your work and correct errors in grammar, spelling, mechanics, and punctuation.

> *Mistakes obviously show us what needs improving. Without mistakes, how would we know what we had to work on?*
>
> PETER McWILLIAMS,
> *American author*

Revising for Unity

Unity means that the ideas in an essay clearly support the focus of the essay. All information heads in the same direction, and there are no forks in the road. If an essay lacks unity, then some ideas drift away from the main idea a writer has expressed in the essay. To check for unity in an essay, consider the following:

- Ensure that all topic sentences in the body paragraphs support the thesis statement of the essay.
- Ensure that all sentences within a body paragraph support the topic sentence of that paragraph.

Essay Without Unity

The next essay plan looks at the reasons for deforestation. The third topic sentence veers away from the writer's central focus that deforestation has implications for the quality of life.

Thesis Statement: Deforestation in the Amazon has tremendous implications for people's quality of life.

Topic Sentence 1: First, logging, mining, and agriculture displace indigenous people in the Amazon.

Topic Sentence 2: Also, scientists believe that deforestation in the Amazon will lead to a rapid increase in global climate change, which will affect people worldwide.

This topic sentence ➤ strays from the thesis of this essay.

Topic Sentence 3: Many development experts are trying to find methods to have sustainable development in the Amazon.

PRACTICE I The following thesis statements have three supporting points that can be developed into body paragraphs. Circle the point that does not support the thesis statement.

1. Thesis Statement: North America is developing a culture of victimization.
   a. First, many people blame their personal and professional problems on addiction.
   b. Furthermore, the increase in personal injury lawsuits suggests that more people see themselves as victims.
   c. In addition, lobbyists are petitioning on behalf of special interest groups.
2. Thesis Statement: International adoptions should be banned.
   a. An internationally adopted child will often lose contact with his or her culture.
   b. Too many celebrities have adopted internationally.
   c. By adopting from poor countries, westerners are complicit in the exploitation of poor people forced to give up their babies due to poverty.

Paragraph Without Unity

Not only must your essay have unity, but each body paragraph must have unity. The details in the paragraph must support the paragraph's topic sentence. The next paragraph is part of a larger work. In it, the writer drifted away from his main idea. Some sentences do not relate to the topic sentence. If the highlighted sentences are removed, then the paragraph has unity.

Americans should not fear the practice of outsourcing by businesses. First, outsourcing is the same practice as subcontracting. In the past, many companies subcontracted work to companies within the same country. Now, businesses simply subcontract to other nations. Furthermore, outsourcing usually leads to higher profits because the product or service is produced more cost effectively. Therefore, the head company's profit margin increases, allowing it to reinvest in domestic markets. In addition, when a company increases its profit, not only do the stockholders benefit, but so do the employees of the company. The stockholders receive more value for their stock, and the employees receive more salaries and benefits. My sister worked in computers and her job became obsolete when her company outsourced the work to India. Now my sister is devastated. She has lost her house and car, and she cannot find another job in her field. Thus, with more disposable incomes, people can help the domestic economy by buying more products.

≺ The writer detours here.

PRACTICE 2   Paragraphs A and B contain problems with unity. In each paragraph, underline the topic sentence and cross out any sentences that do not support the controlling idea.

Paragraph A

The gated community is an attempt to create a modern utopia. First, many people are buying property in gated communities because they want to feel more secure. Gated communities are surrounded by fences and guarded entrances. Therefore, tenants feel that crime will stop at the gate. People also buy homes in gated communities because they do not want to spend time maintaining the yard. Most gated communities have lawn mowing or snow clearing services available. In fact, home maintenance services are becoming very popular in all types of neighborhoods. Such services are not only meant for the elderly, but they are also meant for busy young families. For some people, gated communities give them a lifestyle choice. Since there are rules to follow in a gated community, some homeowners feel that they will be able to live in a community with likeminded neighbors. For example, people with similar religious values may want to live in one community. Thus, gated communities seem to be an attempt at creating utopian living conditions.

Paragraph B

The electric car is not as good for the environment as many people think. First, many people buy electric cars thinking that such vehicles produce no carbon dioxide emissions. Consumers forget how electricity is produced. Most electricity plants generate power by burning coal, oil, or diesel fuel. In fact, burning coal releases many contaminants into the air, which create a great deal of air pollution. Moreover, electric car batteries contain toxic ingredients. If these are not properly recycled, they could contaminate landfill sites. My friend is in the market for a car, and we are going to test-drive a few on the weekend. He is considering both new and used cars. So think carefully about environmental concerns before buying your next car.

Revising for Adequate Support

An arch is built using several well-placed stones. Like an arch, an essay requires **adequate support** to help it stand on its own.

When revising an essay for adequate support, consider the following:

- Ensure that your thesis statement is broad enough to develop several supporting points. It may be necessary to revise the thesis statement to meet the length requirements of the essay.
- When you write the body paragraphs of the essay, insert specific details and try to include vivid descriptions, anecdotes, examples, facts, or quotations.

Avoid Circular Reasoning

Circular reasoning means that a paragraph restates its main point in various ways but does not provide supporting details. Like driving aimlessly around and around a traffic circle, the main idea never seems to progress. Avoid using circular reasoning by directing your paragraph with a clear, concise topic sentence and by supporting the topic sentence with facts, examples, statistics, or anecdotes.

Paragraph with Circular Reasoning

The following paragraph contains circular reasoning. The main point is repeated over and over. The writer does not provide any evidence to support the topic sentence.

This writer leads the ➤
reader in circles.

> Traveling is a necessary educational tool. Students can learn a lot by visiting other places. Many schools offer educational trips to other places for their students. Students may benefit from such cultural introductions. Clearly, traveling offers students an important educational opportunity.

In the second version of this paragraph, the paragraph contains specific examples that help to illustrate the main point.

Revised Paragraph

Traveling is a necessary educational tool. Students can learn a lot by visiting other places. Many schools and colleges offer educational trips. On such trips, students visit museums, art galleries, and historical sites. For example, the art department of our college sponsored a trip to Washington, D.C., and the students visited the Smithsonian. Other travel programs are work programs. Students may travel to another region or country to be involved in a community project. Students in the local high school, for example, helped build a community center for children in a small town in Nicaragua. The students who participated in this project all said that they learned some very practical lessons, including organizational and construction skills. Clearly, traveling offers students an important educational opportunity.

< Anecdotes and examples provide supporting evidence.

PRACTICE 3   Read the following paragraphs and write OK next to the ones that have adequate support. Underline the specific details in those paragraphs. Then, to the paragraphs that lack adequate support, add details such as descriptions, examples, quotations, or anecdotes. Use arrows to indicate where you should place specific details.

The next example is from an essay. In the first paragraph, the writer was repetitive and vague. After the writer added specific examples and vivid details, the paragraph was much more interesting.

Weak Support

   To become a better dresser, follow the next steps. First, ask friends or family members what colors suit you. Also, don't be a slave to the latest fashion. Finally, spend money on a few good items rather than filling your closet with cheap outfits. My closet is half-full, but the clothing I have is of good quality.

Better Support with Details

   To become a better dresser, follow the next steps. First, ask friends or family members what colors suit you. *I love green, for instance, but when I wore an olive green shirt, a close friend said it brought out the green in my skin and made me look ill.* Also, don't be a slave to the latest fashion. *Although tank tops and low-waist jeans were popular for several years, I didn't have the right body type for that fashion because my belly spilled over the tops of my jeans. Instead, I wore longer shirts with my jeans, so I looked stylish but not ridiculous.* Finally, spend money on a few good items rather than filling your closet with cheap outfits. My closet is half-full, but the clothing I have is of good quality.

1. **Many cyclists are inconsiderate.** Some
think that they don't have to obey traffic rules
and that traffic signs are just for car drivers.
Also, some cyclists are pretty crazy and do
dangerous things and risk their lives or the
lives of others. People have ended up in the
hospital after a run-in with these two-wheeled
rebels. Cyclists should take safety courses
before they ride on public roads.

Write OK or add details

2. **During my first job interview, I managed
to overcome my fright.** I sat in a small,
brightly lit room in front of four interviewers.
A stern woman stared at me intently and curtly
asked me why I wanted the job. Perspiration
dripped into my eyes as I stammered that I
had seen an advertisement. She smirked and
asked me to be more specific. Feeling that I
didn't have a chance anyway, I relaxed and
stopped worrying about the faces gazing at
me. I spoke about my first experience in a
hospital, and I described the nurses who took
care of me and the respectful way the orderlies
treated me. I expressed my heartfelt desire to
work as an orderly, and I got the job.

Write OK or add details

3. **Hollywood producers should stop making
movies based on old television shows.** Many
of the original series were on television in the
1960s or 1970s, and younger audiences cannot
relate to movies based on those television shows.
Even when those programs were first on
the air, they were mediocre. The remakes are
boring for young people even when studios hire
stellar actors and spend fortunes on special
effects. Then the studio bosses are surprised
when the remakes are not successful. Hollywood
studios should realize that the public doesn't
want any more remakes of old television shows.

Write OK or add details

Revising for Coherence

Make your writing as smooth as possible by using expressions that logically guide the reader from one idea to the next. When revising an essay for **coherence**, consider the following:

- Ensure that sentences within each body paragraph flow smoothly by using transitional expressions.
- Ensure the supporting ideas of an essay are connected to each other and to the thesis statement by using paragraph links.

Transitional Expressions

Just as stepping stones can help you cross from one side of the water to the other, **transitional expressions** can help readers cross from idea to idea in an essay.

Here are some common transitional expressions.

Function	Transitional Word or Expression
Addition	again, also, besides, finally, first (second, third), for one thing, furthermore, in addition, in fact, last, moreover, next, then
Comparison and contrast	as well, equally, even so, however, in contrast, instead, likewise, nevertheless, on the contrary, on the other hand, similarly
Concession of a point	certainly, even so, indeed, of course, no doubt, to be sure
Effect or result	accordingly, as a result, consequently, hence, otherwise, then, therefore, thus
Emphasis	above all, clearly, first, especially, in fact, in particular, indeed, least of all, most important, most of all, of course, particularly, principally
Example	for example, for instance, in other words, in particular, namely, specifically, to illustrate
Reason or purpose	because, for this purpose, for this reason, the most important reason
Space	above, behind, below, beneath, beside, beyond, closer in, farther out, inside, near, nearby, on one side/the other side, on the bottom, on the left/right, on top, outside, to the north/east/south/west, under
Summary or conclusion	in conclusion, in other words, in short, generally, on the whole, therefore, thus, to conclude, to summarize, ultimately
Time	after that, at that time, at the moment, currently, earlier, eventually, first (second, etc.), gradually, immediately, in the beginning, in the future, in the past, later, meanwhile, months after, now, one day, presently, so far, subsequently, suddenly, then, these days

> ## Hint   Use Transitional Expressions with Complete Sentences
>
> When you add a transitional expression to a sentence, ensure that your sentence is complete. Your sentence must have a subject and a verb, and it must express a complete thought.
>
> **Incomplete:** For example, violence on television.
>
> **Complete:** For example, violence on television is very graphic.

Adding Transitional Words Within a Paragraph

The next paragraph shows transitional words linking sentences within a paragraph.

GRAMMAR LINK

For more practice using transitions in sentences, see Chapter 17, Compound Sentences, and Chapter 18, Complex Sentences.

   Learning a new language provides invaluable benefits to a person's life. **First**, researchers have found that learning a foreign language is a kind of exercise for the brain. It improves the area in the brain that processes information. Such people display better problem-solving abilities. **Furthermore**, people who know a second language can communicate with more people. **Therefore**, they can use this skill to acquire greater understanding of different cultures. **For example**, knowing a foreign language may give them more personal satisfaction when they are traveling because it allows them more opportunities to communicate with other people. **In addition**, bilingual people are more competitive in the job market. Because they know another language, they may be more mobile in their careers. They may **also** be able to take advantage of more job opportunities. In their spare time, people should learn a second language. They won't regret it.

PRACTICE 4   Add appropriate transitional expressions to the following paragraph. Choose from the following list, and use each transitional word once. There may be more than one correct answer.

in addition	therefore	in fact	for instance
first	then	for example	moreover

Counterculture is a pattern of beliefs and actions that oppose the cultural norms of a society. _____ hippies are the best-known counterculture group in the recent past, and they are known for rebelling against authority. _____ they rejected the consumer-based capitalist society of their parents in favor of communal living arrangements.

_____ the hippie generation valued peace and created a

massive antiwar movement. _____ there were mass protests

against the Vietnam War. _____ small religious groups belong

to the countercultural current. These groups live with other like-minded

people and turn away from widely accepted ideas on lifestyle.

_____ the Amish are pacifists, and they reject modern

technology. _____ militant groups and anarchist groups

reject conventional laws. Some of these groups want to eliminate legal,

political, and social institutions. Countercultural social patterns will always

remain part of the mainstream society.

PRACTICE 5 The next paragraph lacks transitional expressions. Add
appropriate transitional expressions wherever you think they are necessary.

People in our culture tend to idolize notorious gangsters. Al Capone operated

during Prohibition, selling alcohol and building a criminal empire. He became

infamous and his name is instantly recognizable. The Gotti family's patriarch was

the head of a large and vicious crime family in New Jersey. The family members

are celebrities and one of the daughters, Victoria Gotti, had her own reality

television show. Filmmakers contribute to the idealization of criminals. Movies

such as _The Godfather_ and _Live Free or Die Trying_ celebrate gangsters and criminals.

Gangsters appear to have exciting and glamorous lives. It is unfortunate that our

culture elevates criminals to heroic status.

Making Links in Essays

To achieve coherence in an essay, try the following methods to transition from one
idea to the next.

1. **Repeat words or phrases from the thesis statement in the topic sentence
   of each body paragraph.** In this example, _giftedness_ and _ambiguity_ are repeated
   words.

Thesis Statement:	Although many schools offer a program for <u>gifted</u> children, there continues to be <u>ambiguity</u> concerning the definition of <u>gifted</u>.
Body Paragraph 1:	One <u>ambiguity</u> is choosing the criteria for assessing the <u>gifted</u>.
Body Paragraph 2:	Another <u>ambiguity</u> pertains to defining the fields or areas in which a person is <u>gifted</u>.

2. **Refer to the main idea in the previous paragraph, and link it to your current topic sentence.** In the topic sentence for the second body paragraph, the writer reminds the reader of the first point (*insomnia*) and then introduces the next point.

Thesis Statement:	Sleeping disorders cause severe disruption to many people's lives.
Body Paragraph 1:	<u>Insomnia</u>, a common <u>sleep disorder</u>, severely limits the <u>sufferer's quality of life</u>.
Body Paragraph 2:	The <u>opposite condition of insomnia</u>, narcolepsy also causes <u>mayhem as the sufferer struggles to stay awake</u>.

3. **Use a transitional word or phrase to lead the reader to your next idea.**

Body Paragraph 3:	<u>Moreover</u>, when sufferers go untreated for their sleep disorders, they pose risks to the people around them.

Revising for Style

When you revise for sentence **style**, you ensure that your essay has concise and appropriate language and sentence variety. You can ask yourself the following questions.

- Have I used a variety of sentence patterns? (To practice using sentence variety, see Chapter 11.)
- Are my sentences parallel in structure? (To practice revising for parallel structure, see Chapter 14.)
- Have I used exact language? (To learn about slang, wordiness, and overused expressions, see Chapter 22.)

Alicia's Revision

In Chapter 3, you read Alicia's essay plan about college dropouts. After writing her first draft, she revised her essay. Look at her revisions for unity, support, coherence, and style.

Dropping Out of College   ◄ Add title.

I live in a small coastal town on the Atlantic. The town attracts

tourists from all over the country. Because of its beautiful beach.

My college roommate, Farrad, works as a cook at the local pizza

stand. Last year, Farrad started working a few hours per week,

but then because of his efficiency, his boss increased Farrad's

hours. My roommate then joined a growing group of people. He

became a college dropout. **Students may drop out of college**

because they lack financial support, experience an emotional   ◄ Thesis statement

crisis, or are unprepared.

First   ◄ Add transition.
~~S~~some students drop out because they face overwhelming

financial burdens. Like Farrad, they may have a part-time job to

help pay for tuition and rent. If the job requires students to work for

many hours, they might not have time to study or to do homework.
According to an Indiana government Web site, Investment Watch, "Teenagers and young   ◄ Add detail.
adults often find themselves in high debt with little knowledge of basic savings and budg-
eting concepts. About 40 percent of Americans spend 110 percent of their income."
Nadia, for exemple, works in the computer lab four nights a week.
The number of hours is overwhelming and she may drop out of college.   ◄ Add detail.
                                                              ◄ Clarify pronoun.
Some students
~~They~~ also drop out because they live far from campus, and

transportation may be too expensive or inconvenient.
                                        events, and they
Furthermore, some students undergo life-changing events. ~~They~~   ◄ Combine sentences.

must leave college. A college student may get married or a
In an interview with CNN, Dr. William Pepicello, President of the University of Phoenix,
stated that one reason that students drop out is "life gets in the way."
female student may become pregnant and taking care of a

baby may consume all of her time and energy. ~~There are public~~   ◄ Revise for unity.

~~and private daycare centers. But parents must choose very carefully.~~
In addition, an   ◄ Add transition.
~~An~~ illness in the family may cause a student to miss too many

classes. A student may feel emotionaly fragile because of a broken relationship. The student may not be able to cope with their

feelings and wanted to leave college.

Find better word. ➤

adapt to
Moreover, some students may be unable to ~~get into~~

college life. Some have poor study skills and fall behind in

homework assignments. Students may not be able to organize there

time. Or a student might be unused to freedom in college and skip

too many classes. For instance, my lab partner has missed about

Add transition. ➤

In addition, not
six classes this semester. ~~Not~~ every student has clear career goals.

Add detail. ➤

According to the National Academic Advising Association (NACADA) Web site,
75 percent of first-year students do not have clear career goals.
Those who are unsure about their academic futur may drop

out rather than continue to study in a field they do not enjoy.

Add detail. ➤

For instance, my cousin realized she did not want to be an engineer, so she left school
until she could figure out what she really wanted to do.
Even though students drop out of college for many good

Add transition. ➤

For example,
reasons, some decide to return to college life. Farrad hopes to

Improve conclusion. ➤

finish his studies next year. *He knows he would have to find a better balance*
between work and school to succeed, but he is motivated to complete his education.

> ## Hint **Enhancing Your Essay**
>
> When you revise, look at the strength of your supporting details. Ask yourself the
> following questions.
>
> - Are my supporting details interesting and will they grab my reader's attention?
>   Should I use more vivid vocabulary?
> - Is my concluding sentence appealing? Could I end the paragraph in a more
>   interesting way?

Editing for Errors

GRAMMAR LINK
To practice your editing skills, try the practices in Chapter 28.

When you **edit**, you reread your writing and make sure that it is free of errors.
You focus on the language, and you look for mistakes in grammar, punctuation,
mechanics, and spelling.

There is an editing guide on the inside back cover of this book. It contains some
common error codes that your instructor may use. It also provides you with a list of
errors to check for when you proofread your text.

Editing Tips

The following tips will help you to proofread your work more effectively.

- Put your text aside for a day or two before you do the editing. Sometimes, when you have been working closely with a text, you might not see the errors.
- Begin your proofreading at any stage of the writing process. For example, if you are not sure of the spelling of a word while writing the first draft, you could either highlight the word to remind yourself to verify it later, or you could immediately look up the word in the dictionary.
- Use the grammar and spelling checker that comes with your word processor. However, be vigilant when accepting the suggestions. Do not always choose the first suggestion for a correction. For example, a grammar checker cannot distinguish between when to use *which* and *that*. Make sure that suggestions are valid before you accept them.
- Keep a list of your common errors in a separate grammar log. When you finish a writing assignment, consult your error list and make sure that you have not repeated any of those errors. After you have received each corrected assignment from your instructor, you can add new errors to your list. For more information about a grammar and spelling log, see Appendix 5.

Alicia's Edited Essay

Alicia edited her essay about college dropouts. She corrected errors in spelling, punctuation, and grammar.

Dropping Out of College

I live in a small coastal town on the Atlantic. The town attracts

tourists from all over the country. ~~Because~~ *country because* of its beautiful beach.

My college roommate, Farrad, works as a cook at the local pizza

stand. Last year, Farrad started working a few hours per week, but

then because of his efficiency, his boss increased Farrad's hours.

My roommate then joined a growing group of people, and he

became a college dropout. Students may drop out of college

because they lack financial support, experience an emotional

crisis, or are unprepared.

First, some students drop out because they face overwhelming

financial burdens. Like Farrad, they may have a part-time job to help pay for tuition and rent. According to an Indiana government Web site, *Investment Watch*, "Teenagers and young adults often find themselves in high debt with little knowledge of basic savings and budgeting concepts. About 40 percent of Americans spend 110 percent of their income." If the job requires students to work for many hours, they might not have time to study or to do homework. Nadia, for ~~exemple~~ *example*, works in the computer lab four nights a week. The number of hours is overwhelming, and she may drop out of college. Some students also drop out because they live far from campus, and transportation may be too expensive or inconvenient.

Furthermore, some students undergo life-changing events, and they must leave college. In an interview with CNN, Dr. William Pepicello, President of the University of Phoenix, stated that one reason that students drop out is "life gets in the way." A college student may get married or a female student may become pregnant *, [add comma]* and taking care of a baby may consume all of her time and energy. In addition, an illness in the family may cause a student to miss too many classes. A student may also feel ~~emotionaly~~ *emotionally* fragile because of a broken relationship. The student may not be able to cope with ~~their~~ *his or her* feelings and ~~wanted~~ *want* to leave college.

Moreover, some students may be unable to adapt to college life. Some have poor study skills and fall behind in homework assignments. Also, students may not be able to organize ~~there~~ *their* time. Or a student might not be used to freedom in college and skip too many classes. For instance, my lab partner has missed about six classes this semester. In addition, not every student has clear career goals. According to the *National Academic Advising Association* (NACADA) Web site, 75 percent of first-year students do not have clear career goals. Those who are unsure about their academic ~~futur~~ *future* may drop out rather than continue to study in a field they do not enjoy. For instance, my cousin realized she did not want to be an engineer, so she left school until she could figure out what she really wanted to do.

Even though students drop out of college for many good reasons, some decide to return to college life. Farrad, for example, hopes to finish his studies next year. He knows he ~~would~~ *will* have to find a better balance between work and school to succeed, but he is motivated to complete his education.

Writer's Desk Revise and Edit Your Paragraph

Choose an essay that you have written for Chapter 4, or choose one that you have written for another assignment. Carefully revise and edit the essay. You can refer to the Revising and Editing checklists on the inside covers.

Peer Feedback

After you write an essay, it is useful to get peer feedback. Ask a friend, family member, or fellow student to read your work and give you comments and suggestions on its strengths and weaknesses.

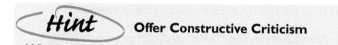

Hint **Offer Constructive Criticism**

When you peer edit someone else's writing, try to make your comments useful. Phrase your comments in a positive way. Look at the examples.

Instead of saying . . .	**You could say . . .**
You repeat the same words.	Maybe you could find synonyms for some words.
Your paragraphs are too short.	You could add more details here.

You can use this peer feedback form to evaluate written work.

Peer Feedback Form

Written by _____   Feedback by _____

Date: _____

1. What is the main point of the written work? _____

_____

_____

2. Which details effectively support the thesis statement? _____

_____

_____

3. What, if anything, is unclear or unnecessary? _____

_____

_____

4. Give some suggestions about how the work could be improved. _____

_____

_____

5. What is the most interesting or unique feature of this written work? _____

_____

_____

Writing the Final Draft

When you have finished making revisions on the first draft of your essay, write the final draft. Include all the changes that you have made during the revising and editing phases. Before you submit your final draft, proofread it one last time to ensure that you have caught any errors.

Writer's Desk **Write Your Final Draft**

You have developed, revised, and edited your essay. Now write the final draft.

 **Spelling, Grammar, and Vocabulary Logs**

• **Keep a Spelling and Grammar Log.** You probably repeat, over and over, the same types of grammar and spelling errors. You will find it very useful to record your repeated grammar mistakes in a Spelling and Grammar Log. You can refer to your list of spelling and grammar mistakes when you revise and edit your writing.

• **Keep a Vocabulary Log.** Expanding your vocabulary will be of enormous benefit to you as a writer. In a Vocabulary Log, you can make a list of unfamiliar words and their definitions.

See Appendix 5 for more information about spelling, grammar, and vocabulary logs.

 **Essay Topics**

Writing Activity 1

Choose an essay that you have written for this course or for another course. Revise and edit that essay, and then write a final draft.

Writing Activity 2

Choose any of the following topics, or choose your own topic, and then write an essay. Remember to follow the writing process.

General Topics

1. online shopping
2. heroes in sports
3. a problem in politics
4. unfair gender roles
5. making the world better

College and Work-Related Topics

6. something you learned in college
7. bad work habits
8. reasons to accept a job
9. unpleasant jobs
10. a funny co-worker

CHECKLIST: REVISING AND EDITING

When you revise and edit your essay, ask yourself the following questions.

Does my essay have **unity**? Ensure that every paragraph relates to the main idea.

Does my essay have **adequate support**? Verify that there are enough details and examples to support your main point.

Is my essay **coherent**? Try to use transitional expressions to link ideas.

Does my essay have good **style**? Check for varied sentence patterns and exact language.

Does my essay have any errors? **Edit** for errors in grammar, punctuation, spelling, and mechanics.

Is my **final draft** error-free?

Peer Review Worksheet

Work together with a classmate to analyze the writing of another pair of students. Read each paper with your partner, discussing and agreeing on whether it meets the criteria in the peer feedback form below. When you have finished writing your comments for each paper, meet with the other pair of students to give the authors feedback on their work.

Student Whose Essay is Being Reviewed: _____

Student Reviewer(s): _____

Part I: Introduction

1. Does the introduction provide the reader with sufficient background on the topic?

2. What is the thesis of the essay? State it in your own words by completing the following statement: "The main point of the essay is "

3. Does the writer take a clear stand on the issue being discussed?

4. Do you have any suggestions about how the writer could improve the introduction and/or the thesis?

Part II: The Body Paragraphs

5. Does the essay offer logical reasons that support the writer's thesis? If not, which paragraphs need help?

6. Consider the support the writer uses for his reasons. Where could the writer provide better evidence?

7. Do the body paragraphs do a good job integrating quotations/paraphrases/summaries? Mark the paragraphs that need help integrating sources.

8. Does the writer refute/concede to an opposing viewpoint? What is that viewpoint?

9. What does the student writer argue in response to the opposing viewpoint? Is it clear?

Part III: Conclusion

11. Has the writer done an effective job of showing his audience why the issue is an important one?

12. Do you have any suggestions for the conclusion?

Revision Checklist for essays in which summary and introduction paragraphs are separate

Does my essay have a summary, an introduction with a thesis statement at the end, three body paragraphs, and a conclusion? ☐ Yes   ☐ No

Does the first sentence of my summary include the required information? ☐ Yes   ☐ No

Does my summary cover the major arguments and reasons for those arguments given by the author? ☐ Yes   ☐ No

Does my summary stay away from random details? ☐ Yes   ☐ No

Does my essay use the simple present tense whenever I refer to what the author has written? ☐ Yes   ☐ No

Does my introduction paragraph "connect" to the issues raised in the summary? ☐ Yes   ☐ No

Does my thesis statement appear towards the end of the introduction paragraph? ☐ Yes   ☐ No

Does my thesis statement state clearly whether I agree and/or disagree with the author and why? ☐ Yes   ☐ No

Does each body paragraph begin with my making a claim that I can then prove with examples, observations, and logic? ☐ Yes   ☐ No

Do I give reasons and evidence for each opinion claim that I make? ☐ Yes   ☐ No

Do I make clear connections between the evidence that I give and the topic sentence that evidence is supposed to support? ☐ Yes   ☐ No

Is my conclusion clearly a conclusion without my adding the words "in conclusion?" ☐ Yes   ☐ No

Do I answer all questions and address all issues posed in the essay prompt or assignment sheet? ☐ Yes   ☐ No

Within paragraphs, do I avoid including any ideas or sentences that do not fit with the topic sentence of each or with the sentences around it? ☐ Yes   ☐ No

Are my sentences clearly worded? Do they avoid using words and phrases that I would have to explain later? ☐ Yes   ☐ No

Do I stay away from repeating words or ideas? ☐ Yes   ☐ No

Do I avoid run-ons, comma-splices, and sentence fragments? ☐ Yes   ☐ No

Do I spell as many words correctly as I can? ☐ Yes   ☐ No

Do I avoid subject/verb agreement errors? ☐ Yes   ☐ No

If you answered "no" to any of these questions, you will need to revise those areas of your essay.

Revision Checklist for essays in which the summary is within the introduction paragraph:

Does my essay have an introduction paragraph (which contains a summary and a thesis statement at the end), three body paragraphs, and a conclusion? ☐ Yes   ☐ No

Does the introduction paragraph begin with a "hook" that catches the reader's attention?
☐ Yes   ☐ No

Does the introduction contain some "lead-in" sentences?   ☐ Yes   ☐ No

Does the first sentence of my summary include the required information?   ☐ Yes   ☐ No

Does my summary cover the major arguments and reasons for those arguments given by the author?   ☐ Yes   ☐ No

Does my summary stay away from random details?   ☐ Yes   ☐ No

Does my essay use the simple present tense whenever I refer to what the author has written?
☐ Yes   ☐ No

Does my thesis statement appear towards the end of the introduction paragraph?   ☐ Yes   ☐ No

Does my thesis statement state clearly whether I agree and/or disagree with the author and why?
☐ Yes   ☐ No

Does each body paragraph begin with my making a claim that I can then prove with examples, observations, and logic?   ☐ Yes   ☐ No

Do I give reasons and evidence for each opinion claim that I make?   ☐ Yes   ☐ No

Do I make clear connections between the evidence that I give and the topic sentence that evidence is supposed to support?   ☐ Yes   ☐ No

Is my conclusion clearly a conclusion without my adding the words "in conclusion?"   ☐ Yes   ☐ No

Do I answer all questions and address all issues posed in the essay prompt or assignment sheet?
☐ Yes   ☐ No

Within paragraphs, do I avoid including any ideas or sentences that do not fit with the topic sentence of each or with the sentences around it?   ☐ Yes   ☐ No

Are my sentences clearly worded? Do they avoid using words and phrases that I would have to explain later?   ☐ Yes   ☐ No

Do I stay away from repeating words or ideas?   ☐ Yes   ☐ No

Do I avoid run-ons, comma-splices, and sentence fragments?   ☐ Yes   ☐ No

Do I spell as many words correctly as I can?   ☐ Yes   ☐ No

Do I avoid subject/verb agreement errors?   ☐ Yes   ☐ No

If you answered "no" to any of these questions, you will need to revise those areas of your essay.

A Final Word from Truman

Students should remember that writing is a process and that they will not learn everything all in one class period (or even in one semester). It will take time for students to learn how best to improve their papers, and as the course continues, they will learn ways to move their papers beyond the basic patterns laid out here. As students learn, they should go back to earlier papers and make changes to them. Students should get feedback from their teachers during their office hours or should go see a tutor. A student will improve most if he or she uses all of the time and resources available to you to learn how to write good academic papers.

Two-Source Summary/Response Essay

CHAPTER 7

CONTENTS

Writing Skill Focus: Two-Source Summary/Response Essay

In this type of essay, you will respond in writing to *two* sources you have read, rather than one.

There are various writing prompts for this type of essay. A common one is to compare or contrast two situations or characters you have read about. Another one is to discuss how a theory/position/set of guidelines proposed by one author applies to *another* situation. In this case, when you read the theory, argument, position, or guidelines being proposed, you might also analyze the author's **purpose, tone, and bias.** When you read the second source, you might examine to what degree the theory, argument, position, or guidelines from the *first* source are being followed, OR you may assess whether or not the theories, arguments, etc. from the first source are applicable to the situation in the second source.

This type of writing requires you to read critically and thoroughly understand these *two* sources before you respond!

Author's Purpose:
Why has the author written his/her text?
- To inform
- To persuade
- To instruct
- To entertain

Author's Tone:
How does the author feel about the topic? (Some examples)
- Neutral
- Critical
- Supportive

Author's Bias:
What is the author's attitude toward the topic?
- Unbiased (the author does not take one side or the other)
- Positive about the topic
- Negative about the topic

NOTE: For a thorough discussion of purpose, tone, and bias, see *Making Reading Relevant*, chapter 4, Part b.

Writing in the Real World

Comparing two sources or applying information from one source to another is not just required in writing class. It's important in other courses, too. Here are some examples of how you might be asked to do this in different academic areas:

- Discuss to what extent the argument anthropologist Margaret Mead makes in her article "Grandparents Have Copped Out" has affected the Indian-

American family in Jhumpa Lahiri's short story "Unaccustomed Earth" (Anthropology)
- Read the discussion of the tools for diagnosis in your nursing textbook. Then look at a case study and explain how you should work with the patient. (Nursing)
- Read the chapter in your textbook on the periodic table of the elements. Then read the attached description of a new, mystery element. Based on the description of the new element, explain where you think it belongs in the periodic table and support your opinion. (Chemistry)

Example Essay

Here, you will see the "full cycle" of a student's two-source summary/response essay assignment. You will read the articles that the student was assigned to read. Then, you will see the essay that the student wrote, and you will analyze how the student composed the essay.

Articles

An Introduction to Meeting the Needs of English Language Learners

by Manka M. Varghese

In this article, I aim to provide an overview of some of the critical information that teachers in U.S. public schools would find helpful to know about their students whose first language is not English. I first provide a synopsis of the nature of today's immigrant student population, and then summarize some of the major legal guidelines for teachers to be cognizant of in relation to these students. In the last two sections, I look at some programmatic options for teachers to be aware of, and finally some specific strategies and resources for teachers to consider when planning their instruction.

In recent years, there has been a rapid increase of students in K-12 classrooms who are designated as Limited English Proficient (L.E.P.) or English Language Learners, ELLs, as they will be referred to in this article. From 1997–2000, ELL student enrollment grew by almost 30% (Kindler, 2002) and state educational agencies reported that in the 1999–2000 school year, almost 10% of all U.S. school children were classified as ELLs.

According to the U.S. Department of Education, nearly one in 12, almost 4 million public school children, received special assistance to learn English in 2001–2002. Many school districts have 50 or more languages represented although more than 90% of immigrant students are from the following language groups: Spanish, Tagalog, Chinese and Hmong.

Although the United States has always been a land of immigrants, the nature of immigration in the recent past is markedly different from early waves of immigration (Suarez-Orozco & Suarez-Orozco, 1995; Gibson). Most importantly, the "new immigrants," people who have immigrated since the 1970s, are people of color, coming from Central and South America, the Caribbean and Southeast Asia. There is also a greater range in terms of languages spoken and in educational level, social class, economic capital represented in this groups. Perhaps paradoxically, many of today's immigrants are more likely than their native born counterparts to have family members who graduated from college and also more likely to have not graduated from high school themselves.

What is also dramatically different at present is the nature of employment trends in the U.S., where there are fewer manufacturing jobs and more service and technology-related jobs, which in turn require skilled labor and a college degree. Therefore, immigrants of today face a job market which requires higher educational accomplishments than their earlier predecessors. It is also important to note that one third of ELL students were born in the United States (and therefore, were not recent arrivals) to families in which English is not regularly spoken in the home (Fleischman & Hopstock, 1993).

As we all know, all teachers are responsible in a moral, ethical and legal sense for all their students, including their ELL students. But often, many teachers ask what the specific legal requirements are that their school districts and schools must meet in relation to these students. These students, like all others, are protected by Title VI (of the Civil Rights Act), stating that "school systems . . . (are) responsible for assuring that students of a particular race, color, or national origin are not denied the opportunity to obtain the education generally obtained by other students in the system" (quoted in Lyons, 1990, p.70). A section of the U.S. Equal Educational Opportunities Act (EEOC), the federal agency responsible for interpreting and enforcing Title VI, adds that states are mandated also to protect and help students "overcome language barriers that impede equal participation by its students in its instructional programs."

The protection and assistance for students whose first language is not English were legislated through the landmark case of Lau vs. Nichols (1974), where a class-action suit was filed by the parents of Chinese speaking students in San Francisco Public Schools who stated that their children were not given equal educational opportunities because of the linguistic barriers they faced.

From this court case and several subsequent ones, three specific guidelines need to be met by all school districts: (i) all ELL students need to be identified and assessed throughout their educational program, (ii) a program of specific instruction, based on sound educational research, needs to be provided for these students, implemented effectively, and evaluated after a trial period, and (iii) parents whose first language is not English must have all documents which are sent home translated into their native language.

One of the major complaints of advocates for ELL students has been that these guidelines are not specific enough, especially the fact that there is a lack of a mandate for the specific instructional approach that schools and districts must follow. Other legal specifications that are important to know about are those passed in the Plyer vs. Doe case (1982) where the following was ruled: (i) public schools were prohibited from denying immigrant students access to K-12 public education, (ii) immigrant students residing in the United States cannot be denied resident status by public schools solely on the basis of their immigration status, and (iii) making inquiries that might expose the undocumented status of a student or the parents is prohibited.

Since there have not been specific mandates concerning the type of instructional program or approach, the natural question to ask is what programs are available and which program has yielded the best results for ELL students. The six major program types (e.g. ESL, two way bilingual education) can be found in August & Hakuta's (1997) seminal summary report on research on ELL students, although it is important to keep in mind that often these programs are implemented in a hybrid form. Critics and advocates of bilingual education have reviewed these programs to prove either the strength of ESL or bilingual programs.

In a recent study by Thomas & Collier (2001) on studies involving over 24,000 language minority children, these researchers found that children bilingual programs (maintenance and two way) had the highest academic and English language achievement. In general, ELL students who have the highest achievement in both these areas are students who come from a higher socioeconomic status, are literate in their first language, and have had high quality exposure and instruction in English, their primary language and in academic subject areas.

August & Hakuta (1997), in the same report mentioned above, also review the research on characteristics and optimal conditions in schools and classrooms rather than on program types, which can provide us a list of "best practices" for schools and districts. These practices are stated as the following:

A supportive school-wide climate, school leadership, a customized learning environment, articulation and coordination within and between schools, use of native language and culture in instruction, a balanced curriculum that includes both basic and higher-order skills, explicit skill instruction, opportunities for student-directed instruction, use of instructional strategies that enhance understanding, opportunities for practice, systematic student assessment, staff development, and home and parent involvement. (August & Hakuta, 1997, p. 171)

Teachers can be involved in attempting to make their schools more like environments described above. In their classrooms, they obviously must provide a meaning-based, context-rich and cognitively demanding curriculum. An example of this can be found in a recent piece published by the American Educational Research Association (2004), on boosting academic achievement of ELLs in terms of literacy, where the following critical components of reading instruction for these students are provided:

1. Explicit instruction in word recognition through phonological awareness, practice reading, phonics and frequent in-class assessments.
2. Explicit instruction in skills that are needed to understand text, such as vocabulary building in context, strategies to aid comprehension, academic oral language.

Other specific guidelines that would be useful to attempt to adopt are provided in this section. One of the major understandings that practitioners and scholars have reached is that ELL students cannot be provided special assistance only in the English language. They must be provided assistance also in acquiring subject-specific knowledge in several ways. It can be done with bilingual education (subject specific knowledge through their primary language), with richer and more sustained collaborations between content area teachers and English language specialists so that pullout classes do not only focus on decontextualized skills and language. Many content area teachers need training in making language and content more accessible to ELL students (as with SDAIE specifically designed academic instruction in English.) It can also be done by training these teachers in Sheltered English through a more comprehensive program called the Sheltered Instruction Observation Protocol, S.I.O.P. See resource list at the end of the article.

Teachers must also be aware that learning another language, especially becoming academic competent in it, is a lengthy process, that can take from 7–10 years (Cummins, 1981a, Cummins 1981b), as compared to conversational proficiency in a language which can take from 1–5 years. The rationale behind this is that academic, decontextualized language or content offers few clues for learners and is therefore much more difficult to learn.

This is especially true for students who start this process in the later grades (Collier, 1989; Cummins & Swain, 1986,) for students who are not literate or academically skilled in their first language, and for many who come from war torn countries. Therefore, the process for learning a second language is generally idiosyncratic, and dependent on different variables, which need to be considered.

Teachers must attempt to provide ELLs with explicit instruction in different strategies for gaining academic competence—cognitive, metacognitive and social (Chamot & O'Malley, 1992). For example, when asking students to write a summary, teachers (even content teachers, such as Social Studies or Science) cannot assume that students will know how to write a summary and must either teach them the necessary steps to write a summary or collaborate with an English language specialist to accomplish this.

Finally, the classroom and the environment must be a welcoming place for students and their families. Implicit rules must be made explicit. The cultural and linguistic resources that students come with (especially with the involvement of parents and community partners) must be integrated and celebrated in the classroom. A last word of caution for teachers is that although this issue has been framed mainly as a "language" issue, we must always remember that the education of linguistically diverse students is always situated in larger issues about immigration, distribution of wealth and power, and the empowerment of students. It is thus essential for teacher professional development to encompass knowledge, skills and dispositions to meet the needs of ELLs.

Since this article is only a brief introduction to meeting the needs of English Language Learners, I conclude by providing a list of useful resources for teachers and other practitioners to look up as a "starter kit". These resources are divided into books, professional associations, and web sites.

References

American Educational Research Association. (2004). English Language Learners: Boosting Academic Achievement. Essential Information for Education Policy, 2(1). Washington, D.C. : Author.

August, D. & Hakuta, K. (Eds). (1997). Improving Schooling for Language Minority Students: A Research Agenda. Washington, D.C.: National Academy Press.

Chamot, A. U. & O'Malley, J. M. (1992). The CALLA Handbook: Implementing the Cognitive Academic Language Learning Approach: Reading. MA: Addison-Wesley.

Collier, V. (1989). "How Long? A Synthesis of Research on Academic Achievement in a Second Language." TESOL Quarterly, 21(4), 617–641.

Cummins, J. (1981a). "Four Misconceptions about Language Proficiency in Bilingual Education." NABE Journal, 5(3), 31–45.

Cummins, J. (1981b). "The Role of Primary Language Development in Promoting Educational Success for Language Minority Students." In California State Department of Education (Ed.), Schooling and Language Minority Students: A Theoretical Framework, (pp. 3–49). Los Angeles: Evaluation, Dissemination and Assessment Center.

Cummins, J. & Swain, M. (1986). Bilingualism in Education. New York: Longman.

Fleischman, H. L. & Hopstock, P.J. (1983). Descriptive Study of Services to Limited English Proficient Students. Arlington, VA: Development Associates, Inc.

Gibson, M. A. (1997). "Complicating the Immigrant/Involuntary Minority Typology." Anthropology & Education Quarterly, 28(3), 431–454.

Kindler, A. L. (2002). Survey of the L.E.P. Students and Available Educational Programs and Services, 2000–2001 Survey Report. Washington, D.C.: National Clearinghouse for English Language Acquisition and Language Instruction Educational Programs.

Lyons, J. J. (1990). "The Past and Future Directions of Federal Bilingual-Education Policy." In C.B. Cazden & C.E. Snow (Eds.), Annals of the American Academy of Political and Social Science: Volume 508. English Plus: Issues in bilingual education (pp. 66–80). Newbury Park, CA: Sage.

Suarez-Orozco, C. & Suarez-Orozco, M. M. (1995). Transformations: Immigration, Family Life, and Achievement Motivation Among Latino Adolescents. Stanford, CA: Stanford University Press.

Thomas, W. P. & Collier, V. P. (2001). A National Study of School Effectiveness for Language Minority Students' Long Term Academic Achievement. Center for Research on Education, Diversity and Excellent.

The Positive Impact of English Language Learners at an Urban School

By Ted Appel & Larry Ferlazzo

Luther Burbank High School, Sacramento's (CA) largest inner-city high school with 2,000 students, and the school with the largest number of English Language Learners in the entire region (over half of our students are ELL's), recently became one of the few high schools in the nation to come out of Program Improvement (PI) status after having been a PI school for six years. Program Improvement is the designation assigned schools by the No Child Left Behind Act (NCLB) if they have not met a number of academic benchmarks. Approximately forty percent of our student body is Asian (largely, but not exclusively, Hmong, including 200 pre-literate refugees who came to our school three years ago and whose scores are included in NCLB rankings), twenty percent is African-American, and twenty-seven percent is Latino.

There were many causes for this turn-around, including dividing our school into Small Learning Communities with about 300 students each who stayed together, and with the same group of teachers, for their four-year high school career.

It's also important to highlight what we **did not** do—we didn't "teach to the test." Instead, we specifically focused on developing life-long learners recognizing that while there might be short-term pain in terms of test scores, there would ultimately be long-term gain for students and the school.

We believe that having large numbers of English Language Learners did not inhibit our escaping NCLB sanctions. On the contrary, we believe that having to address the needs of our large number of English Language Learners had a very positive impact on instruction for *all* of our students. Looking at ELL's through this *asset* lens is very different from the *deficit* lens through which they are usually perceived.

Professional Development

All of our teachers have had to learn how to effectively teach English Language Learners simply because all of our classes have significant numbers of ELL's in them. Graphic organizers, visual supports, cooperative learning, modeling, and accessing prior knowledge are just a few of the instructional strategies that are used school-wide.

Of course, all of these teaching methods are effective with any type of struggling student, whether they are struggling because of language or because of some other challenge.

Our large number of English Language Learners pushed our school and faculty to invest in professional development so that our teachers would learn and refine these skills. Time and resources have been made for extensive in-service training and peer-to-peer support, including observations and weekly "study teams" where groups of teachers meet to enhance their professional practice.

Creating Life-Long Learners

As we mentioned earlier, we have been very intentional about not "teaching to the test." We are committed to having our entire curriculum both accessible and academically stimulating and challenging.

All of our incoming ninth graders, for example, immediately begin to learn *strategies* and not just *skills* in their classes. Someone once said that a skill is knowing how to put your key in a lock and turn it. A strategy is knowing what to do when you can't find your keys. This is emphasized from our Beginning ESL classes to our advanced International Baccalaureate ones. Because of this school-wide commitment to higher-order thinking development, our teachers need to use effective ELL teaching strategies to ensure that all our students—ELL and non-ELL—develop this capacity.

Our ESL program (know in California schools as ELD—English Language Development) has hundreds of students at Beginning and Intermediate English levels. Teachers and students in those classes initiated educational technology projects (see Language Magazine, August 2007) and international online collaborations that are now not just being considered for replication by other non-ELD classes in our school, but by schools around the world. In addition, The Write Institute () writing curriculum for English Language Learners was found to be so effective in our ELD classes that portions are now used in a number of other classes on campus.

Burbank also has an International Baccalaureate (IB) program, and we do not recruit students to participate in IB from outside our attendance boundaries. We are committed to making the IB curriculum accessible to all our students, including our English Language Learners.

Student & Parent Relationships

Social capital, the value placed on trusting and valuable interpersonal relationships, is being recognized more and more by researchers as a key component of a successful school. Burbank prides itself on the supportive relationships teachers develop with their students, and those that students can develop with each other, through being connected in the same Small Learning Community for four years.

There are other ways where those relationships are nurtured, specifically connected to English Language Learners.

A number of our ELD classes have "sister classes" within our school— connections to classes that have more native English speakers. For example, one ELD class uses a Dialogue Journal, a tried and true ELL teaching tool where students typically write to their teacher and then the teacher writes a response. Somewhere within that response the teacher includes something the student wrote, but in the correct " form." The idea is that the student will learn without feeling that he/she has been corrected, and will continue to feel comfortable taking writing risks.

The difference in this case is that the Dialogue Journal is written to a pen pal in an eleventh and twelfth grade class whose teacher uses it as a component of writing instruction for her students. Both classes get together periodically as well, and work together on a variety of other projects.

Burbank has also developed parent engagement programs particular to the needs of English Language Learners. Working with parents and a local university, one hundred parents, many monolingual in their native language, meet regularly to learn and discuss topics that they choose, ranging from immigration issues to how they can best help their children succeed academically. The meetings/workshops are run in multiple languages through a simultaneous translation system with headphones.

In addition, ELL parents and students worked with Burbank staff to develop a family literacy effort where we provide home computers and wireless Internet service to assist in English study at home, which was awarded the 2007 International Reading Association Presidential Award For Reading and Technology. Finally, hundreds of home visits are made with interpreters by teachers and other Burbank staff each year.

School Support of Heritage Cultures

Hmong for Hmong speakers and Spanish for Spanish speakers are popular classes on campus, and research shows that increased academic mastery of a heritage language leads to higher academic achievement.

In addition, we have student leadership classes (for credit) both during and after-school that are multi-racial as well also culturally-specific, including Latino/Latina Leadership, Hmong (and Men's) Women's Circles, Hmong Cultural Club, and the Pacific Islanders club. We have similar classes for African-American students.

We do not have specific data that points to which of these elements have contributed to a larger or smaller degree to our academic success. However, we can say that our rate of absenteeism compares quite favorably to other high schools, and we can say that we are no longer a Program Improvement school.

So, we can say we must be doing something right. . . .

Ted Appel is the principal of Luther Burbank High School in Sacramento, California. Larry Ferlazzo teaches English and Social Studies at Burbank.

ASSIGNMENT: Write an essay in which you summarize the article "An Introduction to Meeting the Needs of English Language Learners" and then evaluate how well Luther Burbank High School (in the article "The Positive Impact of English Language Learners at an Urban School") is meeting the needs of its English Language Learners.

When immigrants come to the US, they bring their children with them, and it is the responsibility of public schools to meet the language and educational needs of these new, young Americans. Nevertheless, although schools are required by law to serve these students, it is often hard to determine which types of instructional programs are most effective. In the article "An Introduction to Meeting the Needs of English Language Learners," published by New Horizons for Learning, Manka M. Varghese proposes guidelines for what schools and teachers can do to help these students and their families adjust to the new language and community. Recommended strategies include involving the entire school in educating English Language Learners, offering a challenging academic environment, and engaging in family outreach. Luther Burbank High School, as described in the article "The Positive Impact of English Language Learners at an Urban School," is an outstanding example of how a school can help English Language Learners (ELLs) and their families not only adjust but thrive in their new environment.

Varghese reports that English language learners have the best chances for success when the entire school supports them, which means that the education of ELLs should involve not only ESL teachers but content teachers and the native-English speaking students as well. Varghese recommends that teachers use instructional strategies to help make it easier for ELL students to learn content, and Burbank High School has firmly embraced this philosophy by making sure that all teachers use special techniques such as "graphic organizers, visual supports, cooperative learning, modeling, and accessing prior knowledge" in their classrooms. Varghese also proposes the need for staff development and providing "richer and more sustained collaborations between content area teachers and English language specialists," and Burbank High School actively incorporates this practice by giving its teachers frequent in-service training and having teachers form groups and meet regularly in order to discuss teaching techniques. In addition to having the support of teachers in other disciplines, Burbank also involves native-English-speaking students in helping ELL students. In its "sister classes," ELL students are paired with native-English speaker students for writing activities and other projects. These aspects of Burbank High School reflect the fact that English Language Learners occupy a central focus at this school.

Burbank High School is also engaging in best practice for English Language Learners by providing these students with an academically challenging environment. Varghese argues for a "meaning-based, context-rich and cognitively demanding curriculum" and Burbank High School demonstrates this with its "school-wide commitment to higher-order thinking development." Their emphasis on having students develop strategies for solving problems rather than simply teaching students how to do something is a clear example of this. Moreover, their extensive use of technology from even the earliest level of ESL instruction demonstrates their high expectations for ELLs. They report that their online participation with schools in other countries has become a model for schools around the world. Perhaps most impressive in their high academic standards for ELLs is their inclusion of English Language Learners in the rigorous International Baccalaureate program, which has traditionally been geared toward native-English-speaking students.

In addition to putting English language learners at the forefront of their school and challenging them to excel academically, the most innovative programming for English Language Learners at Burbank High School is its extensive involvement of parents. Varghese emphasizes the importance of making the students' families a part of the learning community, and Burbank High School has gone way beyond that recommendation. Using the school's resources, Burbank teachers and staff bring interpreters along with them when they visit parents at home every year, thus enabling them to involve parents who are not fluent in English in their children's learning process. Furthermore, Burbank staff helps these parents become literate in English by providing computers and internet programs for home study. Moreover, Burbank feels so strongly about educating parents along with ELL students that they have gone outside their institution and teamed up with a local university to provide the parents with high-interest workshops offered in their native languages. Although Burbank already excels at supporting the ELL students at their school, these parent outreach programs demonstrate how Burbank High School exceeds expectations in order make the students and their families feel fully integrated into the school.

Burbank High School is clearly a model of successful support for immigrant students. Through its many high-quality programs, particularly its comprehensive parental education initiatives, it fulfills many of the suggestions provided by Varghese. With the strong presence of English Language Learners in classrooms across the country, it is essential that more schools embrace these practices and enable these students to reach their highest potential in our ethnically diverse nation.

Genre Analysis Questions

1. What did the student writer do in the first paragraph?
2. Is there a thesis? Where is it?
3. How many points does the student writer use to develop his/her thesis?
4. Where do these points appear?
5. How does the student writer support each point?
6. What does the student writer do in the final paragraph?
7. How is this essay similar to the essays we read in previous chapters? How is it different?

Consider how well the student writer consistently applied one source to another.

Note how the student writer connects one body paragraph to another.

Prewriting (matrix)

For essays where you must apply information from one source to another, it is often helpful to create a "matrix," which provides a visual display of the "connection" between the two sources.

For instance, in the example essay, the student writer listed the key ways mentioned in the first article to help English Language Learners succeed and then filled in the evidence of this, from the second article:

"An Introduction to Meeting the Needs of English Language Learners"	"The Positive Impact of English Language Learners at an Urban School"
"Supportive school-wide climate" (p. 3, par. 3)	"Sister Classes" "Dialogue Journals" (p. 3) "School support of heritage cultures"— ethnic clubs, leadership classes (p. 4)
Use of native language/bilingual instruction (p. 3, par. 3, par. 4)	Heritage language classes (p. 4)
Curriculum—"basic and higher-order skills" (p. 3, par. 3, par. 4)	"creating life-long learners" (p. 2) Technology in curriculum (p. 2) IB program (pp. 2–3)
Instructional strategies (p. 3, par. 3; p. 4, par. 3)	"graphic organizers, visual supports, cooperative learning, modeling, and assessing prior knowledge" (p. 1, par. 5)
Staff development (p. 3, par. 3, par. 5)	"professional development" (p. 1, par. 5); "in-service training, peer-to-peer support, study teams" (p. 2, par. 2)
Assessment (p. 3, par. 3)	
Home and parent involvement (p. 3, par. 3; p. 4, par. 4)	"Student & Parent Relationships" meetings & workshops for parents, family literacy program (p. 3)

- Pay attention to quoting and paraphrasing when you fill in the matrix; if you copy something directly (word-for-word) from the source, put it in quotation marks.
- Include page and paragraph numbers so that you can quickly find this information.

Thesis Statement/Outline

After the student writer completed the matrix, she then studied it in order to come up with a thesis statement (in response to the prompt) and outline the key points that would support her thesis.

Review the student's matrix and compare it to the outline below. Notice how she "grouped" the information from the matrix into three key points, which formed the support for her thesis. Also notice what information from the matrix she wound up NOT using in her essay.

ACTIVITY: Fill in the missing parts of the outline for the response section of the example essay, which you have read previously.

THESIS STATEMENT

Luther Burbank High School, as described in the article "The Positive Impact of English Language Learners at an Urban School," is an outstanding example of how a school can help English Language Learners (ELLs) and their families not only adjust but thrive in their new environment.

I. Support of entire school
   A. Instructional strategies
      Detail/Example _____
   B. _____
      Detail/Example: <u>in-service training, group meetings</u>
   C. Involvement of native-speaker Students
      Detail/Example _____

II. Academically challenging environment
   A. "School-wide commitment to higher-order thinking development"
      Detail/Example _____
   B. _____
      Detail/Example: <u>online participation with schools from other countries</u>
   C. IB program
      Detail/Example _____

III. Innovative involvement of parents
   A. Using the school's resources
      Detail/Example _____
      Detail/Example: <u>literacy program</u>
   B. With a university partner
      Detail/Example _____

Writing Assignments

Article: How to Bring Our Schools Out of the 20th Century
http://www.time.com/time/magazine/article/0,9171,1568480,00.html

Article: Building a New Student in Michigan
http://www.time.com/time/nation/article/0,8,599,1568853,00.html

Prompt: Write an essay in which you summarize the article "How to Bring Our Schools Out of the 20th Century" and then *rank* (1st place, 2nd place, 3rd place) the three high schools discussed in the article "Building a New Student in Michigan" according to the criteria for preparing students for the 21st Century (discussed in the 1st article). Be sure to explain WHY each school is at this ranking.

Article: The Future of Education: Textbooks vs. eBooks
http://www.bookhitch.com/archives/082009a-future.aspx

Article: Toward an All E-Textbook Campus
http://www.insidehighered.com/news/2009/01/14/ebooks

Prompt: Write an essay in which you summarize the article "The Future of Education: Textbooks vs. eBooks and then argue whether Northwest Missouri State University, discussed in the article "Toward an All E-Textbook Campus," is making the right decision about e-books for their students.

Prewriting

Choose one of the assignments and make sure you fully understand the prompt. Then, use the "matrix" strategy to explore ideas for your essay.

For example, to create a matrix for assignment 1, you might follow these steps:

1. List the important competencies from the "How to Bring Our Schools Out of the 20th Century" article in the first column of the matrix.
2. List the three schools from the "Building a New Student in Michigan" in the next three columns.
3. Fill in what each school is doing to meet the competencies listed in the first column.

The matrix might start out like this:

How to Bring Our Schools Out of the 20th Century	Henry Ford Academy	Farmington H.S.	Roosevelt High
"Knowing more about the world" "Global trade literate, sensitive to foreign cultures, conversant in different languages"		Internationally-focused studies—Model U.N., debates, rigorous curriculum	
"Thinking Outside the Box" ability to be creative & innovative; ability to see connections among disciplines	Connects academic world with real word (e.g., learning about economics by working in the school's "village")	Independent student research; student-produced multimedia presentations	

Now, create a matrix (on a separate sheet of paper), for the two sources you will be using in your assignment.

Organizing Your Writing Through Outlining

After you have generated ideas through the matrix, you must organize those ideas in a way that will effectively present your argument to your reader. Once you've completed your matrix, do the following steps:

1. Re-read the writing prompt for the assignment.
2. Review the matrix to see which items can be "grouped" into key points, which items are details/examples for these key points, and (if possible) which information won't be included in your essay.
3. Develop a thesis statement, in response to the prompt.
4. On a sheet of paper, write the thesis statement at the top of page and make an outline for the RESPONSE section of the paper (see the outline for the example essay).

Writing the First Draft of Your Essay

The following grid will help you outline the ENTIRE essay (including introductory and concluding paragraphs).

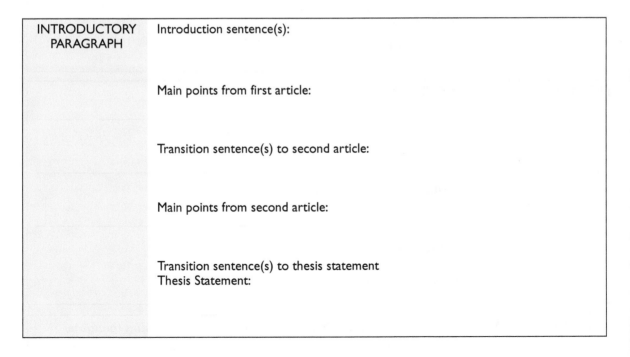

INTRODUCTORY PARAGRAPH	Introduction sentence(s):
	Main points from first article:
	Transition sentence(s) to second article:
	Main points from second article:
	Transition sentence(s) to thesis statement Thesis Statement:

BODY PARAGRAPH 1   KEY POINT I:

A. _____

Detail/Example:

B. _____

Detail/Example:

C. _____

Detail/Example:

Concluding sentence:

BODY PARAGRAPH 2   KEY POINT II:

A. _____

Detail/Example:

B. _____

Detail/Example:

C. _____

Detail/Example:

Concluding sentence:

BODY PARAGRAPH 3   KEY POINT III:

A. _____

Detail/Example:

B. _____

Detail/Example:

C. _____

Detail/Example:

Concluding sentence:

CONCLUSION *(At least 3 sentences, connecting thesis, key points, and closing thoughts)*

Instructor's Rubric

Your instructor will be grading your essay based on the following rubric.

Category	Exceeds expectations	Meets expectations	Does not yet meet expectations
Source Material	Included authors' names (if applicable) and titles in well-integrated sentences which clearly and correctly articulate main ideas of the articles.	Included authors' names (if applicable) and titles; sentences may be awkwardly or unclearly connected to main ideas of articles	Authors' names or titles are missing, or source information is not connected to main ideas of articles.
	Clearly and correctly articulated main ideas of articles; preceded main idea with an interesting, creative introduction	Correctly articulated main ideas of articles; preceded main idea with a general introduction.	Did not correctly articulate main ideas of articles; general introduction is missing or connection to main idea is not evident.
	Clearly and correctly articulated key supporting points of articles without unnecessary details; points are unified, making the structure of the original articles clear.	Correctly articulated key supporting points of articles without unnecessary details. Some points may not be clearly connected.	Did not correctly identify key supporting points, may have misinterpreted some ideas or included unnecessary minor details.
	Clearly and consistently attributed information from sources, using reporting phrases as necessary.	Attempt at attribution is evident, but effort may be required to infer attribution in some places.	Failed to use paraphrases and quotes or failed to attribute them.
Focus	Thesis responds in a thorough and original way to the prompt and enables reader to anticipate supporting argument (and counter-argument, if applicable).	Thesis responds to the prompt but may be formulaic or awkward.	Thesis does not respond to the prompt, is missing or is incomprehensible.
	There is a clear, effective transition from summary to thesis.	The ideas in the articles as summarized clearly relate to the ideas in the thesis, but the connection may not be explicitly stated.	The thesis and summary seem unrelated.
	Clearly connected own key supporting points to thesis	Almost all key supporting points are clearly connected to thesis but in some places, connection may need to be inferred.	Many key supporting points are not clearly connected to the thesis or seem totally unrelated.

Category	Exceeds expectations	Meets expectations	Does not yet meet expectations
Focus (*continued*)	Conclusion neatly ties together thesis, key supporting points, & ideas from both articles without repeating sentences or phrases from earlier in the essay. Conclusion ends with an appropriate generalizing idea.	Conclusion returns to thesis with some reference to ideas from one or both articles and/or key supporting points. Repetition of earlier phrases is minimal.	Conclusion is missing, fails to refer to the thesis, fails refer to either of the articles, or largely consists of sentences repeated from elsewhere in the essay. Ideas more suited to an additional body paragraph may be present.
Support	Body contains 3+ key supporting points which all connect to thesis.	Body contains two key supporting points that connect to thesis. It may contain an additional point that does not connect.	Body contains one or no key supporting points that connect to the thesis, the key supporting points are redundant, or it may not be apparent what the key supporting points are.
	All key supporting points are excellent, logical support that would be difficult to refute.	Some key supporting points may be simplistic but all are sensible.	Key supporting points are illogical.
	Used appropriate facts, examples, and other details to explain each key supporting point.	Used some appropriate facts, examples, and other details to explain most key supporting points. There may be a few lapses in which details do not clearly support points.	Facts, examples, and other details do not adequately explain each key supporting point.
	Consistently used paraphrases and quotes from article (s) effectively.	Used paraphrases and quotes from article (s) effectively most of the time.	Did not use paraphrases or quotes from article(s) effectively.
Organization	Divided essay appropriately into introductory paragraph(s), body paragraphs, and concluding paragraph.	Essay is appropriately divided into introduction, body, and conclusion, but body may not be optimally paragraphed.	Essay is not appropriately divided into introduction, body, and conclusion.
	Organized own key supporting points logically, using transitions as necessary to show relationship between paragraphs.	Generally organized own key supporting points logically, but some relationships may not be totally clear in every case.	There are many places where connections between key supporting points are not clear.
	Produced cohesive body paragraphs with clear topic sentences, using transitions as necessary to show relationship between sentences within the paragraph.	Body paragraphs are generally organized around one clear point, but connections between ideas may not be totally clear in every case.	Body paragraphs contain many disconnected ideas.

Category	Exceeds expectations	Meets expectations	Does not yet meet expectations
Vocabulary & Mechanics	Used academic vocabulary words and expressions consistently and correctly.	Used some academic vocabulary words and expressions; when used, they are generally correct. Extremely casual language is not evident.	No academic vocabulary or consistent incorrect use of vocabulary or inappropriate use of casual language.
	There are very few minor grammar, spelling or punctuation problems.	There are consistent minor problems with grammar, spelling or punctuation or a few major problems.	Grammar errors interfere with meaning or demonstrate a pattern of lack of control.
	Formatted paper appropriately (double-spaced, 12pt font, paragraphs indented, 1" margins, header).	Most formatting is correct but there may be one or two lapses.	There are multiple significant problems with formatting.

Peer Feedback

After you've written the first draft of your paper, work together with a classmate to analyze the writing of another pair of students. Read each paper with your partner, discussing and agreeing on whether it meets the criteria in the peer feedback form below. When you have finished writing your comments for each paper, meet with the other pair of students to give the authors feedback on their work.

Student Whose Essay Is Being Reviewed:

_____

Student Reviewer(s):

_____

1. In the introduction, did the student include the titles and authors of the original sources?

    ____ YES   ____ NO   If not, explain what the student is missing.

2. In the introduction, is there a summary that contains only the important ideas from the original sources?

 ____ YES   ____ NO   If not, explain which ideas are missing or unnecessary.

3. In the introduction, does the essay have a thesis statement that answers the prompt (teacher's question)?

 ____ YES   ____ NO   If it does, write the student's thesis statement below. If not, write what you think the thesis should be and what the problem is (No thesis? Thesis doesn't answer teacher's question?).

4. Does the body of the essay have at least two paragraphs, and do all of these paragraphs support the thesis?

 ____ YES   ____ NO   If it does, write the key point of each body paragraph. If not, explain the problem— fewer than two body paragraphs? The paragraphs don't support the thesis?

5. Do *all* of the parts of each body paragraph support its key point?

 ____ YES   ____ NO   If not, explain which paragraphs have problems and what those problems are.

6. Do the body paragraphs have ADEQUATE support (details, examples) for each key point?

   ____ YES   ____ NO   If not, explain which body paragraphs need MORE support.

7. Does the body of the essay include BOTH ideas from the reading sources AND the student's own ideas?

   ____ YES   ____ NO   If not, explain which is missing.

8. Does the essay use an acceptable amount of quotes and/or para-phrases properly?

   ____ YES   ____ NO   If not, explain what the problem is. Are there no quotes or paraphrases? Are they plagia-rized? Are they not logical support for the claims the student-writer is making?

9. Does the essay have a conclusion that ties the supporting arguments back to the thesis and the original sources?

   ____ YES   ____ NO   If not, explain what the problem is. Is the conclusion missing? Or does it fail to tie back to the thesis?

10. Rate this essay from 1–10 (9–10=A, 7-8=B, 5-6=C, 3-4=D, 1–2=F) and explain your rating (What did you like best? What needs improvement?)

Checklist for Draft 2

Now that you have received feedback from others, write draft 2 of your essay. Use this checklist to help you revise:

Revision Checklist: Your revision isn't complete until you can answer YES to ALL of the questions.

_____ 1. Does the essay open with a "hook" that engages the reader's interest while leading naturally into the subject of the essay?

_____ 2. Does the first line of the summary of EACH source introduce the article title and author(s) in a grammatically clear statement? *In the article "   ," author X argues that . . . In the article "   ," the issue of . . . is discussed.*

_____ 3. Is the summary of the EACH source accurate and complete, featuring only the most important ideas and not unnecessary details? Have you re-read the articles to help clarify the ideas?

_____ 4. Have you paraphrased the articles' ideas in your own words, sometimes quoting brief passages that have special meaning or are hard to paraphrase?

_____ 5. Have you shown that the articles' ideas are INDEED from the articles, by consistently using reporting phrases such as *The author finds that. . . . The article reports that. . . .*

_____ 6. Is there a transitional sentence which connects the summary of first source to the summary of the second source?

_____ 7. Is YOUR THESIS STATEMENT clear?

_____ 8. Does your thesis statement immediately follow the summary?

_____ 9. Does each BODY paragraph begin with a clear topic sentence that identifies the key point you're making?

_____ 10. Do you support each of your key points with specific and relevant evidence?

_____ 11. Do you support each of your key points with *adequate* evidence? Could you *add more* to strengthen your point?

_____ 12. Have you explained your evidence as fully as necessary for the reader to understand it and to see how it proves your point?

_____ 13. Does each body paragraph end with a conclusion that re-emphasizes its key point?

_____ 14. Have you revised for UNITY, making sure that each paragraph addresses only ONE key point and that there is no off-point information in that paragraph?

_____ 15. Have you revised for COHERENCE, making sure that ideas flow from one idea to the next within each paragraph? Between paragraphs?

_____ 16. Have you fixed grammar mistakes such as run-ons, fragments, and agreement errors?

_____ 17. Have you carefully edited and proofread for clarity? Have you read it aloud? Checked verb tenses? Spelling? Punctuation?

_____ 18. Have you corrected or addressed EVERY suggestion you've received from your peers, a tutor, etc.?

_____ 19. (If applicable) Have you looked at the sample essays and used them as models?

Writing About Literature

CHAPTER 8

CONTENTS

Writing Skills Focus: Writing from Literature

In many ways writing a paper about literature is no different than writing an essay in response to an article. You are still required to read the material thoroughly and make an argument of some kind. It might seem that the stories do have specific meanings, and your instructor has already decided what that meaning is. Not true! Even the most well-informed instructor rarely arrives at conclusions that someone else wouldn't disagree with—and often for good reasons. Interpretations of fiction are often opinion, but not all opinions are equal, valid, or interesting.

What makes a valid and interesting opinion? A good interpretation of fiction will:

- Avoid the obvious (in other words, it won't argue a conclusion that most readers could reach on their own from a general knowledge of the story).
- Support its main points with strong evidence.
- Use careful reasoning to explain how that evidence relates to the student writer's interpretation.

When you write a literary essay, you are essentially making an argument. You are arguing that your perspective (an interpretation, an evaluative judgment, or a critical evaluation) is valid.

Like any argumentative essay, you will need a debatable "working" thesis. You will also need to gather evidence. Look over the notes you have made in the margins of the text. Which of them say something about your main point? Keep your topic and your thesis about your topic constantly in your mind as you reread and take notes. It might help you come up with more evidence if you also take into account some of the broader components that go into making fiction, things like plot, point of view, character, setting, and symbols.

Suggested Readings and Prompts

Reading: "Ambush" by Tim O'Brien

Prompt: Do you agree with O'Brien's decision not to tell Kathleen this story until she is older?

Reading: "Teenage Wasteland" by Anne Tyler

Prompt: Do you believe Donny's version of events? Why or why not?

Reading: "The Life You Save May Be Your Own" by Flannery O'Connor

Prompt: If the story ended with Mr. Shiftlet's leaving The Hot Spot and before he meets the hitchhiker, how might your perceptions of him be different?

Prompt: How do you interpret the story's title?

Reading: "Sonny's Blues" by James Baldwin

Prompt: What is the significance of jazz to Sonny

Prompt: Harlem is a powerful presence in the story. How has this world positively and negatively shaped each brother?

Reading: "Everyday Use" by Alice Walker

Prompt: Which sister is in touch with her roots? Why do you think so?

Prompt: How does the quilt become an image that encapsulates the conflict of the story?

Reading: "A&P" by John Updike

Prompt: Define the word "hero" and discuss whether or not Sammy is a hero.

When you speak, you have tools such as tone of voice and body language to help you express your ideas. When you write, however, you have only words and punctuation to get your message across. If your writing includes errors in style, grammar, and punctuation, you may distract readers from your message, and they may focus, instead, on your inability to communicate clearly. You increase your chances of succeeding in your academic and professional life when you write in clear, standard English.

This Editing Handbook will help you understand important grammar concepts, and the samples and practices in each chapter offer interesting information about many themes. Before you begin working with these chapters, review the contents and themes shown here.

Identifying Subjects and Verbs

CHAPTER 9

CONTENTS

Section Theme **CONFLICT**

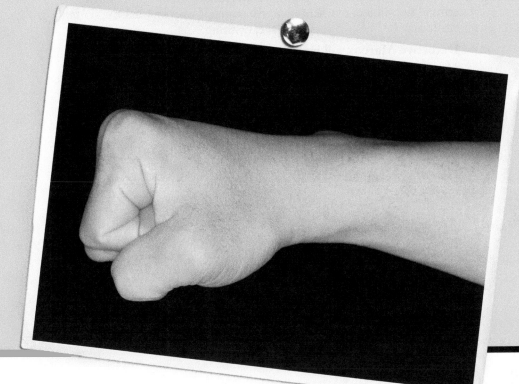

Is behavior learned or genetic? In this chapter, you will learn about the sources of aggressive behavior.

Grammar Snapshot

Looking at Subjects and Verbs

Psychologist Ken Low has given seminars on dealing with aggression. In the following excerpt from a seminar, he discusses the source of anger. Notice that subjects are in bold and verbs are underlined. Also observe that some sentences have no visible subjects.

Understand the source of your anger. Examine your feelings of unhappiness. In my case, the **cause** of the unhappiness was my sense of worthlessness. **Everyone** was succeeding, in my mind, and **I** was not. **I** wanted to blame my boss, my parents, or my wife. **I** was prepared to blame anybody and anything outside of myself. **Recognizing** my unhappiness gave me insight into the source of my anger. **I** held a mistaken conviction: the **world** owed me a good life.

In this chapter, you will identify subjects and verbs.

Identifying Subjects

A **sentence** contains one or more subjects and verbs, and it expresses a complete thought. The **subject** tells you who or what the sentence is about. A **verb** expresses an action or state. If a sentence is missing a subject or a verb, it is incomplete. You will use your ability to identify subjects and verbs in the editing process.

- Subjects may be **singular** or **plural**. A subject can also be a **pronoun**. To determine the subject of a sentence, ask yourself who or what the sentence is about. It may be about a person, place, or thing.

    Detective Marcos will interview the suspects.
    Many **factors** cause people to break laws.
    It is an important case.

- A **compound subject** contains two or more subjects joined by *and*, *or*, or *nor*.

    Reporters and **photographers** were outside the prison gates.

- Sometimes a **gerund** (*-ing* form of the verb) is the subject of a sentence.

    Listening is an important skill.

Hint > **Here and There**

Here and *There* are not subjects. In sentences that begin with *Here* or *There*, the subject follows the verb.

There are several **ways** to find a criminal.

Here is an interesting **brochure** about the police academy.

How to Find the Subject

To find the subject, ask yourself *who* or *what* the sentence is about. The subject is the noun or pronoun or the complete name of a person or organization.

The **Federal Bureau of Investigation** is a large organization. **It** has branches in every state.

When you are identifying the subject, you can ignore words that describe the noun.

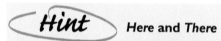

adjectives   subject

The pompous and rude **sergeant** left the room.

PRACTICE I   Circle the subject in each sentence. Sometimes there may be more than one subject.

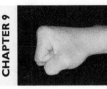

EXAMPLE: A behavioral (study) examines genetics and behavior.

1. Research psychiatrist Carl E. Schwartz works in the Department of Psychiatry at Massachusetts General Hospital.

2. He conducted a study to determine hereditary factors in behavior.

3. There were over one hundred children in his study.

4. Infants and toddlers were classed into two groups.

5. Objects, strange people, and unfamiliar settings were used to test the children.

6. Talking was not permitted.

7. The outgoing toddlers easily interacted in new surroundings.

8. The inhibited children were more likely to show signs of stress in unfamiliar surroundings.

Prepositional Phrases

A **preposition** is a word that links nouns, pronouns, and phrases to other words in a sentence. It expresses a relationship based on movement or position. A **prepositional phrase** is made up of a preposition and its object (a noun or a pronoun).

Because the object of a preposition is a noun, it may look like a subject. **However, the object in a prepositional phrase is never the subject of the sentence.**

prepositional phrase   subject
With the parents' approval, the **experiment** began.

Common Prepositions

about	among	beside	during	into	onto	toward
above	around	between	except	like	out	under
across	at	beyond	for	near	outside	until
after	before	by	from	of	over	up
against	behind	despite	in	off	through	with
along	below	down	inside	on	to	within

To help you identify the subject, put parentheses around prepositional phrases. In each of the following examples, the prepositional phrase is in parentheses. Notice that a sentence can contain more than one prepositional phrase.

(In spite of the storm), **they** drove to the hospital.

The **clinic**, (after 1971), expanded greatly.

(In the late 1990s), (during a period of cost cutting), high-tech **cameras** were placed in the room.

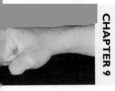

> ### Hint   **Using of the**
>
> In most expressions containing *of the*, the subject appears before *of the*.
>
> subject
> **Each** (of the parents) agreed to participate.
>
> **One** (of the fathers) was uncomfortable with the process.

PRACTICE 2   Circle the subject in each sentence. Also add parentheses around any prepositional phrases that are near the subject.

EXAMPLE: (For many years), (Schwartz) has studied genetics and behavior.

1. In Schwartz's study, half of the babies were classified as shy. The others in the group were classified as outgoing. In unfamiliar surroundings, the shy and outgoing children reacted differently. For example, in the presence of a stranger, the shy toddlers would freeze. The outgoing toddlers would approach the stranger and interact.

2. The differences in reactions occurred in their heart rate, in the dilation of their pupils, and in the levels of the stress hormone, cortisone. Generally, the differences in the temperament of children persisted to adulthood.

3. After the first study, Carl Schwartz tracked down twenty-two of the original subjects. About one-third of the uninhibited adults showed impulsive and aggressive behavior. Some of the shy children became extremely shy adults. However, not all outgoing infants become bold or aggressive adults. In fact, most individuals in the study did not develop behavioral problems.

Identifying Verbs

Every sentence must contain a verb. The **verb** expresses what the subject does, or it links the subject to other descriptive words.

An **action verb** describes an action that a subject performs.

> Detective Rowland <u>attended</u> a seminar. He <u>spoke</u> to some officials.

A **linking verb** connects a subject with words that describe it, and it does not show an action. The most common linking verb is *be*, but other common linking verbs are *appear*, *become*, *look*, and *seem*.

> Kim Rossmo <u>is</u> a former detective. His methods <u>seem</u> reliable.

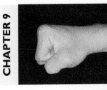

When a subject performs more than one action, the verbs are called **compound verbs.**

In 2003, Rossmo <u>wrote</u> and <u>spoke</u> about his methods.

Helping Verbs

The **helping verb** combines with the main verb to indicate tense, negative structure, or question structure. The most common helping verbs are forms of *be*, *have*, and *do*. **Modal auxiliaries** are another type of helping verb, and they indicate ability (*can*), obligation (*must*), and so on. For example, here are different forms of the verb *ask*, and the helping verbs are underlined.

<u>is</u> asking	<u>had</u> asked	<u>will</u> ask	<u>should have</u> asked
<u>was</u> asked	<u>had been</u> asking	<u>can</u> ask	<u>might be</u> asked
<u>has been</u> asking	<u>would</u> ask	<u>could be</u> asking	<u>could have been</u> asked

The **complete verb** is the helping verb and the main verb. In the following examples, the main verb is double underlined. In **question forms**, the first helping verb usually appears before the subject.

Criminal profiling techniques <u>have been</u> <u>spreading</u> across the continent.

<u>Should</u> the detective <u>have</u> <u>studied</u> the files?

Interrupting words such as *often*, *always*, *ever*, and *actually* are not part of the verb.

Rossmo <u>has</u> often <u>returned</u> to Vancouver.

> **Hint** **Infinitives Are Not the Main Verb**
>
> **Infinitives** are verbs preceded by *to* such as *to fly, to speak,* and *to go.* An infinitive is never the main verb in a sentence.
>
> infinitive
> The network <u>wanted</u> **to produce** a show about geographic profiling.

PRACTICE 3 In each sentence, circle the subject and underline the complete verb. Remember to underline the helping verbs as well as the main verbs. You could also place prepositional phrases in parentheses to help you identify the other parts of the sentence.

EXAMPLE: (According to Professor Saundra K. Ciccarelli,) many (factors) <u>contribute</u> to aggressive behavior.

1. The amygdala is located near the base of the brain. Studies have shown the amygdala's role in fear responses. In a 1939 experiment, the temporal lobe was removed from the brains of several monkeys. The lobe contains the amygdala. After the surgery, the monkeys showed absolutely no fear of snakes and humans. This anecdote illustrates the role of the brain in fearful or aggressive behavior.

2. Why do people harm others? In her book *Psychology*, Ciccarelli discusses the connection between the brain and aggressive behavior. She gives an example of a specific case. In 1966, Charles Whitman shot and killed fourteen people. Before his death in a shootout with police, Whitman wrote a note and asked doctors to examine the state of his brain. In fact, a later examination revealed the presence of a tumor next to his amygdala.

3. There are also chemical links to aggression, according to Ciccarelli. Testosterone, in high levels, has been shown to cause aggressive behavior. Also, certain substances have an impact on the brain. Alcohol affects the amount of some brain chemicals and reduces a person's inhibitions.

FINAL REVIEW

Circle the subjects and underline the complete verbs in the following sentences. Underline *all* parts of the verb. To avoid misidentifying subjects, you can place prepositional phrases in parentheses.

EXAMPLE: (One)(of the most interesting influences on behavior) is social roles.

1. Many psychologists and social scientists believe in the importance of social roles on behavior. Thus, children can be influenced by aggressive characters on television. Young adults may be pressured or manipulated by peers. Basically, people can learn to be aggressive.

2. Most interesting of all, people of all ages can modify their behavior due to their social roles. Psychologist Philip Zimbardo demonstrated the importance of social roles in his prison experiment at Stanford University. He recruited about seventy volunteers and gave half of them guard roles and the other half prisoner roles. Many volunteers in the guard roles exhibited violent behavior. Other volunteers in the prisoner roles became meek. Therefore, the behavior of the students changed due to their roles.

3. History is filled with examples of people behaving badly, often during times of conflict. Soldiers, especially, are in stressful situations and fulfill

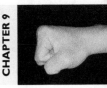

the obligations of their roles. The prison abuse scandal at Abu Ghraib in Iraq is a real-life example. Prison guards beat and humiliated prisoners. Why did the guards act so cruelly? According to psychologists, a uniform and a specific social role have powerful influences on people's behavior.

The Writer's Room Topics for Writing

Write about one of the following topics. After you finish writing, identify your subjects and verbs.

1. List various ways in which social roles influence people's behavior. Support your points with specific examples.

2. Some experts suggest that personality traits are partly inherited. Are your character traits similar to a family member's traits? Compare and contrast yourself with someone else in your family.

CHECKLIST: SUBJECTS AND VERBS

Review this chapter's main points.

To identify **subjects,** look for words that tell you who or what the sentence is about.

To identify **verbs,** look for words that do the following:

- **action verbs** describe the actions that the subject performs.
- **linking verbs** describe a state of being or link the subject with descriptive words.
- **helping verbs** combine with the main verb to indicate tense, negative structure, or question structure.

To identify **prepositional phrases,** look for words that consist of a preposition and its object. Note: the object of a prepositional phrase cannot be the subject.

prepositional phrase   subject   helping verb   verb

In spite of criticism, the police chief has released the suspect.

10
CHAPTER

Sentence Combining

Section Theme **CONFLICT**

In this chapter, you will read about eyewitness testimony, profiling techniques, and wrongful convictions.

Grammar Snapsh•t

Looking at Compound and Complex Sentences

The following excerpt is from *Criminal Justice Today* by Frank Schmallager. The underlined sections are called dependent clauses.

> Defendants may choose to be represented in Chinese courts by an attorney, a relative, or a friend, or they may choose to represent themselves. If they desire, a lawyer will be appointed for them.... While they work to protect the rights of the defendant, attorneys have a responsibility to the court. Defense lawyers are charged with helping the court render a verdict.

In this chapter, you will identify and write compound and complex sentences.

Understanding Key Words

When you use sentences of varying lengths and types, your writing flows more smoothly and appears more interesting. You can vary sentences and create relationships between ideas by combining sentences.

Before you learn about the types of sentences, it is important to understand some key terms.

A **phrase** is a group of words that is missing a subject, a verb, or both, and is not a complete sentence.

in the morning   acting on her own   the excited witness

A **clause** is a group of words that contains a subject and a verb. There are two types of clauses.

- An **independent clause** is a complete sentence. It stands alone and expresses one complete idea.

  The victims asked for compensation.

- A **dependent clause** has a subject and a verb, but it cannot stand alone. It "depends" on another clause to be complete. A dependent clause usually begins with a subordinator such as *after, although, because, unless,* and *when.*

  . . . because they had lost a lot of money.

PRACTICE 1   Write S next to each complete sentence. If the group of words is not a complete sentence—perhaps it is a phrase or a dependent clause—then write X in the blank.

EXAMPLE: Circumstantial evidence is discounted.   _S_

Although it may be reliable.   _X_

1. Circumstantial evidence is often very reliable.   _____

2. Blood, for example.   _____

3. It may match with the DNA of the victim.   _____

4. Pieces of clothing, hair fibers, and other types of evidence.   _____

5. Unless somebody altered it.   _____

6. Such evidence is usually very good.   _____

7. A credit card may place a criminal at the crime scene.   _____

8. Although the suspect may have an alibi.   _____

Making Compound Sentences
Combining Sentences
Using Coordinating Conjunctions

A **coordinating conjunction** joins two complete ideas and indicates the connection between them. The most common coordinating conjunctions are *for, and, nor, but, or, yet,* and *so.*

Complete idea   **, coordinating conjunction**   complete idea.

The detective collected the evidence, **and** the lab analyzed it.

Review the following chart showing coordinating conjunctions and their functions.

Conjunction	Function	Example
and	to join two ideas	Anna went to school, **and** she became a forensics expert.
but	to contrast two ideas	The courses were difficult, **but** she passed them all.
for	to indicate a reason	She worked very hard, **for** she was extremely motivated.
nor	to indicate a negative idea	The work was not easy, **nor** was it pleasant.
or	to offer an alternative	She will work for a police department, **or** she will work for a private lab.
so	to indicate a cause and effect relationship	She has recently graduated, **so** she is looking for work now.
yet	to introduce a surprising choice	She wants to stay in her town, **yet** the best jobs are in a nearby city.

   **Recognizing Compound Sentences**

To be sure that a sentence is compound, place your finger over the coordinator, and then ask yourself if the two clauses are complete sentences. In compound sentences, always place a comma before the coordinator.

Simple: The witness was nervous **but** very convincing.

Compound: The witness was nervous, **but** she was very convincing.

PRACTICE 2 Insert coordinating conjunctions in the blanks. Choose from the following list, and try to use a variety of coordinators. (Some sentences may have more than one answer.)

but   or   yet   so   for   and   nor

EXAMPLE: In 1969, the FBI introduced criminal profiling as an investigative strategy, _____*and*_____ it has been quite successful.

1. Kim Rossmo is a renowned geographic profiler, _____ he is also an excellent detective. In the early 1990s, Detective Rossmo could either work in Canada, _____ he could take a job in the United States. The Vancouver Police Department did not try to keep Rossmo, _____ he moved south.

2. Rossmo examines the movements of criminals, _____ he searches for specific patterns. According to Rossmo, criminals attack places they know, _____ they generally don't work in their own neighborhoods. Most people don't want to travel long distances for their jobs, _____ they are lazy. Criminals work the same way, _____ they stay relatively close to home.

3. Rossmo developed a fascinating mathematical formula, _____ many police departments were skeptical about his ideas. He tried to convince others, _____ he believed strongly in his computer program. Basically, he inputs the addresses of suspects into a computer, _____ he also inputs details about the crime scenes. His program can process a ten-square-mile area, _____ it looks for a "hot" area. Suspects may live directly in the center of the hot area, _____ they may live within a few blocks.

4. For example, in the late 1990s, there were several sexual assaults in a town in Ontario, Canada, _____ Rossmo and his associates created a profile map. One particular suspect's home was compared to the location of the crime scenes, _____ it was placed in Rossmo's computer program. Originally, the main offender's name was low on a list of 316 suspects, _____ it rose to number 6 on the list after the

profiling. The suspect did not admit his guilt, _____ other evidence tied him to the crime scenes. He was eventually tried and convicted for the crimes, _____ he went to prison.

Combining Sentences Using Semicolons (;)

Another way to form a compound sentence is to join two complete ideas with a semicolon. The semicolon replaces a coordinating conjunction.

GRAMMAR LINK

For more practice using semicolons, see Chapter 13, Run-Ons.

Complete idea   ;   complete idea.

The eyewitness was certain; she pointed at the suspect.

Hint   **Use a Semicolon to Join Related Ideas**

Use a semicolon to link two sentences when the ideas are equally important and closely related. Do not use a semicolon to join two unrelated sentences.

Incorrect: Some eyewitnesses make mistakes; I like to watch criminal trials.
(The second idea has no clear relationship with the first idea.)

Correct: One eyewitness misidentified a suspect; the witness was not wearing contact lenses that day.
(The second idea gives further information about the first idea.)

PRACTICE 3   Make compound sentences by adding a semicolon and another complete sentence to each simple sentence. Remember that the two sentences must have related ideas.

EXAMPLE: Last year, Eric joined a gang; *he regretted his decision.*

1. Eric rebelled against his parents _____

   _____

2. Some people don't have supportive families _____

   _____

3. At age fifteen, I acted like other teens _____

   _____

4. She didn't commit the crime _____

   _____

5. His friends tried to influence him _____
   _____

6. Eric entered the courtroom _____
   _____

Combining Sentences Using Transitional Expressions

A **transitional expression** links two complete ideas and shows how they are related. Most transitional expressions are **conjunctive adverbs** such as *however* or *furthermore*.

Some Transitional Expressions

Addition	Alternative	Contrast	Time	Example or Emphasis	Result or Consequence
additionally	in fact	however	eventually	for example	consequently
also	instead	nevertheless	finally	for instance	hence
besides	on the contrary	nonetheless	frequently	namely	therefore
furthermore	on the other hand	still	later	of course	thus
in addition	otherwise		meanwhile	undoubtedly	
moreover			subsequently		

If the second sentence begins with a transitional expression, put a semicolon before it and a comma after it.

Complete idea   **; transitional expression,**   complete idea

Truscott was not guilty**; nevertheless,** he was convicted.

PRACTICE 4   Combine sentences using the following transitional expressions. Choose an expression from the list, and try to use a different expression in each sentence.

in fact   ~~frequently~~   however   of course   for instance
therefore   moreover   nevertheless   thus   eventually

                                              ; frequently, it
EXAMPLE: DNA evidence is useful. ~~It~~ has helped clear many innocent people.

1. In the past, many technicians looked at evidence through a microscope. They might examine a strand of hair.

2. In the early 1990s, a comparison of hair samples could deliver a conviction. Scientists developed more sophisticated techniques.

3. Dr. Edward Blake is a leading authority on DNA evidence. He often testifies at trials.

4. According to Dr. Blake, microscopic hair analysis is subjective. It has secured convictions in many cases.

5. Billy Gregory's hair matched a hair found at a crime scene. Both strands of hair appeared identical.

6. The strands of hair had exactly the same color and width. They were genetically different.

7. In 1993, Gregory was convicted of the crime. He was sentenced to life in prison.

8. In 2000, a DNA test cleared him. He was able to go home.

9. Today, conventional hair comparison evidence is no longer allowed in most courtrooms. It may become an obsolete science.

Making Complex Sentences

When you combine a dependent and an independent clause, you create a **complex sentence.** An effective way to create complex sentences is to join clauses with a **subordinating conjunction.** "Subordinate" means secondary, so subordinating conjunctions are words that introduce secondary ideas.

CHAPTER 10

If you use a subordinator at the beginning of a sentence, put a comma after the dependent clause. Generally, if you use a subordinator in the middle of the sentence, you do not need to use a comma.

| Main idea | **subordinating conjunction** | secondary idea |

The police arrived **because** the alarm was ringing.

| **Subordinating conjunction** | secondary idea | , | main idea |

Because the alarm was ringing, the police arrived.

Meanings of Subordinating Conjunctions

Subordinating conjunctions create a relationship between the clauses in a sentence.

Subordinating Conjunction	Indicates	Example
as, because, since, so that	a reason, cause, or effect	He paid a lot because he wanted a reliable alarm system.
after, before, since, until, when, whenever, while	a time	After he drove home, he parked on the street.
as long as, even if, if, provided that, so that, unless	a condition	The alarm won't ring unless someone touches the car.
although, even though, though	a contrast	Although the alarm began to wail, nobody looked at the car.
where, wherever	a location	Wherever you go, you will hear annoying car alarms.

> ## Hint More About Complex Sentences
>
> Complex sentences can have more than two clauses.
>
> 1
> Although males commit most violent crimes, more and more females engage
>
> 3
> in violent acts after they have joined gangs.
>
> You can also combine compound and complex sentences. The next example is a **compound-complex sentence.**
>
> complex
> Although Alicia is tiny, she is strong, and she is a dedicated police officer.
> compound

PRACTICE 5   Add a missing subordinating conjunction to each sentence. Use each subordinating conjunction once.

although	when	because	since
even though	if	unless	whenever

1. _____ a new television program about crime scene investigations is announced, many people watch it. Real-life lawyers and prosecutors get annoyed _____ members of the jury expect to see the same expensive, sophisticated crime-solving techniques used in average cases. _____ the members of the jury are not experts, they believe they know a lot about crime investigations because they have picked up tidbits from crime shows.

2. It is very expensive and difficult to get DNA analyses _____ the case is a very high profile and important one. _____ there is no DNA evidence, the case can still be very strong.

3. According to actor Robert Blake's defense lawyer, jurors will listen to detailed scientific evidence _____ they are used to watching those crime shows on television. The jury will find the defendant guilty _____ the evidence is solid. _____ the jury is unconvinced, the defendant might be released.

PRACTICE 6   Combine the sentences by adding a subordinating conjunction. Use a different subordinating conjunction in each sentence. Properly punctuate your sentences.

EXAMPLE: He entered the courtroom. Photographers snapped photos.

As he entered the courthouse, photographers snapped photos.

Or   *The photographers snapped photos as he entered the courthouse.*

1. Stephen was fourteen years old. He was arrested.

   _____

   _____

2. He proclaimed his innocence. The police refused to believe him.

   _____

   _____

3. He was extremely nervous. He appeared to be guilty.

   _____

   _____

4. He was in jail. He finished high school.

   _____

   _____

5. New evidence surfaced. He was released.

   _____

   _____

FINAL REVIEW

The following paragraphs only contain simple sentences. When sentences are not varied, the essay is boring to read. To give the paragraphs more sentence variety, combine at least fifteen sentences. You will have to add some words and delete others.

EXAMPLE: ~~The~~ *When the* witness is traumatized. ~~She~~ *, she* might not remember her assailant's face.

1. Each day, you may see many faces. How many will you remember? You

   might recall the ones you see repeatedly. You will forget the others.

   Dr. Rod Lindsay works at Queen's University. He is an expert on

   eyewitness testimony. Dr. Lindsay says that it is not easy to remember

   faces. During a traumatic moment, the brain almost shuts down.

   Dr. Lindsay is worried. He does not trust the methods used to collect

   eyewitness testimony.

2. In 1986, the police showed a crime victim a set of six photos. She felt a strong pressure to make a choice. One photo looked different from the others. It was in color. The other photos were black and white. She picked the color photo. It was not the guilty man. According to Dr. Lindsay, all photos of suspects should have similar color and lighting to avoid biasing witnesses.

3. The best way to show photos is to show them sequentially. The witness must look at each photo. The witness must say "yes" or "no." He or she cannot go back to a previous picture. The witness must compare each photo to his or her memory. Dr. Lindsay contacted thirty-three police departments. Only nine showed photos of suspects sequentially.

4. According to experts, more police departments should use the "double blind" procedure. Sometimes, police officers know about the main suspect. They might cue the witness unconsciously. The double blind procedure ensures that the person showing the photos does not know the main suspect. Dr. Lindsay contacted thirty-three police departments. Only six used the double blind procedure.

5. Marvin Anderson spent fifteen years in jail. He was convicted of rape. The witness pointed at him during the trial. She identified him as her rapist. Many years later, DNA evidence cleared Anderson. He was released. Today, the lawyers see problems with the ways the photos of suspects were presented to the victim. Also, the officer may have "cued" the victim.

6. According to Dr. Lindsay, many people are wrongfully convicted. Witnesses misidentify them. It is unfortunate. The jury tends to believe eyewitness testimony. It can be seriously flawed.

The Writer's Room   **Topics for Writing**

Write about one of the following topics. Include some compound and some complex sentences.

1. Do you watch crime shows or read about crime? Describe a crime show, movie, or book.
2. What can people do to reduce the risk of being robbed? List several steps that people can take.

✔ CHECKLIST: COMBINING SENTENCES

When you edit your writing, ask yourself these questions.

Are my compound and complex sentences complete?

He was arrested because
~~Because~~ of the scandal.

Are my sentences correctly punctuated?

- In compound sentences, place a comma before the coordinator.
- In complex sentences, place a comma after a dependent introductory clause.

Comma: The case was dismissed, and the suspect was freed.

Comma: After she was released, she tried to find a job.

No comma: She tried to find a job after she was released.

Sentence Variety

CONTENTS

- What Is Sentence Variety?
- Varying the Opening Words
- Combining Sentences with an Appositive
- Combining Sentences with Relative Clauses
- Writing Embedded Questions

Section Theme **CONFLICT**

In this chapter, you will read about crime and prisons.

Grammar Snapshot

Looking at Sentence Variety

The next selections from *Crime, A Normal Phenomenon* by sociologist Emile Durkheim were translated from the original French. The first translation sounds choppy because the sentences are short and uniform in length. When the passage is rewritten with sentence variety, it flows more smoothly.

No Sentence Variety

Crime is normal. It exists in all societies. The type of crime may change. The form of crime may change. Everywhere and always there have been criminals.

Sentence Variety

Crime, which is normal, exists in all societies. The type or form of crime may change, but everywhere and always there have been criminals.

In this chapter, you will vary the length and structure of sentences to produce sentence variety.

164

What Is Sentence Variety?

In Chapter 10, you learned about writing different types of sentences. In this chapter, you will learn to vary your sentences by consciously considering the length of sentences, by altering the opening words, and by joining sentences using different methods.

Hint   Be Careful with Long Sentences

If your sentence is too long, it may be difficult for the reader to understand. Also, you may accidentally write run-on sentences. If you have any doubts, break up a longer sentence into shorter ones.

Long and complicated:	In his book *Criminal Justice Today,* Frank Schmalleger describes a practice of the ancient Hebrews who sometimes punished a tribe by sending a sacrificial goat into the wilderness, and the goat, which was supposed to symbolically contain the tribe's sins, became the source of the modern word *scapegoat.*
Better:	In his book *Criminal Justice Today,* Frank Schmalleger describes a practice of the ancient Hebrews. They sometimes punished a tribe by sending a sacrificial goat into the wilderness. The goat, which was supposed to symbolically contain the tribe's sins, became the source of the modern word *scapegoat.*

PRACTICE I   Edit each long sentence by breaking it into smaller, more easily understood segments. Each segment must be a complete sentence.

1. Many early punishment methods were designed to publicly humiliate criminals, and one of the most common methods was to force an offender to stand in a public square with his or her head and hands secured so that everyone in the community would see that person, and often the local citizens would throw eggs and tomatoes at the offender, but sometimes they would throw rocks which could end the offender's life, so such retribution was permitted by the community, and ultimately citizens had the power to exact extreme punishment if they believed that the criminal deserved it.

2. In the eighteenth century, England sent convicts to the American colonies and to Australia, and the program, which was known as transportation, had two purposes, which included ridding Britain of undesirable criminals but

also of providing a captive force of workers who could help build roads, bridges, and housing for the people who were developing the colonies, so although many criminals had to go on long journeys and would never see their families again, they also had a much better life than they would have had if they had remained in Great Britain's damp and overcrowded prisons, so some may have been grateful for the chance to build a new life in a different country.

Varying the Opening Words

An effective way to make your sentences more vivid is to vary the opening words. Instead of beginning each sentence with the subject, you could try the following strategies.

Begin with an Adverb (-*ly* word)

An **adverb** is a word that modifies a verb, and it often (but not always) ends in -*ly*. *Quickly* and *frequently* are adverbs. Non -*ly* adverbs include words such as *sometimes* and *often*.

<u>Quickly</u>, the criminal left the scene.

Begin with a Prepositional Phrase

A **prepositional phrase** is a group of words made up of a preposition and its object. *In the morning* and *at dawn* are prepositional phrases.

<u>On the courtroom steps</u>, the defendant covered his head with his jacket.

Begin with a Present Participle (-*ing* Verb)

You can begin your sentence with a **present participle** or -*ing* word. Only combine sentences using an -*ing* modifier when the two actions happen at the same time.

<u>Reaching for her identification</u>, she asked the officer why she had been pulled over.

GRAMMAR
LINK

For a list of irregular past participles, see Appendix 2.

Begin with a Past Participle (-*ed* Verb)

You can begin your sentence with a **past participle**, which is a verb that has an -*ed* ending. There are also many irregular past participles such as *gone*, *seen*, and *known*.

<u>Shocked</u>, she stepped into the police cruiser.

PRACTICE 2 Combine the sets of sentences using the indicated words.

EXAMPLE: The attacker was nervous.   (*-ly* word)
            He grabbed the purse.

Nervously, the attacker grabbed the purse.

1. The bystanders watched the police cruiser arrive.   (*-ly* word)
   They were anxious.

   _____

2. The bystanders were relieved.   (*-ed* verb)
   They left the scene.

   _____

3. The officers saw the people leave.   (*-ed* verb)
   They were annoyed.

   _____

4. One witness gave the officers his name.   (*-ly* word)
   He was reluctant.

   _____

5. The officers looked at the injured woman.   (*-ing* verb)
   They felt upset.

   _____

6. The guilty man raised his hands.   (prepositional phrase)
   He did this with a grin.

   _____

Combining Sentences with an Appositive

An **appositive** is a word or phrase that gives further information about a noun or pronoun. You can combine two sentences by using an appositive. In the example, the italicized phrase could become an appositive because it describes the noun *Mr. Zlatko*.

> **Two sentences:** Mr. Zlatko was *a middle-aged male.*
>   He lost his savings.

You can place the appositive directly before the word that it refers to or directly after that word. Notice that the appositives are set off with commas.

appositive

Combined: A middle-aged male, **Mr. Zlatko** lost his savings.

appositive

Mr. Zlatko, a middle-aged male, lost his savings.

PRACTICE 3 Combine the following pairs of sentences. In each pair, make one of the sentences an appositive. Try to vary the position of the appositive.

EXAMPLE: The man, ~~was~~ an extravagant spender,~~. He~~ owed money to many people.

Charles Dickens

1. Charles Dickens was a British novelist. He often wrote about Debtor's Prison.

2. Dickens lived in the 1800s. It was a time when laws were very harsh.

3. His father was John Dickens. John Dickens was a poor businessman who often owed money to others.

4. When Charles was twelve years old, his father was taken to Marshalsea Debtor's Prison. It was an event that changed the life of the boy.

5. The prison was a filthy, crowded place. It had no separate sections for males and females.

6. For the next six months, Charles left school and went to work in a shoe factory. The school was a place where he had been receiving a good education.

7. When he was released from prison, John Dickens paid for Charles to return to school. John Dickens was a thinner, tired man.

8. Charles Dickens wrote about Debtor's Prison in many of his novels. He was a talented writer.

Combining Sentences with Relative Clauses

A **relative pronoun** describes a noun or pronoun. You can form complex sentences by using relative pronouns to introduce dependent clauses. Review the most common relative pronouns.

who   whom   whomever   whose   which   that

Which

Use **which** to add nonessential information about a thing. Generally use commas to set off clauses that begin with *which*.

> The crime rate, **which peaked in the 1980s**, has fallen in recent years.

That

Use **that** to add information about a thing. Do not use commas to set off clauses that begin with *that*.

> The car **that was stolen** belonged to a police officer.

GRAMMAR LINK

For more information about punctuating relative clauses, refer to Chapter 24.

Who

Use **who** (*whom, whomever, whose*) to add information about a person. When a clause begins with *who,* you may or may not need a comma. Put commas around the clause if it adds nonessential information. If the clause is essential to the meaning of the sentence, do not add commas. To decide if a clause is essential or not, ask yourself if the sentence still makes sense without the *who* clause. If it does, the clause is not essential.

> The woman **who committed the theft** did not use a gun.
> (The clause is essential. The sentence would not make sense without the *who* clause.)

> The female thief, **who spent a lot on legal fees**, was sentenced to ten years in prison.
> (The clause is not essential.)

Hint   **Using *That* or *Which***

Both *which* and *that* refer to things, but *which* refers to nonessential ideas. Also, *which* can imply that you are referring to the complete subject and not just a part of it. Compare the next two sentences.

The shirts **that** had stains provided DNA evidence.
(This sentence suggests that some shirts had no stains.)

The shirts, **which** had stains, provided DNA evidence.
(This sentence suggests that all of the shirts had stains.)

PRACTICE 4   Using a relative pronoun, combine each pair of sentences. Read both sentences before you combine them. Having the full context will help you figure out which relative pronoun to use.

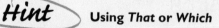

EXAMPLE: Sociologist Emile Durkheim was from France. He believed that deviant behavior can be good for societies.

1. Crime can vary from culture to culture. It sometimes forces societies to change and adapt.

2. In many countries, people express their opinions about the government. These people are breaking the law.

3. Last year, some citizens in China criticized government policies. They were arrested and imprisoned.

4. Some rigid governments enact questionable laws. Those governments may eventually collapse.

5. Definitions of criminal behavior are agreed on by citizens. The definitions can change over time.

6. For instance, in the 1960s, Americans broke Jim Crow laws. They were arrested.

7. The activists were treated as criminals. But they actually helped change society.

8. Durkheim reflects about crime.Sometimes there are positive consequences to criminal behavior.

9. However, Durkheim also warns people. Deviance beyond a certain level can threaten the social order.

PRACTICE 5   Add dependent clauses to each sentence. Begin each clause with a relative pronoun (*who*, *which*, or *that*). Add any necessary commas.

EXAMPLE: The case _____*that involved an adolescent boy*_____ was made into a documentary.

1. The boy _____ did not commit the crime.

2. His lawyers _____ did not have all of the evidence.

3. The jury came to a conclusion _____

4. The judge sentenced the boy _____ to a long prison term.

5. The wrongfully convicted _____ are sometimes never exonerated.

6. Sometimes mistakes _____ can change the lives of individuals.

7. The case _____ brought attention to the wrongfully convicted.

Writing Embedded Questions

It is possible to combine a question with a statement or to combine two questions. An **embedded question** is a question that is set within a larger sentence.

Question: How old was the victim?

Embedded question: The detectives wondered <u>how old the victim was</u>.

CHAPTER 11

In questions, there is generally a helping verb before the subject. However, when a question is embedded in a larger sentence, remove the helping verb or place it after the subject. As you read the following examples, pay attention to the word order in the embedded questions.

1. **Combine two questions.**

   Separate: Why **do** people commit crimes? Do you know?

   (In both questions, the helping verb is *do*.)

   Combined: Do you know <u>why people commit crimes?</u>

   (The helping verb *do* is removed from the embedded question.)

2. **Combine a question and a statement.**

   Separate: How **should** society treat young offenders? I wonder about it.

   (In the question, the helping verb *should* appears before the subject.)

   Combined: I wonder <u>how society should treat young offenders.</u>

   (In the embedded question, *should* is placed after the subject.)

Hint   **Use the Correct Word Order**

When you edit your writing, ensure that you have formed your embedded questions properly.

Dr. Alvarez wonders why ~~do~~ people commit crimes. I asked her what
she thought
~~did she think~~ about the issue.

PRACTICE 6   Edit six errors in embedded questions.

                                   people can
EXAMPLE: The writer explains how ~~can people~~ become criminals.

1. Many experts wonder why is the crime rate so high? Parents may ask how

   are role models a factor. They question how do negative models influence

   youths. Some blame icons in youth culture. For example, a recent

newspaper report linked the hateful words found in some gangsta rap songs to youth crime.

2. However, it is unclear how can people only criticize singers or other celebrities from youth culture. In fact, they should really ask why are so many "pillars" of society deviant. Corporate executives have stolen from shareholders, and prominent religious figures have promoted intolerance and hatred. A reporter from San Diego asks why have so many people in highly regarded positions of authority abused their power. Psychologists, sociologists, and criminologists are trying to find answers.

FINAL REVIEW

The next essay lacks sentence variety. Use the strategies that you have learned in this chapter, and create at least ten varied sentences.

EXAMPLE: Criminal profilers study crime scenes. *, believing* ~~They believe~~ that they can determine the personality of the perpetrator.

1. Two people were at a bus stop. A large man tried to take a woman's purse. He was very aggressive. An innocent bystander intervened. He asked the man to leave the woman alone. The thief pushed the bystander. This action caused the bystander to fall and crack his head on the pavement. The woman got onto the next bus.

2. The police arrived. The action witnesses left the scene. They thought that the situation was under control. Susan Helenchild is a prosecutor. She has advice for witnesses. They should give their names and addresses to police

officers. They should remain at the crime scene. A court cannot easily convict a guilty person. The court needs evidence.

3. A girl arrived after the crime had occurred. She was interviewed by the police. She said nothing important. The prosecutor asked the police to interview her again. The girl had seen the thief earlier in the day. He was drunk and aggressive. In court, the thief claimed to be calm and gentle. He blamed the victim for the crime. He called the victim aggressive. The girl's testimony helped the prosecution. Her testimony contradicted the words of the accused.

4. Why do witnesses leave crime scenes? Officers often wonder. Sometimes witnesses believe they have nothing useful to add. Helenchild feels frustrated with such witnesses. She says that any evidence can help the prosecution. Witnesses should always give contact information to police officers.

READING LINK

Conflict

The following essays contain more information about law, order, and conflict.

The Writer's Room **Topics for Writing**

Write about one of the following topics. Use a variety of sentence lengths.

1. What are some categories of criminals? Classify criminals into different types.

2. Why does criminal life seem exciting to some people? What factors contribute to make crime appealing?

CHECKLIST: SENTENCE VARIETY

When you edit your writing, ask yourself the following questions.

Are my sentences varied? Check for problems in these areas:

- too many short sentences
- long sentences that are difficult to follow

> Police departments examine strategies to lower the crime rate
> because they want to show they are being effective in
>   *. Sometimes*
> the fight against crime ~~and sometimes~~ they present those
> strategies to the media.

Do I have any embedded questions? Check for problems in these areas:

- word order
- unnecessary helping verbs

> I don't know why ~~do~~ people break the law.

12 Fragments

CHAPTER

Section Theme **URBAN DEVELOPMENT**

In this chapter, you will read about the development of suburbs and cities.

Grammar Snapshot

Looking at Sentence Fragments

In his essay "Every Day Carless," Ewan Schmidt argues for a motorized vehicle–free downtown. The sentence fragments are underlined.

   The downtown core is very quiet each Friday. There are no car horns. No screeching of the brakes. No yelling. No loud motor noises. Because there are no cars. People can walk anywhere they want without worrying about traffic. Even in the middle of the street.

In this chapter, you will identify sentence fragments and write complete sentences.

What Are Fragments?

A **fragment** is an incomplete sentence. It lacks either a subject or a verb, or it fails to express a complete thought. You may see fragments in newspaper headlines and advertisements (*overnight weight loss*). You may also use fragments to save space when you are writing a text message. However, in college writing, it is unacceptable to write fragments.

CHAPTER 12

Sentence: More and more people are moving to urban centers.

Fragment: In developing countries.

Phrase Fragments

Phrase fragments are missing a subject or a verb. In each example, the fragment is underlined.

No verb: <u>The history of cities.</u> It is quite interesting.

No subject: Ancient civilizations usually had one major city. <u>Specialized in trades.</u>

How to Correct Phrase Fragments

To correct phrase fragments, add the missing subject or verb, or join fragment to another sentence. The following examples show how to correct the previous phrase fragments.

Join sentences: The history of cities is quite interesting.

Add words: Ancient civilizations usually had one major city. **The citizens in that city** specialized in trades.

Hint   **Incomplete Verbs**

The following example is a phrase fragment because it is missing a helping verb. To make this sentence complete, you must add the helping verb.

Fragment: Modern cities growing rapidly.

Sentence: Modern cities <u>are</u> growing rapidly.

CHAPTER 12

PRACTICE I Underline and correct ten phrase fragments.

It was founded

EXAMPLE: Damascus is one of the world's oldest cities. ~~Founded~~ in the third millenium B.C.

1. The first cities began in ancient civilizations. Mesopotamia, the Indus Valley, and China. Those were large ancient civilizations. Ancient cities such as Jericho, Harappa, and Mohenjo-daro had small populations. Compared to modern cities. For example, the first cities had only around 150,000 people. Eventually, ancient empires grew. Rome reached a population of one million. Baghdad. It exceeded that number.

2. During the Middle Ages, some European cities became powerful city-states. Venice and Genoa even had their own military and maritime institutions. Around that time. London became the largest city in the world. Paris as populated as Beijing and Istanbul.

3. The Industrial Revolution was an important phenomenon for the growth of cities. In the eighteenth and nineteenth centuries. Many people migrated from the countryside to the urban centers. Urbanization led to many social problems. Child labor, low wages, and unsanitary living conditions. Those were some common problems. Many reformers worked hard to improve the living conditions. Of the urban poor.

4. By the 1930s, the Great Depression raised the unemployment rate. In rural areas. Many people had to leave their farms and look for work in the cities. After World War II. Economic prosperity helped to increase the migration to the cities. Most of today's cities are growing and prospering.

Fragments with *-ing* and *to*

A fragment may begin with a **present participle**, which is the form of the verb that ends in *-ing* (*running, talking*). It may also begin with an **infinitive**, which is *to* plus the base form of the verb (*to run, to talk*). These fragments generally appear next to another sentence that contains the subject. In the examples, the fragments are underlined.

-*ing* fragment: <u>Reacting to urban sprawl.</u> City planners started a new movement in the 1980s and 1990s.

***to* fragment:**   Urban designers believe in the new urbanism. <u>To help people live better lives.</u>

How to Correct *-ing* and *to* Fragments

To correct an *-ing* or *to* fragment, add the missing words or join the fragment to another sentence. The following examples show how to correct the two previous fragments.

Join sentences: Reacting to urban sprawl, city planners started a new movement in the 1980s and 1990s.

Add words: Urban designers believe in the new urbanism. **They want** to help people live better lives.

Hint   When the *-ing* Word Is the Subject

Sometimes a gerund (*-ing* form of the verb) is the subject of a sentence. In the example, *cycling* is the subject of the sentence.

Correct sentence: <u>Cycling</u> is a great form of exercise in urban areas.

A sentence fragment occurs when the *-ing* word is part of an incomplete verb string or when you mention the subject in a previous sentence. In the example, the fragment is underlined.

Fragment: Many city dwellers get exercise. <u>Cycling on bike paths.</u>

 **PRACTICE 2**   Underline and correct ten *-ing* and *to* fragments.

One principle is designing

EXAMPLE: The new urbanism movement has many principles. ~~Designing~~ walkways in neighborhoods.

1. New urbanism is a suburban planning movement. To create people-friendly neighborhoods. To limit the use of cars. Urban planners design self-contained neighborhoods. Believing in the need to curtail urban sprawl. Architects pattern areas where people can walk to work and choose recreational activities close to home.

2. The new urbanism movement is a reaction against older suburban areas. After World War II, architects designed suburbs that relied heavily on the use of cars. Therefore, most people living in traditional suburbs have to commute to city centers. Creating problems such as traffic congestion and air pollution.

3. Driving to work, school, and shopping areas. Suburban dwellers waste a lot of time traveling in their cars. In addition, urban sprawl creates difficulties for people who cannot drive. Limiting their daily activities. To do errands downtown or at a mall. Nondrivers must find other means of transport.

4. To answer such concerns. Urban designers reconsidered traditional suburban models. Since 1990, the new urbanism movement has become very popular. To improve the quality of suburban life. City planners design

beautiful areas for living, working, shopping, and playing. They hire innovative architects who insert skylights and green spaces in their designs. Presently, there are many communities in North America. Using the principles of the new urban movement.

Explanatory Fragments

An **explanatory fragment** provides an explanation about a previous sentence and is missing a subject, a complete verb, or both. These types of fragments begin with one of the following words.

also	especially	for example	including	particularly
as well as	except	for instance	like	such as

In the examples, the explanatory fragment is underlined.

Fragment: Planners in the 1960s influenced the new urbanism movement. <u>For example, Jane Jacobs.</u>

Fragment: New urbanism planners take into consideration many factors. <u>Especially reducing the use of the automobile.</u>

How to Correct Explanatory Fragments

To correct explanatory fragments, add the missing words, or join the explanation or example to another sentence. The following examples show how to correct the previous explanatory fragments.

Add words: Planners in the 1960s influenced the new urbanism movement. For example, Jane Jacobs **was an important authority on urban planning**.

Join sentences: New urbanism planners take into consideration many factors, especially reducing the use of the automobile.

PRACTICE 3   Underline and correct ten explanatory fragments. You may need to add or remove words.

EXAMPLE: Some new urbanism towns are famous. ~~Such as~~ *, such as* Celebration.

1. New urbanists plan communities with a central downtown area that is

   walking distance from all neighborhoods. The first community built on the

   new urbanism principles is Seaside, Florida. It was started in 1981 and

   became very famous. For example, *The Atlantic Monthly*. It featured Seaside

   on its cover. Robert Davis bought the land to build the community. He

hired many people who followed the principles of the new urbanism philosophy. Such as architects and urban planners.

2. Seaside was relatively easy to build because the area did not have the traditional rules for developing land. For instance, no zoning regulations. The buildings in the town have uniform designs. Particularly the houses. They all have certain features, including porches that must be sixteen feet from the sidewalk. Also, the streets. They must be made of bricks so cars cannot speed.

3. There are many other towns. Like Seaside. The most famous of these is the one Disney has built in Florida called Celebration. It also has strict rules for conformity. For example, the windows. They must be decorated with white or off-white curtains. The houses are built close together. For instance, only twenty feet apart. In Celebration, if neighbors complain about a barking dog, the dog can be evicted from the town.

4. Many people criticize those types of communities. Especially regarding the conformity of the design. On the other hand, people moving to those towns hope to live in an ideal community. For example, no crime or social problems. However, critics point out that all communities have some social problems.

Dependent-Clause Fragments

A **dependent clause** has a subject and verb, but it cannot stand alone. It literally depends on another clause to be a complete sentence. Dependent clauses may begin with subordinating conjunctions or relative pronouns. The following list contains some of the most common words that begin dependent clauses.

Common Subordinating Conjunctions				**Relative Pronouns**
after	before	though	whenever	that
although	even though	unless	where	which
as	if	until	whereas	who(m)
because	since	what	whether	whose

In each example, the fragment is underlined.

> **Fragment:** In the city, houses are close together. <u>Whereas in the suburbs, houses have large yards.</u>

> **Fragment:** <u>Before William Levitt built Levittown.</u> Many people lived in congested neighborhoods.

How to Correct Dependent-Clause Fragments

To correct dependent-clause fragments, join the fragment to a complete sentence, or add the necessary words to make it a complete idea. You could also delete the subordinating conjunction. The following examples show how to correct the previous dependent-clause fragments.

> **Delete subordinator:** In the city, houses are close together. In the suburbs, houses have large yards.

> **Join sentences:** Before William Levitt built Levittown, many people lived in congested neighborhoods.

PRACTICE 4 Underline and correct ten dependent-clause fragments.

EXAMPLE: William Levitt and his brother built Levittown. ~~Because~~ *because* of a shortage of affordable housing.

1. In 1948, developer William Levitt built a community in

   Pennsylvania. Which has been designated the first traditional suburb.

   Levitt wanted to give returning soldiers the opportunity to participate in

   the American dream. He called his community Levittown. This town

   consisted of similarly built single-family homes. That attracted young

families. People wanted to escape the crowds of big cities like New York and Philadelphia. Homes in large cities were very expensive. Levittown contained affordable housing. The community grew to approximately 17,000 houses. Which led to the beginning of urban sprawl.

2. Some people criticized the idea of Levittown. Because all of the houses looked similar. Even though the town had four different house styles. The first residents sometimes got lost trying to find their homes. Although it began with the premise of affordable housing for everyone. Levittown initially discriminated against nonwhites and did not permit them to buy houses in the community. Eventually, Levittown abandoned its "whites-only" policy. In 1957, the first African Americans to buy a house there were Bill and Daisy Meyers. Who had rocks thrown at them by the other residents.

3. Because Levittown is getting older. It has become a more attractive suburb. Many homeowners have remodeled their homes, and the saplings have grown into mature trees. Although many other suburbs have developed. Levittown remains a model of traditional suburban living.

FINAL REVIEW

The following paragraphs contain the four types of fragments: phrase, explanatory, *-ing* and *to*, and dependent clause. Correct fifteen fragment errors.

EXAMPLE: Tourists have been coming to Tokyo. ~~Since~~ *since* World War II.

1. Tokyo, the world's largest city. It was originally called Edo. The Edo warrior

   family inhabited a marshy region of

   Japan. Where there were a few villages.

   Eventually, the town of Edo grew. It

   started to gain prominence in the 1600s.

   In 1603, Edo warrior Tokugawa Ieyasu

   became shogun or warlord of the region. He was so powerful that he moved

   the government from Kyoto to Edo. Thinking that he would have more

   control over politics. He acquired complete control over Japan. Quelling any

   opposition. His government promoted an isolationist policy. Japan had no

   contact with other nations. Until the nineteenth century.

2. From the seventeenth century to the nineteenth century, Japan was

   politically stable, allowing Edo's population to grow rapidly to about one

   million people. Both London and Paris had a smaller population. At that

   time. Edo became the economic center of Japan. Prospering greatly due

   to industry. Also at that time, Japanese society developed a class

   system. Based on four levels of hierarchy. The samurai or warriors

   were at the top of the social system.

3. The Tokugawa Ieyasu family's power collapsed by the 1850s. Because of

   corruption within its government. At the same time, the Western powers

   were pressuring Japan. To open trade. England and the United States

   wanted Japan as a trading post. For example, in 1853, Matthew Perry. He

   forced Japan to open trade relations with America. Japan westernized

rapidly. After its contact with Europe and America. In 1867, Edo's name was changed to Tokyo.

4. Since the late 1800s. Tokyo has modernized like other Western capitals. In 1923, a great earthquake destroyed much of the city, and rebuilding became a priority. Many structures were built. Such as a subway system in 1927, an airport in 1931, and a port in 1941. After World War II, Tokyo greatly expanded. Today, it is a mega metropolis. Inviting visitors from all around the world.

The Writer's Room   Topics for Writing

Write about one of the following topics. Check that there are no sentence fragments.

1. Write about where you live. Describe your neighborhood.
2. What are some similarities and differences between living in a city and living in a suburb?

Patricia Schwimmer (Canadian, b. 1953) "My San Francisco", 1994, Tempera, Private Collection. © Patricia Schwimmer/SuperStock.

CHECKLIST: SENTENCE FRAGMENTS

When you edit your writing, ask yourself this question.

Are my sentences complete? Check for the next types of fragments.

- phrase fragments
- *-ing* and *to* fragments
- explanatory fragments
- dependent-clause fragments

Los Angeles and San Francisco are moving closer

because

together. ~~Because~~ of the San Andreas fault. The two cities

if

will make the largest urban area in the world. ~~If~~ the movement

continues.

CHAPTER 13 Run-Ons

Section Theme **URBAN DEVELOPMENT**

In this chapter, you will read about architects and architecture.

Grammar Snapshot

Looking at Run-Ons

Darius Knightley is a freelance travel writer. The next excerpt about his recent trip to Barcelona contains a sentence error. The underlined error is a run-on.

> Barcelona is a city of contrasts. Visitors see medieval buildings, narrow streets, and <u>grandiose churches they also see grid-like neighborhoods, modernist architecture, and glass and steel places of worship.</u> The modern sections of the city contrast with the older areas.

In this chapter, you will learn to correct run-on sentences.

What Are Run-Ons?

A **run-on sentence** occurs when two or more complete sentences are incorrectly joined. In other words, the sentence runs on without stopping.

There are two types of run-on sentences.

1. A **fused sentence** has no punctuation to mark the break between ideas.

   Incorrect: Skyscrapers are unusually tall buildings the Taipei 101 tower is among the tallest.

2. A **comma splice** uses a comma incorrectly to connect two complete ideas.

   Incorrect: The CN Tower is located in Toronto, it is the world's tallest communication structure.

> **PRACTICE I**   Read the following sentences. Write C beside correct sentences, FS beside fused sentences, and CS beside comma splices.

EXAMPLE: Gustave Eiffel was born in 1832 he designed the Eiffel
Tower and the Statue of Liberty.   _FS_

1. One of the most recognizable modern structures is the Eiffel Tower, it was built at the end of the eighteenth century.   _____

2. The French government wanted to celebrate the centennial anniversary of the French Revolution, which took place in 1789.   _____

3. The government held a competition it invited architects to submit designs to commemorate the anniversary of the revolution.   _____

4. Winners of the competition would have their designs displayed at the World's Fair of 1889.   _____

5. Many architects submitted designs, Gustave Eiffel's tower design won.   _____

6. The tower took twenty-six months to complete it was the tallest structure in the world at that time.   _____

7. It was 1,051 feet tall and weighed 70,000 tons.   _____

8. Many Parisians did not like the look of the tower, they wanted to destroy it.   _____

9. But it proved to be a very popular tourist attraction people from all over the world visit Paris and climb the tower.   _____

10. In fact, tourism experts consider the Eiffel Tower as the number one tourist attraction in the world.   _____

Correcting Run-Ons

You can correct both fused sentences and comma splices in a variety of ways. Read the following run-on sentence, and then review the four ways to correct it.

> **Run-On:** Antoni Gaudi began his career as a secular architect he eventually became very religious.

1. Make two separate sentences by adding end punctuation, such as a period.

   > Antoni Gaudi began his career as a secular architect. **He** eventually became very religious.

2. Add a semicolon (;).

   > Antoni Gaudi began his career as a secular architect**;** he eventually became very religious.

3. Add a coordinating conjunction such as *for, and, nor, but, or, yet,* or *so.*

   > Antoni Gaudi began his career as a secular architect**, but** he eventually became very religious.

4. Add a subordinating conjunction such as *although, because, when, before, while, since,* or *after.*

   > **Although** Antoni Gaudi began his career as a secular architect, he eventually became very religious.

PRACTICE 2 Correct the run-ons by making two complete sentences.

EXAMPLE: Antoni Gaudi designed very interesting works~~,~~ ̲.̲ ̲H̲e̲ ~~he~~ is considered to be a genius.

1. Antoni Gaudi was born in 1852 in Tarragona, Spain he is considered to be

   Catalonia's greatest architect.

2. Gaudi became a Catholic he also believed in Catalan nationalism.

3. Gaudi designed the *Sagrada Familia* he wanted to express his Catholic faith

   in his work.

4. Nature fascinated Gaudi, he incorporated nature's images into his

   creations.

5. Classical design used geometric shapes Gaudi's designs mimicked shapes from nature.

6. Gaudi's style evolved from Gothic influences, he created intricate, flowing, asymmetrical shapes.

7. Businessmen in Barcelona commissioned Gaudi to design a modern neighborhood, he constructed many buildings like the Casa Mila.

8. His work used the *trencadis* style this style involves the use of broken tiles to decorate surfaces.

9. One of Gaudi's most famous designs is Park Guell, the park has dragon-shaped benches and tree-shaped columns.

10. Many people initially laughed at Gaudi's vision eight of his creations are now recognized as World Heritage Sites.

 **Semicolons and Transitional Expressions**

Another way to correct run-ons is to connect sentences with a transitional expression. Place a semicolon before the expression and a comma after it.

> **Example:** The construction costs were too high**; therefore,** the town abandoned plans to build city hall.
>
> The design was beautiful**; nevertheless,** it was rejected.

Some common transitional expressions are:

additionally	meanwhile	of course
furthermore	moreover	therefore
however	nevertheless	thus

To practice combining sentences with transitional expressions, see Chapter 10.

PRACTICE 3   Correct the run-ons by joining the two sentences with a semicolon.

EXAMPLE: I. M. Pei has designed many famous buildings *; the* the John F. Kennedy Library is just one.

1. The Louvre Palace is one of the most recognized buildings in Paris, it was built in the Renaissance style for French monarchs.

2. The French Revolution abolished the monarchy the Louvre became a museum.

3. French officials wanted to expand the Louvre, they hired a famous architect to modify the building.

4. I. M. Pei was born in China in 1917 he immigrated to the United States to study architecture.

5. The French government commissioned Pei to enlarge the museum, he designed three pyramids for the entrance.

6. The main pyramid gives light to the underground entrance, it is made of many glass squares.

7. The pyramid is about seventy feet high, it has two smaller pyramids on each side.

8. The pyramids were completed in 1989 many people thought the entrance was unattractive.

9. I. M. Pei is an outstanding architect his innovative designs have won many prizes.

PRACTICE 4   Correct the run-ons by joining the two sentences with a comma and a coordinator (*for, and, nor, but, or, yet, so*).

EXAMPLE: Arthur Erickson is a Canadian architect $\overset{, and}{}$ his designs are world famous.

1. The University of British Columbia has many beautiful buildings Arthur Erickson's Museum of Anthropology is the most beautiful.

Museum of Anthropology

2. The museum rooms are high and spacious they can house large totems of the northwest First Nations.

3. The museum contains unusual artifacts, its totem pole collection is very interesting.

4. Architect Arthur Erickson considers the environment important his designs must fit into the landscape.

5. Erickson was an inexperienced architect his design won first place in a competition.

6. Many architects entered the competition Erickson's design was the most innovative.

7. The first-place winner was asked to design Simon Fraser University Erickson evaluated the surroundings.

8. The site was on top of a mountain it overlooked the ocean.

9. Erickson could follow the design trend of the time he could design according to his personal vision.

10. Simon Fraser University fits into the landscape its buildings are built into the mountainside.

PRACTICE 5 Correct the run-ons by joining the two sentences with a **subordinator.** Use one of the following subordinators: *because, before, although, when, even though,* and *although.* If the dependent clause comes at the beginning of the sentence, remember to add a comma.

Even though
EXAMPLE: European ideas have influenced African architecture, many indigenous designs reveal beauty and practicality.

1. African architecture is not that well known it is very rich and diverse.

2. African architecture was influenced by Arabs they colonized North Africa.

3. Europeans arrived in the sixteenth century Islam provided inspiration for architectural design.

4. Until the twenty-first century, there were very few famous African architects African countries were controlled by European powers.

5. Modern African buildings are beautiful they are not appreciated as World Heritage Sites.

6. The Aswan Dam, one of the most famous dams in the world, was constructed in the twentieth century the Nile River no longer flooded each year.

7. The construction of the Aswan Dam was controversial people were concerned about its impact on the environment.

8. The Eastgate Centre was built in Harare it became the world's first modern building to use natural cooling methods.

9. Modern African architecture is gaining momentum architects are considering the unique needs of Africa.

PRACTICE 6   Use a variety of methods to correct ten run-on errors. Add commas when necessary.

EXAMPLE: Many new buildings are being erected all over China, *and* modern building designs are very popular.

1. The Chinese Revolution dominated politics China's government developed policies to minimize class differences. As a result, new buildings were designed for utility with no regard for beauty.

2. Now, China is industrializing at a great rate businesses are asking architects to design practical but beautiful buildings. The National Theatre building, for example, is controversial, it is also extremely intriguing. It was designed by French architect Paul Andreu, many people have criticized its design. It is shaped like an egg. It has three halls and a lake, it has a bridge. Another highly discussed building in Beijing is the CCTV tower. It looks like the letter Z, many Chinese think it is an eyesore.

3. The cost of building these edifices is very expensive, some members of the public complain that such designs are too foreign. Others believe that

CHAPTER 13

designing interesting buildings is very important China built a fabulous stadium for the 2008 Olympics. The Olympic Stadium is a necessity, the cost was prohibitive.

4. The Beijing skyline has changed, not everybody has liked the changes. Some say that such change is the price for industrialization. Average citizens are eager for Beijing to join the ranks of the most beautiful cities in the world.

FINAL REVIEW

Correct ten run-on errors.

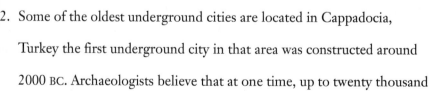

EXAMPLE: The construction industry is the largest in the world, ~~publie~~ *and public* and private buildings consume a lot of energy.

1. When most people envision cities, they think about houses, roads, and skyscrapers built above ground they do not think about subterranean cities. However, many people use underground public and private buildings every day. In North America, there are at least five hundred public and private underground buildings for example, the Engineering Library at the University of Berkeley and the Vietnam Veterans Memorial Education Center are only two such subterranean structures. More and more underground structures are being built every day.

Entrance to tunnels in Cappadocia.

2. Some of the oldest underground cities are located in Cappadocia, Turkey the first underground city in that area was constructed around 2000 BC. Archaeologists believe that at one time, up to twenty thousand

people lived in those underground Turkish cities the early Christians used them as a means to escape persecution.

3. Montreal, Canada, contains an extremely large modern underground city. It was designed by I. M. Pei in the 1960s other architects have contributed to its expansion. It is located downtown and has around 26 miles of tunnels with about 120 exterior access points. More than 500,000 people use the underground city each day they want to avoid Montreal's very cold temperatures in the winter.

4. There are many reasons to build underground. First, underground buildings benefit from better climate control architects say that such buildings can be heated and cooled more efficiently than above-ground buildings. Also, building underground reduces the impact on the environment, forests and fields do not have to be cleared. Moreover, the wind, snow, and rain do not erode the walls, well-constructed underground buildings are resistant to fire and earthquakes.

5. Perhaps in the future, there will be more underground public and private buildings, they are more environmentally friendly and more energy efficient. Certainly it is time to rethink how urban planners design cities.

The Writer's Room Topics for Writing

Write about one of the following topics. Edit your writing and ensure that there are no run-ons.

1. Are there any buildings or areas in your neighborhood, town, or country that you find attractive or unattractive? Describe these buildings and explain why you believe they are beautiful or unsightly.

2. Are there any changes or additions that you would make to the town or city where you live, such as adding a new park or a museum? What suggestions would you make to city planners?

✔ CHECKLIST: RUN-ONS

When you edit your writing, ask yourself this question.

Are my sentences correctly formed and punctuated? Check for and correct any fused sentences and comma splices.

One of the most successful architects in the world is Frank Lloyd
Wright. His
~~Wright his~~ famous house design "Falling Water" is a national

monument.

Faulty Parallel Structure

CONTENTS

Section Theme **URBAN DEVELOPMENT**

In this chapter, you will read about landscapes and gardens.

Grammar Snapshot

Looking at Parallel Structure

The Royal Botanic Gardens in Kew, England, supports research on conservation of the environment. The following paragraph summarizes one of the conservation schemes in Peru. Review the underlined ideas to see how they are parallel.

The Huarango (*Prosopis pallida*) forests of the south coast of Peru are among the most highly threatened ecosystems on earth. The remaining trees are important primary producers, forming soil, preventing desertification, and providing the only refuge for biodiversity in large areas of hyperarid desert. They also furnish an extraordinary cornucopia of food, forage, and other products used by local people for thousands of years.

In this chapter, you will identify and correct faulty parallel structure.

What Is Parallel Structure?

Parallel structure occurs when pairs or groups of items in a sentence are balanced. Notice how the following sentences repeat grammatical structures but not ideas.

Parallel Nouns:	Books, stores, and catalogs give gardeners information.
Parallel Tenses:	Gardeners dig and plant in the soil.
Parallel Adjectives:	Kew Garden is large, colorful, and breathtaking.
Parallel Phrases:	You will find the public garden down the road, over the bridge, and through the field.
Parallel Clauses:	There are some gardens that have just trees, and some that have only flowers and plants.

Correcting Faulty Parallel Structure

Use parallel structure for a series of words or phrases, for paired clauses, for comparisons, and for two-part constructions. If you see "//" or simply "faulty parallelism" on one of your marked essays, try the following tips for correcting those errors.

Series of Words or Phrases

Use parallel structure when words or phrases are joined in a series.

Not Parallel:	The English, the Chinese, and people from Japan create luxurious gardens.
Parallel Nouns:	The English, the Chinese, and the Japanese create luxurious gardens.
Not Parallel:	I like to read books about gardens, to attend lectures about gardening, and buying plants for my garden.
Parallel Verbs:	I like to read books about gardens, to attend lectures about gardening, and to buy plants for my garden.

Paired Clauses

Use parallel structure when independent clauses are joined by *and*, *but*, or *or*.

Not Parallel:	I am allergic to grass seed, and ragweed also gives me allergies.
Parallel Word Order:	I am allergic to grass seed, and I am also allergic to ragweed.

Not Parallel:	The tourists were dazzled, but they also had a feeling of fatigue.
Parallel Adjectives:	The tourists were <u>dazzled</u>, but they were also <u>fatigued</u>.

Hint Use Consistent Voice

When joining two independent clauses with a coordinating conjunction, use a consistent voice. For example, if the first part of the sentence uses the active voice, the other part should also use the active voice.

Not parallel: The bees <u>flew</u> to the flowers, and then the nectar <u>was tasted</u> by them.

Parallel active voice: The bees <u>flew</u> to the flowers, and then they <u>tasted</u> the nectar.

PRACTICE I Underline and correct the faulty parallel structure in each sentence.

EXAMPLE: The Hermitage, which was the Winter Palace of the Russian Tsars, has a collection of valuable paintings,
antique furniture
rare books, and <u>furniture that is antique</u>.

The Winter Palace

1. Tsar Peter the Great was cosmopolitan, educated, and he had great determination.

2. In 1703, Peter created plans and workers were ordered to build a new city.

3. The Tsar commissioned a summer palace and a palace for the winter.

CHAPTER 14

4. The Tsar designed parks, flower gardens, and he was also creating arboretums.

5. The summer garden contains large, exotic trees that are rare.

6. The landscaper, Domenico Trezzini, worked fastidiously, diligently, and he was creative.

7. Tourists can stroll down paths, over bridges, and walking by marble statues.

8. St. Petersburg is called the "window to the west," "the city of the white nights," and people also view it as "the northern Venice."

Comparisons

Use parallel structure in comparisons containing *than* or *as*.

Not Parallel:	Designing an interesting garden is easier than to take care of it.
Parallel -ing Forms:	Designing an interesting garden is easier than taking care of it.
Not Parallel:	The rock garden looks as colorful as the garden where there are roses.
Parallel Noun Phrases:	The rock garden looks as colorful as the rose garden.

Two-Part Constructions

Use parallel structure for the following paired items.

either . . . or	not . . . but	both . . . and
neither . . . nor	not only . . . but also	rather . . . than

Not Parallel:	The lecture on landscaping was both enlightening and of use.
Parallel Adjectives:	The lecture on landscaping was both enlightening and useful.

Not Parallel: I could either see the bonsai exhibit or going to
                         a film.

Parallel Verbs: I could either <u>see</u> the bonsai exhibit or <u>go</u> to a
                         film.

PRACTICE 2   Correct ten errors in parallel construction.

EXAMPLE: Cities need parks to create green areas, to prevent overcrowding,
                        to develop recreational facilities
           and <u>people can use them for recreation.</u>

1. During the Industrial Revolution, urban life changed rapidly and

   with completion. City planners realized that more people were moving to

   the cities. Planners, politicians, and people who immigrated saw city life

   changing. Urban designers wanted to create green space rather than

   filling cities with concrete buildings.

2. One of the most important advocates of city beautification was Frederick

   Law Olmsted. He was born in 1822, in Hartford, Connecticut. He not

   only promoted urban planning, but he also was designing beautiful city

   gardens. He and collaborator Calvert Vaux designed New York's Central

   Park. Olmsted wanted the park to reflect his personal philosophy, so in it

   he created open spaces, beautiful views, and paths that wind.

3. Olmsted and Vaux designed many other projects. An important design

   was the Niagara Falls project. At that time, the falls were not completely

   visible to tourists. Olmsted wanted to create a harmonious landscape,

   to allow greater tourist accessibility, and conservation of the area

was important to him. Such a park required a great deal of planning. Goat Island separates Canada from the United States. Either the landscapers could buy Goat Island or Goat Island was continuing to be an eyesore. Olmsted and Vaux bought the island and restored it.

4. For Olmsted, contributing to the community was more important than to have fame. He designed Mount Royal Park in Montreal, and the 1893 World Fair in Chicago was also planned by him. He was known as much for his sense of beauty as for respecting the environment. Olmsted died in 1903, but thousands of people continue to enjoy his legacy.

FINAL REVIEW

Correct fifteen errors in parallel construction.

EXAMPLE: Walking through Kew Gardens is more relaxing than
reading
~~to read~~ a book.

1. One of London's most famous sites is the Royal Botanic Gardens. Kew Gardens contains flower beds, greenhouses, and there are stone sculptures. In the 1700s, King George III commissioned and was supporting the garden's expansion. Since then, not only has Kew been enlarged, but it was becoming a World Heritage site. To visit Kew Gardens, travel over the Thames, along the edge of Kew village, and you must go past the Kew Gardens subway station.

2. Today, at Kew Gardens, botanical research is as important as attracting people who are tourists. The site is important for storing seeds, cataloguing plants, and professional gardeners go there for training. But, modernization is creating problems for Kew. Being so close to London, Kew experiences air pollution, hot weather, and the rainfall is in small amounts. Even with such problems, Kew is truly beautiful, very innovative, and it is also extremely impressive.

3. Another famous European garden is the Versailles garden near Paris, France. King Louis XIV moved his court from Paris to Versailles in 1682, and he asked the great landscaper Andre Le Notre to design the gardens. Le Notre worked carefully, intuitively, and with passion. Le Notre not only had to plan a garden, but water also had to be brought to the site by him. The original soil was neither rich and it was not fertile.

4. Le Notre succeeded in his design. It is perfectly laid out, adhering to Renaissance principles. The gardens have walkways, fountains, statues, and there are ponds. The gardens reflect the glory of the king, the beauty of nature, and human creativity. Le Notre received great fame, honor, and was wealthy. Millions of visitors visit Versailles to enjoy the gardens, to understand a part of history, and seeing the splendor of the age of Louis XIV.

The Writer's Room **Topics for Writing**

Choose one of the following topics, and write a paragraph. Make sure your nouns, verbs, and sentence structures are parallel.

1. If you could be anywhere right now, where would you be? Describe that place. Include details that appeal to the senses.
2. What do you do to relax? List some steps.

CHECKLIST: PARALLEL STRUCTURE

When you edit your writing, ask yourself this question.

Are my grammatical structures balanced? Check for errors in these cases:

- in words or phrases joined in a series
- in independent clauses joined by *and*, *but*, or *or*
- in comparisons

English gardens

We saw Chinese gardens, Japanese gardens, and ~~gardens from England~~.

Mistakes with Modifiers

CONTENTS
- Misplaced Modifiers
- Dangling Modifiers

Section Theme **URBAN DEVELOPMENT**

In this chapter, you will read about pollution and other urban issues.

Grammar Snapshot

Looking at Mistakes with Modifiers

Myles Oka, a student in urban planning, wrote about the consequences of urban sprawl. The next excerpt contains some modifier errors.

> Because I live in a suburb, I drive many miles each day to work. Last night, stuck in traffic, car horns blared constantly. Commuters inched their cars slowly like caterpillars wanting to get home. I was stressed and anxious.

In this chapter, you will identify and correct misplaced and dangling modifiers.

Misplaced Modifiers

A **modifier** is a word, a phrase, or a clause that describes or modifies nouns or verbs in a sentence. To use a modifier correctly, place it next to the word(s) that you want to modify.

modifier   words that are modified

<u>Trying to combat pollution</u>, **city planners** have launched an anti-littering campaign.

A **misplaced modifier** is a word, a phrase, or a clause that is not placed next to the word that it modifies. When a modifier is too far from the word that it is describing, the meaning of the sentence can become confusing or unintentionally funny.

I saw a pamphlet about littering waiting in the mayor's office.

(How could a pamphlet wait in the mayor's office?)

Commonly Misplaced Modifiers

As you read the sample sentences for each type of modifier, notice how the meaning of the sentence changes depending on where the modifier is placed.

Prepositional Phrase Modifiers

A prepositional phrase is made of a preposition and its object.

Confusing: Helen read an article on electric cars <u>in a cafe</u>.

(Who was in the cafe: Helen or the cars?)

Clear: <u>In a cafe</u>, Helen read an article on electric cars.

Participle Modifiers

A participle modifier is a phrase that contains an *-ing* verb or an *-ed* verb.

Confusing: Jamal Reed learned about anti-littering laws <u>touring Singapore</u>.

(Can laws tour Singapore?)

Clear: While <u>touring Singapore</u>, Jamal Reed learned about anti-littering laws.

Relative Clause Modifiers

A modifier can be a relative clause or phrase beginning with *who, whose, which,* or *that.*

Confusing: The woman received a $1,000 fine from the officer <u>who dropped a candy wrapper</u>.

(Who dropped the candy wrapper: the woman or the officer?)

Clear: The woman who dropped a candy wrapper received a $1,000 fine from the officer.

Limiting Modifiers

Limiting modifiers are words such as *almost, nearly, only, merely, just,* and *even.* In the examples, notice how the placement of *almost* changes the meaning of each sentence.

Almost all of the citizens took the steps that solved the littering problem.

(Some of the citizens did not take the steps, but most did.)

All of the citizens **almost** took the steps that solved the littering problem.

(The citizens did not take the steps.)

All of the citizens took the steps that **almost** solved the littering problem.

(The steps did not solve the littering problem.)

 Correcting Misplaced Modifiers

To correct misplaced modifiers, follow these steps:

1. First, identify the modifier.
    Armando saw the oil slick **standing on the pier.**
2. Then, identify the word or words being modified.
    Armando
3. Finally, move the modifier next to the word(s) being modified.
    Standing on the pier, Armando saw the oil slick.

PRACTICE I   Underline and correct the misplaced modifier in each sentence.

who was fined $500
EXAMPLE: The man forgot to flush the public toilet <u>who was fined $500</u>.

1. Experts recognize Singapore as the cleanest city in the world from the United Nations.

2. Singaporean police officers will immediately arrest litterbugs who patrol city streets.

3. After littering, officers give a $1,000 fine to polluters.

4. For a second littering offense, a polluter must clean a public area such as a park or school yard wearing a bright yellow vest.

5. In 1992, Singapore's new law prohibited the importation, selling, or chewing of gum, which caused a large controversy.

6. Because gum was stuck on them, passengers could not close the doors to the subway trains.

7. In 2004, the law was revised to allow gum into the country that has medicinal purposes.

8. Evangeline dropped her gum on a downtown street not seeing the police officer.

9. She nearly cleaned the park for eight hours on the weekend.

10. Singaporeans with no litter are proud of their city.

Dangling Modifiers

A **dangling modifier** opens a sentence but does not modify any words in the sentence. It "dangles" or hangs loosely because it is not connected to any other part of the sentence. To avoid having a dangling modifier, make sure that the modifier and the first noun that follows it have a logical connection.

Confusing: While eating a candy bar, the wrapper fell on the ground.

(Can a wrapper eat a candy bar?)

Clear: While eating a candy bar, Zena dropped the wrapper on the ground.

Confusing: To attend the conference, a background in environmental work is necessary.

(Can a background attend a conference?)

Clear: To attend the conference, **participants need** a background in environmental work.

 **Correcting Dangling Modifiers**

To correct dangling modifiers, follow these steps:

1. First, identify the modifier.
   When traveling, public transportation should be used.
2. Then, decide who or what the writer aims to modify.
   Who is traveling? **People**
3. Finally, add the missing subject (and in some cases, also add or remove words) so that the sentence makes sense.
   When traveling, people should use public transportation.

PRACTICE 2   Underline the dangling modifier in each sentence. Then, rewrite the sentence keeping the modifier. You may have to add or remove words to give the sentence a logical meaning.

EXAMPLE: Enjoying parks, it is difficult when there is a lot of litter.

It is difficult for people to enjoy parks when there is a lot of litter.

1. Believing it is not garbage, cigarette butts are left on city streets.

_____

_____

2. With an unconcerned attitude, the hamburger wrapper ended up on the ground.

_____

_____

3. Unhappy with the garbage in the park, a major cleanup took place.

_____

_____

4. Playing in the sand, there were pieces of glass from broken bottles.

_____

_____

5. Sitting on a park bench, all sorts of plastic bags drifted by.

_____

_____

6. To understand the effects of littering, the cleanup costs must be examined.

_____

_____

7. Seeing no available trash can, the cigarette butt can be wrapped up and carried.

_____

_____

8. While walking barefoot on the grass, a piece of glass cut Pablo's foot.

_____

_____

9. The car alarm was wailing while reading my newspaper in the park.

_____

_____

10. By thinking about litter, parks can be kept clean.

_____

_____

PRACTICE 3   Correct the dangling or misplaced modifiers in the following sentences. If the sentence is correct, write _C_ next to it.

Alicia noticed that

EXAMPLE: Living in Mexico City, the air is extremely bad.

1. Having the highest level of air pollution in the world, people suffer from asthma in Mexico City.

2. Coming mainly from the millions of cars on the streets, the dangers of the air pollution are well known.

3. Situated in a valley surrounded by mountains, pollution gets trapped above Mexico City.

4. Living near Ermita subway, Alicia Gutierrez suffers from pollution-related illnesses.

5. Because they are older models, the latest catalytic converters are not in many cars.

6. Mexico City planners discussed ways to combat the bad air in a meeting.

7. Several years ago, Mexico City's mayor introduced the new fuel-efficient buses in a state of excitement.

8. Because of the law requiring motorists to leave their cars home one day a week, Luis took a bus to work.

9. Trying to combat the pollution, at least five billion dollars has been spent.

10. Appreciating Mexico City's initiatives, the air quality is much better.

FINAL REVIEW

Identify fifteen dangling or misplaced modifier errors in this selection. Then, correct each error. You may need to add or remove words to ensure that the sentence makes sense.

EXAMPLE: Working on his school project, ~~some surprising results were found.~~ *a young boy found surprising results.*

1. Emilio discovered that there are many ways to help the environment in his school project. He sat with his parents to discuss energy-saving strategies drinking coffee. First, there are things people can do to help the environment in their kitchens. When using freezer bags or aluminum foil, washing them can reduce waste. Also, people should use cloth napkins and dishtowels instead of paper products. With airtight lids, Emilio places leftover food in plastic containers.

2. Emilio and his parents also discussed tips for other areas of the home. Families can take measures in the bathroom who want to save energy. For example, people should take shorter showers. While Emilio is brushing his teeth, it is important to leave the faucet turned off as much as possible. People can install a toilet dam to reduce water consumption.

3. For their laundry room, Emilio's parents bought energy-efficient appliances with a smile. After washing shirts, the family hangs them out to dry instead of using a clothes dryer. ~~They~~ also buy phosphate-free detergent doing the shopping.

4. When Emilio's father goes to the grocery store, he makes sensible decisions about products near his house. Trying to do fewer trips and buying in bulk, the gas consumption is reduced. He buys compact fluorescent lightbulbs at the local hardware store that save energy.

5. The family's furnace needs to be upgraded, which is very old. Based on the latest technology, Emilio's parents are planning to buy an energy-efficient heater. Also, watching only one television, there is a reduction in energy consumption and the family spends more time together. Using the techniques mentioned above, Emilio's family has managed to reduce its energy consumption by nearly thirty percent.

The Writer's Room **Topics for Writing**

Write about one of the following topics. Proofread your text to ensure that there are no modifier errors.

1. What are some steps that your neighborhood or town could take to combat a littering or pollution problem?

2. What are some types of polluters? Write about three categories of polluters.

CHECKLIST: MODIFIERS

When you edit your writing, ask yourself these questions.

Are my modifiers in the correct position? Check for errors with the following:

- prepositional-phrase modifiers
- participle modifiers
- relative clause modifiers
- limiting modifiers

> *Wearing overalls, the*
> ~~The~~ urban planner surveyed the garbage ~~wearing overalls~~.

Do my modifiers modify something in the sentence? Check for dangling modifiers.

> *the police officer gave*
> Throwing the plastic bag onto the street, a hefty fine ~~was~~
> ~~given~~ to the tourist.

Subject–Verb Agreement

CHAPTER 16

CONTENTS

- Basic Subject–Verb Agreement Rules
- More Than One Subject
- Special Subject Forms
- Verb Before the Subject
- Interrupting Words and Phrases

Section Theme **INTERNATIONAL TRADE**

In this chapter, you will read about cultural differences in the world of international business.

Grammar Snapshot

Looking at Subject–Verb Agreement

The next excerpt is from "Vacation Policies Around the World," an article that appeared on Jobcircle.com. The subjects and verbs are identified.

> On average, **European employees** get four weeks of vacation. **It** would take the typical American employee fifteen years or longer to attain the same vacation privileges, says **Ann Leeds**, a Hewitt **consultant** who specializes in global benefit practices. And as **job-hopping** becomes more common, fewer **Americans** than ever qualify for such extended vacations.

In this chapter, you will practice making subjects and verbs agree.

Basic Subject–Verb Agreement Rules

GRAMMAR LINK

For more information about the present tense, see Chapter 17.

Subject–verb agreement simply means that a subject and verb agree in number. A singular subject needs a singular verb and a plural subject needs a plural verb.

Simple Present Tense Agreement

Writers use **simple present tense** to indicate that an action is habitual or factual. Review the following rules for simple present tense agreement.

Third-person singular form: When the subject is *he, she, it*, or the equivalent (*Mark, Carol, Miami*), add an *-s* or *-es* ending to the verb.

Maria Orlon works as a marketing researcher.

Base form: When the subject is *I, you, we, they*, or the equivalent (*women, the Rocky Mountains*), do not add an ending to the verb.

Many **businesses** rely on marketing research.

> *Hint* **Be, Have, and Do**
>
> The verbs *be, have*, and *do* have irregular third-person singular forms.
>
> **Be:**　I am　　He is　　We are
> **Have:**　I have　　She has　　They have
> **Do:**　I do　　It does　　You do

Agreement in Other Tenses

In the past tense, almost all verbs have one past form. The only past tense verb requiring subject–verb agreement is the verb *be*, which has two past forms: *was* and *were*.

I was tired. **Edward** was also tired. That day, **we** were very lazy.

In the present perfect tense, which is formed with *have* or *has* and the past participle, use *has* when the subject is third-person singular and *have* for all other forms.

The **travel service** has raised its booking fees. Other **agencies** have not raised their fees.

GRAMMAR LINK

For more information about using the present perfect tense, see Chapter 17.

In the future tense and with modal forms (*can, could, would, may, might* . . .), use the same form of the verb with every subject.

I will work. **She** will work with me. **We** can work together.

> ### *Hint*   **Use Standard English**
> In casual conversations and in movies, you may hear people say *He be cool*, or *She don't have the time*. In professional and academic situations, use the correct forms of *be*, *have*, and *do*: *He is cool* and *She doesn't have the time*.

PRACTICE I   Underline the correct form of the verbs in parentheses.

EXAMPLE: Many businesses (<u>export</u> / exports) products to other nations.

1. Although several countries (share / shares) the English language, the details in the language and culture (be / is / are) different. Business travelers (learn / learns) about these differences.

2. For example, Americans and Canadians (put / puts) gas in their cars, whereas British citizens (use / uses) petrol. In England, you (do / does) not phone people, you "ring" them. Australians also (use / uses) interesting expressions. A "chalkie" (is / are) a teacher, and a "mozzie" (is / are) a mosquito.

3. In England, class-based traditions (is / are) still strong, and many people (support / supports) the monarchy. Australia, on the other hand, (have / has) a very egalitarian culture. Mr. Ian Wynn (have / has) been an Australian real estate agent for seven years, and he (does / do) not like signs of arrogance. Last spring, when some tourists (was / were) arrogant, Wynn said, "Don't be a tall poppy. The tall poppy (get / gets) its head cut off."

4. Spelling also (differ / differs) among English-speaking nations. In countries where people speak British English, common words such as "flavor" or

"color" (have / has) an *our* ending. For example, "color" (become / becomes) "colour" in Canada and Great Britain.

More Than One Subject

There are special agreement rules when there is more than one subject in a sentence.

And

When two subjects are joined by *and*, use the plural form of the verb.

<u>Colleges</u>, <u>universities</u>, and <u>trade schools</u> **prepare** students for the job market.

Or / Nor

When two subjects are joined by *or* or *nor*, the verb agrees with the subject that is the closest to it.

singular

The layout artists or the <u>editor</u> **decides** how the cover will look.

plural

Neither the artist nor her <u>assistants</u> **make** changes to the design.

> ## Hint   As Well As and Along With
>
> The phrases *as well as* and *along with* are not the same as *and*. They do not form a compound subject. The real subject is before the interrupting expression.
>
> <u>Japan</u>, <u>China</u>, and <u>South Korea</u> **develop** high-tech computer products.
>
> <u>Japan</u>, as well as China and South Korea, **develops** high-tech computer products.

PRACTICE 2   Underline the correct verb in each sentence. Make sure the verb agrees with the subject.

EXAMPLE: Japan and China (<u>have</u> / has) interesting types of restaurants.

1. Tokyo and other Japanese cities (have / has) "Maid Cafés."

2. The hostess and the female servers (dress / dresses) in traditional maid uniforms.

3. Recently, in the Otome Road area of Tokyo, a businesswoman and her

    partner (have / has) opened a Butler Café.

4. Every day, Jin or another waiter (serve / serves) customers.

5. The coffee or the tea (come / comes) on a special tray.

6. The host and the waiters (treat / treats) the customers like British royalty.

7. "Mademoiselle" or "Your Highness" (is / are) said to each customer by the

    server in the butler uniform.

8. A crumpet as well as a large scone (appear / appears) on each table.

9. Every day, many young and old women (try / tries) to get a table at the

    Butler Café.

Special Subject Forms

Some subjects are not easy to identify as singular or plural. Two common types
are indefinite pronouns and collective nouns.

Indefinite Pronouns

Indefinite pronouns refer to a general person, place, or thing. Carefully review
the following list of indefinite pronouns.

Indefinite Pronouns

Singular	another	each	nobody	other
	anybody	everybody	no one	somebody
	anyone	everyone	nothing	someone
	anything	everything	one	something
Plural	both, few, many, others, several			

Singular Indefinite Pronouns

In the following sentences, the verbs require the third-person-singular form because the subjects are singular.

Almost <u>everyone</u> **knows** about the Free Trade Agreement.

You can put one or more singular nouns (joined by *and*) after *each* and *every*. The verb is still singular.

<u>Every</u> client **likes** the new rule. <u>Each</u> man and woman **knows** about it.

Plural Indefinite Pronouns

Both, *few*, *many*, *others*, and *several* are all plural subjects. The verb is always plural.

A representative from the United States and another from Mexico are sitting at a table. <u>Both</u> **want** to compromise.

Collective Nouns

Collective nouns refer to groups of people or things. Review the following list

army	class	crowd	group	population
association	club	family	jury	public
audience	committee	gang	mob	society
band	company	government	organization	team

of common collective nouns.

Generally, each group acts as a unit, so you must use the singular form of the verb.

The <u>company</u> **is** ready to make a decision.

> ### Hint   Police Is Plural
>
> Treat the word *police* as a plural noun because the word "officers" is implied but not stated.
>
> The police **have** a protester in custody.

PRACTICE 3   Underline the correct verb in each sentence.

EXAMPLE: The Executive Planet Web site (have / <u>has</u>) tips for business travelers.

1. Each large and small nation (have / has) its own gift-giving rules. For

   example, Singapore (have / has) strict rules against bribery, and the government (pride / prides) itself on being corruption-free. The police (arrest / arrests) officials who accept a bribe.

2. Specific rules (apply / applies) to gift-giving in Singapore. Certainly, everyone (love / loves) to receive a gift. Nobody (like / likes) to be left out while somebody else (open / opens) a present, so in Singapore, every businessman or businesswoman (know / knows) that gifts must be presented to a group. For example, if somebody (want / wants) to thank a receptionist, he or she (give / gives) a gift to the entire department. The group (accept / accepts) the gift graciously.

3. To be polite, most individuals (refuse / refuses) a gift initially. Some (believe / believes) that a refusal (make / makes) them appear less greedy. If the gift-giver (continue / continues) to insist, the recipient will accept the gift.

4. Singaporeans (do / does) not unwrap gifts in front of the giver. It (imply / implies) that the receiver is impatient and greedy. Everyone (thank / thanks) the gift-giver and (wait / waits) to open the gift in privacy.

5. China, as well as Japan, also (have / has) unusual gift-giving rules. In China, nobody (give / gives) a gift in white or green wrapping paper because those colors are unlucky. In Japan, the number four (sound / sounds) like the word meaning "death," so people do not give gifts that contain four items. To avoid insulting their hosts, business travelers should learn about gift-giving rules in other nations.

Verb Before the Subject

Usually the verb comes after the subject, but in some sentences, the verb is before the subject. In such cases, you must still ensure that the subject and verb agree.

There or Here

When a sentence begins with *there* or *here*, the subject always follows the verb. *There* and *here* are not subjects.

V   S   V   S

Here **is** the <u>menu</u>. There **are** many different <u>sandwiches</u>.

Questions

In questions, word order is usually reversed, and the main or helping verb is placed before the subject. In the following example, the main verb is *be*.

V   S   V   S

Where **is** the <u>Butler Café</u>? **Is** the <u>food</u> good?

In questions in which the main verb is not *be*, the subject agrees with the helping verb.

HV   S   V   HV   S   V

When **does** the <u>café</u> **close**? **Do** <u>students</u> **work** there?

PRACTICE 4   Correct any subject–verb agreement errors. If there are no errors, write C for "correct" in the space.

         Have
EXAMPLE: ~~Has~~ you ever visited Turkey? _____

1. Is there etiquette rules about greetings? _____

2. Do each nation have its own rules? _____

3. There be specific rules in each country. _____

4. In Turkey, do older men or women receive preferential treatment? _____

5. If someone enters a room, he or she greet the oldest person first. _____

6. There be tremendous respect for elders. _____

7. Why is the two women holding hands? _____

8. In Turkey, handholding is a sign of respect and friendship. _____

9. In many companies, there have not been enough attention given to business etiquette. _____

10. On the other hand, there is many business professionals who learn about the customs of their foreign clients. _____

Interrupting Words and Phrases

Words that come between the subject and the verb may confuse you. In these cases, look for the subject and make sure that the verb agrees with the subject.

> S   interrupting phrase   V
> Some <u>companies</u> in the transportation sector **lose** money.

> S   interrupting phrase   V
> The <u>manager</u> in my office never **wears** a suit and tie.

Hint   Identify Interrupting Phrases

When you revise your writing, place words that separate the subject and the verb in parentheses. Then you can check to see if your subjects and verbs agree.

> S   interrupting phrase   V
> An <u>employee</u> **(in my brother's company) annoys** his co-workers.

When interrupting phrases contain *of the*, the subject appears before the phrase.

> S   interrupting phrase   V
> <u>One</u> **(of the most common work-related ailments) is** carpal tunnel syndrome.

PRACTICE 5   Identify the subject and place any words that come between each subject and verb in parentheses. Then underline the correct form of the verb. (Two possible verb choices are in bold.)

EXAMPLE: (One) (of the most controversial topics in business circles) **is** / **are** stress.

1. People in this nation **take / takes** very few vacation days. Other nations, including France, England, and Sweden, **have / has** many vacation days. The average employee in France **have / has** about thirty-nine vacation days annually. The typical American, according to numerous studies, only **take / takes** fourteen days off each year.

2. Canada, as well as England and France, **legislate / legislates** vacation days. The United States, unlike most industrialized countries, **do / does** not regulate benefits in the private sector. One of the problems caused by a lack of time off **is / are** stress-related illness.

3. Some Americans, according to JobCircle.com, **is / are** beginning to rebel. Workers increasingly **call / calls** in sick when they really **have / has** family responsibilities or other reasons for missing work. Ted Owens, for example, **have / has** a job as a broker in Los Angeles. Each of the workers in Ted Owens's office **admit / admits** to using sick days for other purposes. Most of the workers **have / has** lied to the boss.

Interrupting Words—*Who, Which, That*

If a sentence contains a clause beginning with *who*, *which*, or *that*, then the verb agrees with the subject preceding *who*, *which*, or *that*.

There is a <u>woman</u> in my neighborhood who **works** as an executive.

Sometimes a complete dependent clause appears between the subject and verb.

interrupting clause
The <u>problem</u>, which we discussed, **needs** to be solved.

PRACTICE 6   Correct nine subject–verb agreement errors.

discusses
EXAMPLE: Jeff Geissler ~~discuss~~ maternity leave in an article for the Associated Press.

1. Elisa Elbert, who works for an accounting firm, is expecting a child. Elisa, like other Australian citizens, receive up to twelve months of paid leave.

Madhuri Datta, a Canadian, is having her baby next month. Datta, who is due in November, want to share her paid leave with her husband. According to a recent poll, one of the Canadian government's best laws are the one that permits parents to divide thirty-five weeks of paid parental leave.

2. The U.S. Family and Medical Leave Act, which only cover workers in large companies, protect new mothers from losing their jobs. The act, according to a Harvard study, only provide for twelve weeks of paid leave.

3. One of the Harvard researchers think that the United States is out of step with most nations. The study showed that 163 out of 168 nations has some sort of paid parental leave. The United States, along with Papua New Guinea and Swaziland, do not.

FINAL REVIEW
Correct fifteen errors in subject–verb agreement.

EXAMPLE: The worker ~~enjoy~~ *enjoys* his afternoon nap.

1. Is afternoon naps beneficial? In Spain, a siesta have been part of the culture for centuries. Many businesses, including shops, restaurants, and offices, close for three hours each afternoon and then opens from 5:00 to 7:00 p.m. During the long break, employees return home and has a siesta. However, this custom is changing.

Mario Carreno (b. 1913/Cuban) La Siesta 1946. Oil on canvas. © Christie's Images/ SuperStock.

2. Some multinational companies that operates in Spain remain open for business in the afternoons. One of the reasons are the companies' desire to increase productivity. To give sleep-deprived Spaniards the siesta that they crave, a new type of business has opened. There is "siesta shops" throughout Spain. Each shop satisfy a need.

3. Jose Luis Buqueras, a computer programmer, work for a British multinational in Madrid, and he has a one-hour lunch break. Luckily for Buqueras, there be several siesta shops in his neighborhood that offers short siestas. If he pays 500 pesetas, he can doze in a darkened room for twenty minutes. One of the attendants massage his neck. Then somebody cover him with a blanket. Quiet music plays in the background.

4. Although many Spanish citizens no longer enjoy three-hour breaks, they have not given up their afternoon siestas. Perhaps other nations can benefit from Spain's example. According to many medical professionals, a short afternoon nap helps reduce stress. There is also studies showing that naps reduce heart disease. David Jenkins, a government employee in Ireland, want siesta shops to open in his country.

The Writer's Room **Topics for Writing**

Write about one of the following topics. Proofread your text to ensure that your subjects and verbs agree.

1. Do you have afternoon naps? Explain why or why not. Compare yourself to someone who has, or does not have, frequent naps.

2. Describe a visit that you made to a culturally different restaurant. What happened? Use language that appeals to the senses.

 CHECKLIST: SUBJECT–VERB AGREEMENT

When you edit your writing, ask yourself these questions.

Do my subjects and verbs agree? Check for errors with the following:

- present tense verbs
- *was* and *were*
- interrupting phrases

                                  are
The clients, whom I have never met, ~~is~~ unhappy with the
       is
new ad. It ~~be~~ too dull.

Do I use the correct verb form with indefinite pronouns? Check for errors with singular indefinite pronouns such as *everybody*, *nobody*, or *somebody*.

            has
Somebody ~~have~~ to modify the photograph.

Do my subjects and verbs agree when the subject is after the verb? Check for errors with the following:

- sentences containing *here* and *there*
- question forms

     Does   *are*
~~Do~~ she watch commercials? There ~~is~~ many funny ads on television.

Verb Tenses

CHAPTER 17

CONTENTS

- What Is Verb Tense?
- Present and Past Tenses
- Past Participles
- Present Perfect Tense
- Past Perfect Tense
- Passive Voice
- Progressive Forms

Section Theme **INTERNATIONAL TRADE**

In this chapter, you will learn about advertising and marketing.

Grammar Snapshot

Looking at Verb Tenses

The following excerpt is from *Business Ethics* by Richard T. De George. Look at the underlined verbs and try to determine what tense the author has used.

> The growth of giant corporations has tended to make competition in many areas very costly. The growth of supermarkets, which began in the 1940s, has forced most small grocers and vegetable and fruit markets out of business. The prices a supermarket was able to charge were lower than those the small operators could charge for equal-quality goods. The consequence has been the elimination of small grocers.

In this chapter, you will write using a variety of verb tenses.

230

What Is Verb Tense?

Verb tense indicates when an action occurred. Review the various tenses of the verb *work*. (Progressive or *-ing* forms of these verbs appear at the end of this chapter.)

Simple Forms

Present	I <u>work</u> in a large company. My sister <u>works</u> with me.
Past	We <u>worked</u> in Cancun last summer.
Future	My sister <u>will work</u> in the Middle East next year.
Present perfect	We <u>have worked</u> together since 2001.
Past perfect	When Maria lost her job, she <u>had worked</u> there for six years.
Future perfect	By 2020, I <u>will have worked</u> here for twenty years.

CHAPTER 17

Hint   Use Standard Verb Forms

Nonstandard English is used in everyday conversation and may differ according to the region in which you live. **Standard American English** is the common language generally used and expected in schools, businesses, and government institutions in the United States. In college, you should write using standard American English.

Nonstandard:	He don't have no money.	She be real tired.
Standard:	He <u>does not</u> have <u>any</u> money.	She <u>is</u> really tired.

Present and Past Tenses

Present Tense Verbs

The simple present tense indicates that an action is a general fact or habitual activity. Remember to add *-s* or *-es* to verbs that follow third-person singular forms.

Fact:	Our fee **includes** mass mail-outs and pamphlet distribution.
Habitual Activity:	Carmen Cruz **takes** drawing classes every Saturday.

GRAMMAR LINK
For more information about subject-verb agreement, see Chapter 16.

PAST	Saturday	Saturday	Saturday	Saturday	FUTURE
▼	▼	▼	▼	▼	▼
	She draws.	She draws.	She draws.	She draws.	

Past Tense Verbs

The past tense indicates that an action occurred at a specific past time. Regular past tense verbs have a standard *-d* or *-ed* ending. Use the same form for both singular and plural past tense verbs.

Yesterday morning, we **discussed** the campaign.

Yesterday morning   Today

▼   ▼

We discussed the campaign.

CHAPTER 17

PRACTICE I Write the present or past form of each verb in parentheses.

EXAMPLE: In the 1960s, some American companies (attempt) _____ *attempted* _____ to enter the Japanese marketplace.

1. General Mills (produce) _____ many food products. Each year, the company (sell) _____ products around the world. Sometimes, a product (succeed) _____ in a foreign marketplace, but occasionally, a product (fail) _____.

2. In 2004, Joyce Millet (publish) _____ an article called, "Marketing in Japan: What History Can Teach Us." To prepare for her article, she (research) _____ examples of product failures.

3. In the late 1960s, General Mills (plan) _____ to market Betty Crocker cake mixes in Japan. They (try) _____ to design a suitable product. Product developers (learn) _____ that very few Japanese homes had ovens, so they (need) _____ to find a new way to bake the cakes.

At that time, most Japanese homes (contain) _____ a

rice cooker, so designers (create) _____ a spongy cake

mix that worked in a rice cooker.

4. At first, sales of the Betty Crocker cake mix were good, but sales quickly

(tumble) _____. What was the problem? In the past,

most Japanese citizens (believe) _____ that rice was

sacred, so they (refuse) _____ to contaminate the rice

with cake flavor.

Irregular Past Tense Verbs

Irregular verbs change internally. Because their spellings change from the present to the past tense, these verbs can be challenging to remember. For example, the irregular verb *go* becomes *went* when you convert it to the past tense.

> The company **sold** the patent. (*sold* = past tense of *sell*)
>
> Consumers **bought** the product. (*bought* = past tense of *buy*)

Be (Was or Were)

Most past tense verbs have one form that you can use with all subjects. However, the verb *be* has two past forms: *was* and *were*. Use *was* with *I, he, she,* and *it*. Use *were* with *you, we,* and *they*.

> The packing box **was** not sturdy enough. The plates **were** fragile.

PRACTICE 2   Write the correct past form of each verb in parentheses. Some verbs are regular, and some are irregular.

EXAMPLE: Long ago, John Pemberton (have) _____*had*_____ a great idea.

1. In 1884, John Pemberton (be) _____ a pharmacist in Atlanta,

Georgia. He (know) _____ about a successful French product

CHAPTER 17

GRAMMAR LINK

See Appendix 2 for a list of common irregular verbs.

called a "coca wine." Pemberton (make) _____ his own version

of the product and called it Pemberton's French Wine Coca. In 1885,

Atlanta (pass) _____ prohibition legislation, so Pemberton

created an alcohol-free version of his drink. He (mix) _____ his

syrup with carbonated water, and he (bring) _____ some

samples to a local pharmacy. Customers (pay) _____ 5 cents a

glass for the drink.

2. Pemberton's bookkeeper (be) _____ a marketing wizard. Frank

M. Robinson (think) _____ of a name for the drink. He also

(feel) _____ certain that the drink required an interesting logo;

thus, Robinson (develop) _____ the handwritten Coca-Cola logo.

In 1886, many stores (have) _____ the red logo on their awnings.

3. Pemberton never (make) _____ a lot of money from his

invention. He (sell) _____ his company to Mr. Asa Candler for

$2,300. Candler (take) _____ the Coca-Cola company to new

heights, and it (become) _____ a highly successful international

company.

4. In 1889, the Coca-Cola Company (do) _____ not patent the

formula for Coca Cola because company executives (do) _____

not want competitors to know the secret formula of the soft drink. It

remains one of the best-kept trade secrets in history.

> ## Hint Use the Base Form After *Did* and *To*
>
> Remember to use the base form:
>
> • of verbs that follow *did* in question and negative forms.
> • of verbs that follow the word *to* (infinitive form).
>
> > *invent*   *promote*
> > Did he ~~invented~~ a good product? Pemberton wanted to ~~promoted~~ his
> > soft drink.

PRACTICE 3   Correct twelve verb tense and spelling errors in the following essay.

like
EXAMPLE: Consumer groups didn't ~~liked~~ the marketing campaign.

1. In past centuries, breastfeeding be the most common method of feeding children. At the end of the eighteenth century, some parents feeded their children cows' milk. In 1838, a German physician analyzed milk from cows and discover that larger proteins and reduced carbohydrates contributed to the increasing infant mortality rate.

2. The search for a healthy alternative to breast milk preoccupied scientists in the nineteenth century. Finally, in the 1870s, Nestle Company produced the first infant formula. Consumers just had to mixed water with the formula.

3. In 1973, Nestle Company wanted to sold the formula in Africa. The company putted advertisements for the product in magazines and on billboards. Nestle also gived free samples to African women as soon as they had their babies. In hospitals, mothers seen their own breast milk dry up

after they gave formula to their babies. When the women returned home,

they did not had enough money to continue buying enough formula. They

added too much water to the formula, and the water was often

contaminated. Babies who drinked formula become malnourished. In

many villages, the level of infant malnutrition and mortality rised.

Past Participles

A **past participle** is a verb form, not a verb tense. The past tense and the past participle of regular verbs are the same. The past tense and the past participle of irregular verbs may be different.

	base form	past tense	past participle
Regular verb:	talk	talked	talked
Irregular verb:	begin	began	begun

GRAMMAR LINK

For a list of irregular past participles, see Appendix 2.

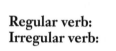 **Using Past Participles**

You cannot use a past participle as the only verb in a sentence. You must use it with a helping verb such as *have, has, had, is, was,* or *were.*

	helping verbs	past participle	
The company	**was**	founded	in 1863.
The products	**have**	become	very popular.

PRACTICE 4   In the next selection, the past participles are underlined. Correct ten past participle errors, and write C above correct past participles.

EXAMPLE: The business ethics students have <u>meeted</u> many times to discuss
            the case.
            met

1. Since 1973, Nestle has <u>faced</u> a lot of criticism for its marketing techniques

   in Africa. According to critics, Nestle should have <u>knew</u> that the advertising

   was dangerous and misleading. For instance, by 1980, Nestle had <u>make</u>

hundreds of billboards showing a white woman feeding her child with a bottle. The African women were <u>teached</u> that good mothers don't breastfeed their children.

2. The method of giving free samples to new mothers was also <u>blamed</u> for the problem. According to critics, a company spokesman has <u>admit</u> that the free samples contributed to the drying up of mothers' breast milk. In addition, the color white was <u>weared</u> by company salespeople when they walked through hospital wards. New mothers could have <u>thinked</u> that the salespeople were nurses.

3. Nestle's business practices have always <u>being</u> legal. In fact, Nestle has successfully <u>used</u> the same techniques in many wealthy nations. Nonetheless, in 1977, a worldwide boycott of Nestle products was <u>organize</u> by a group of concerned citizens.

4. Many business students have <u>studied</u> the Nestle case. Technically, Nestle did the same thing in Africa that it has <u>did</u> in the United States for many years. If a marketing technique has <u>work</u> successfully in wealthy countries, is a company <u>obliged</u> to revise its marketing techniques in less developed countries?

Present Perfect Tense
(*have* or *has* + past participle)

A past participle combines with *have* or *has* to form the **present perfect tense**.

> Kate **has been** a marketing manager for six years.
> Since 2001, the products **have sold** extremely well.

You can use this tense in two different circumstances.

1. Use the present perfect to show that an action began in the past and continues to the present time. You will often use *since* and *for* with this tense.

PAST
(5 years ago, the
factory opened)

NOW

The factory **has flourished** for five years.

2. Use the present perfect to show that one or more completed actions occurred at unspecified past times.

PAST

NOW

? ? ? ?

Mr. Jain **has visited** China four times.
(The time of the four visits is not specified.)

Choosing the Simple Past or the Present Perfect

Look at the difference between the past and the present perfect tenses.

Simple past: In 2002, Kumar Jain **went** to Shanghai.
(This event occurred at a known past time.)

Present perfect: Since 2002, Jain **has owned** a factory in China.
(The action began in the past and continues to the present.)

He **has made** many business contacts.
(*Making business contacts* occurred at unknown past times.)

> ### *Hint*   Use Time Markers
>
> When you try to identify which tense to use, look for time markers. **Time markers** are words such as *since, for,* or *ago* that indicate when an action occurred.
>
> **Simple past:**   Three weeks **ago,** Parker launched her new perfume.
>
> **Present perfect:** **Since then,** her perfume has been selling very well.

PRACTICE 5   Write the simple past or present perfect form of the verb in parentheses.

EXAMPLE: For the last six years, my cousin Mike (be) _____*has been*_____ a sales representative.

1. Since the beginning of the twentieth century, many companies (try)

   _____ to create memorable advertisements for their products.

   Before the 1920s, most ads (be) _____ on billboards and in

   magazines. Then, in 1922, companies (discover) _____ the

   potential of radio advertising. They (sponsor) _____ radio

   shows. For example, the Lucky Strike Cigarette Company sponsored a

   music show. Since then, many companies (sponsor) _____

   artistic and sporting events.

2. In the mid-1920s, radio stations (decide) _____ to give short

   time slots to advertisers so that they could promote their products as an

   alternative to the sponsorship of shows. Ever since, commercials (be)

   _____ an effective way for companies to market their products.

   Most people (see) _____ thousands of commercials.

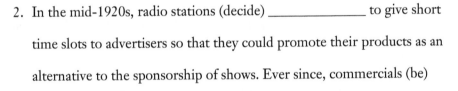

Hint **Simple Past or Present Perfect?**
Use the past tense when referring to someone who is no longer living or to something that no longer exists. Only use the present perfect tense when the action has a relationship to someone or something that still exists.

designed
Leonardo da Vinci ~~has designed~~ many products.

PRACTICE 6 Identify and correct ten verb errors.

began
EXAMPLE: The Coca-Cola Company ~~has begun~~ in 1886.

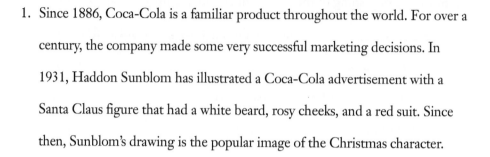

1. Since 1886, Coca-Cola is a familiar product throughout the world. For over a century, the company made some very successful marketing decisions. In 1931, Haddon Sunblom has illustrated a Coca-Cola advertisement with a Santa Claus figure that had a white beard, rosy cheeks, and a red suit. Since then, Sunblom's drawing is the popular image of the Christmas character.

2. Although the Coca-Cola Company been very successful since its inception, occasionally it has made blunders. In 1984, Coca-Cola managers have worried about the increasing popularity of Pepsi. That year, Coke developers modified the original formula and have made the product much sweeter.

3. On April 23, 1985, at a press conference, Coca-Cola's chairman has introduced New Coke by calling it "smoother, rounder, and bolder." Unfortunately, when the product hit store shelves, consumers complained about the taste.

4. On July 29, 1985, the company pulled New Coke from the shelves and reintroduced the original product, calling it Coke Classic. Curiously, Coke Classic is very successful since its reintroduction. Since the New Coke fiasco, other companies learned from Coca-Cola's mistake. If consumers love a product, do not modify it!

Past Perfect Tense
(had + past participle)

The **past perfect tense** indicates that one or more past actions happened before another past action. It is formed with *had* and the past participle.

PAST PERFECT   PAST   NOW

Mr. Lo **had spent** a lot on research when he launched the product.

Notice the differences between the simple past, the present perfect, and the past perfect tenses.

Simple past: Last night, Craig **worked** at Burger Town.
(The action occurred at a known past time.)

Present perfect: He **has owned** the restaurant for three years.
(The action began in the past and continues to the present.)

Past perfect: Craig **had had** two business failures before he bought Burger Town.
(All of the actions happened in the past, but the two business failures occurred before he bought the hamburger restaurant.)

PRACTICE 7 Underline the correct verb form in each sentence. You may choose the simple past tense or the past perfect tense.

EXAMPLE: The Barbosas (were / had been) farmers for ten years when Alex Barbosa decided to sell organic beef.

1. Even though he (never studied / had never studied) marketing, Alex Barbosa decided to promote his organic beef.

2. He printed flyers, and then he (distributed / had distributed) them to private homes.

3. When most residents threw out the flyer, they (did not even read / had not even read) it.

4. The flyer contained a picture that Barbosa (took / had taken) the previous summer.

5. The image of the meat carcass (was / had been) unappealing.

6. After Barbosa received negative feedback about his flyer, he remembered that his daughter (warned / had warned) him about the image.

7. Also, the neighborhood (had / had had) low-income families who could not afford the high price of the organic meat.

8. Finally, in 2005, Barbosa hired a business graduate who (learned / had learned) how to do effective marketing.

9. By December 2006, Barbosa's organic meat (found / had found) a niche in the marketplace.

Passive Voice
(be + past participle)

In sentences with the **passive voice**, the subject receives the action and does not perform the action. To form the passive voice, use the appropriate tense of the verb *be* plus the past participle. Look carefully at the following two sentences.

Active: The boss **gave** documents to her assistant.
(This is active, because the subject, *boss*, performed the action.)

Passive: Several documents **were given** to the assistant.
(This is passive because the subject, *documents*, was affected by the action and did not perform the action.)

Hint   **Avoid Overusing the Passive Voice**

Generally, try to use the active voice instead of the passive voice. The active voice is more direct and friendly than the passive voice. For example, read two versions of the same message.

Passive voice: No more than two pills per day should be ingested. This medication should be taken with meals. It should not be continued if headaches or nausea are experienced. Any side effects should be reported immediately.

Active voice: Do not ingest more than two pills per day. Take this medication with meals. Do not continue taking it if you experience headache or nausea. Immediately report any side effects to your doctor.

PRACTICE 8   Complete the following sentences by changing the passive verb to the active form. Do not alter the verb tense.

EXAMPLE: Each department *will be visited* by the supervisor.
   The supervisor will visit each department.

1. A funny commercial *was created* by the advertising agency.

   _____

2. The ad *will be seen* by many people.

   _____

3. A well-known comedian *was hired* by the company.

   _____

4. Many commercials *are created* by Pedro Guzman.

   _____

5. Complaints about their commercials *are often ignored* by companies.

   _____

> ### Hint ⟩ When *Be* Is Suggested, Not Written
>
> In the passive voice, sometimes the verb *be* is suggested but not written. The following sentence contains the passive voice.
>
>   A man **named** Harley Cobb complained about the car company's decision.
>   ↑
>   (who was)

PRACTICE 9   Underline and correct eight errors with past participles.

                    found
EXAMPLE: A problem was <u>find</u> with the design.

1. When Apple Computer first developed the Macintosh, a pull-down

   screen, or window, was include in the product. The computer also had a

   variety of icons for different tasks. For instance, useless files were drag to a trash can icon. A year later, Microsoft Corporation introduced its popular software program name Windows. The software, create in 1988, looked a lot like Apple's software. Apple sued Microsoft for copyright infringement and argued that Microsoft copied the "look and feel" of Apple software.

2. There are strict rules about copyright. A unique product can be patent. However, people cannot copyright an idea. Therefore, Apple's decision to use specific icons could not be protect. Still, Apple argued that its original concept should not have been copy. The case, which lasted for four years, was win by Microsoft.

Progressive Forms
(-*ing* verbs)

Most verbs have progressive tenses. The **progressive tense**, formed with *be* and the –*ing* form of the verb, indicates that an action is, was, or will be in progress. For example, the present progressive indicates that an action is happening right now or for a temporary period of time. The following time line illustrates both the simple and progressive tenses.

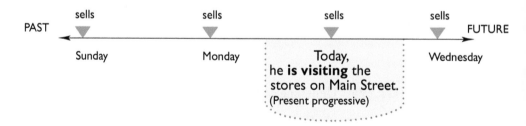

Every day, he **sells** leather wallets. (Simple present)

	sells	sells	sells	sells	
PAST	▼	▼	▼	▼	FUTURE
	Sunday	Monday	Today, he **is visiting** the stores on Main Street. (Present progressive)	Wednesday	

To form the progressive, use the appropriate tense of the verb *be* with the -*ing* verb.

Present progressive:	Right now, I **am working**.
Past progressive:	We **were sleeping** when you phoned us.
Future progressive:	Tomorrow, at noon, I **will be driving**.

Present perfect progressive: The receptionist **has been** <u>working</u> since 8:00 A.M.

Past perfect progressive: She **had been** <u>speeding</u> when the officer stopped her.

Common Errors in the Progressive Form

- Do not use the progressive form when an action happens regularly.

   complains
   Every day he ~~is complaining~~ about his job.

- In the progressive form, use the correct form of the verb *be*.

   is
   Right now, Ron ~~be~~ talking with his manager.

- In the progressive form, always include the complete helping verb.

   is   *have*
   Right now, the manager ˄ discussing the problem. They ˄ been talking

   for hours.

Nonprogressive Verbs

Some verbs do not take the progressive form because they indicate an ongoing state or a perception rather than a temporary action.

Examples of Nonprogressive Verbs

Perception Verbs	Preference Verbs	State Verbs	Possession
admire	desire	believe	have*
care	doubt	know	own
hear	feel	mean	possess
see	hate	realize	
seem	like	recognize	
smell*	look	suppose	
taste*	love	think*	
	prefer	understand	
	want		

*Some verbs have more than one meaning and can be used in the progressive tense. Compare the following pairs of sentences.

Nonprogressive	**Progressive**
He **has** a franchise. (expresses ownership)	He **is having** a bad day.
I **think** it is unethical. (expresses an opinion)	I **am thinking** about you.

PRACTICE 10   Correct one verb error in each sentence.

                  had

EXAMPLE: She ~~been~~ working in the store for ten years when she was

            fired.

1. Ellen Peters was producing and give away her own fragrances when her

    sister suggested that she try to market her perfume.

2. These days, Peters negotiating with a cosmetics company that hopes to

    market her perfume internationally.

3. She been looking for a product name for the last six months.

4. Last May, she be planning to call it Golden Mist when someone told her

    that "mist" means "manure" in German.

5. While her friends were brainstorm to help her, one of them suggested the

    name "Pete," which is a shortened form of Peters.

6. Unfortunately, pété is meaning "release of gassy air" in French.

7. Often, companies are having problems with bad translations.

8. For instance, the owner of the Japanese travel agency called Kinki Nippon

    Tours be complaining about foreign customers who wanted sex tours when

    a customer told him the English meaning of "kinky."

9. In another case, a Scandinavian vacuum cleaner company was making a

    mistake when it created the slogan "Nothing sucks like an Electrolux."

10. Ellen Peters wants her product to sell internationally, so right now she is

    work with a marketing firm to come up with a good product name.

FINAL REVIEW

Underline and correct fifteen errors in verb form or tense.

published

EXAMPLE: The book *Business Ethics* was <u>publish</u> by Prentice Hall in 2006.

1. Since 1900, many products been defective. In his book *Business Ethics*,

   Richard T. De George discusses a famous product defect case. In the early

   1970s, American automakers lose market share because smaller Japanese

   imports be flooding the market.

2. Lee Iacocca, the CEO of Ford Motor Company, was wanting the company

   to produce a lightweight, economical car. Engineers developed the Ford

   Pinto. Because Ford wanted the product on the market quickly, the car was

   not test for rear-end impact during the production period. Then, after the

   Pintos had been produce, they were put in collision tests, and they failed

   the tests. When the Pinto was hitted from behind, a bolt on the bumper

   sometimes punctured the fuel tank. It could cause an explosion.

3. Ford conducted a study and determined that a small baffle, worth about

   $8, could be place between the bumper and the gas tank. The company

   maked a cost–benefit analysis to compare the cost of adding the baffle

   against the estimated cost of lawsuits. The company decided that it was

   less expensive to fight lawsuits than to insert the baffle. For the next seven

years, the design of Ford Pintos did not changed. The company also neglected to offer the baffle to customers.

4. In 1976, Pintos had thirteen explosions from rear-end impacts, whereas comparable cars had far fewer explosions. When it be too late, the Ford Motor Company realized that the lawsuits was much more expensive than the baffle installations.

5. The Pinto was recall in 1978. Since 1978, Ford has make much better business decisions. In the late 1970s, the bad publicity from the Pinto case damaged the company's reputation. Since then, Ford tried to improve its image.

 The Writer's Room **Topics for Writing**

Write about one of the following topics. Proofread your writing and ensure that your verbs are formed correctly.

1. Write a short paragraph describing a useful product that you own. When and where did you get the product? How is it useful?

2. What are the effects of advertising on consumers? How does the deluge of commercials, spam, billboards, and other advertising affect the population?

✓ **CHECKLIST: VERB TENSES**

When you edit your writing, ask yourself these questions.

Do I use the correct present and past tense forms? Check for errors in these cases:

- verbs following third-person singular nouns
- irregular present or past tense verbs
- question and negative forms

               were   *were*
The products that ~~was~~ defective ~~was~~ in his shop.

Do I use the correct form of past participles? Check for errors in the following:

- spelling of irregular past participles
- present perfect and past perfect verbs
- passive and active forms

                          have made
Since the 1970s, some car companies ~~made~~ bad business decisions.

Do I use *-ing* forms correctly? Check for the overuse or misuse of progressive forms. Also ensure that progressive forms are complete.

                     designing
In 1971, while engineers were ~~design~~ the Pinto, nobody

    wanted
~~was wanting~~ to make an unsafe car.

Problems with Verbs

CHAPTER 18

CONTENTS

- Verb Consistency
- Avoiding Double Negatives
- Nonstandard Forms—*Gonna, Gotta, Wanna*
- Problems in Conditional Forms
- Nonstandard Forms—*Would of, Could of, Should of*
- Recognizing Gerunds and Infinitives

Section Theme **INTERNATIONAL TRADE**

In this chapter, you will read about unusual and dangerous jobs.

Grammar Snapshot

Looking at Other Verb Forms

The following excerpt is from a personal letter by Garrett Brice, a student who spent one summer working in a fire tower. Conditional sentences are underlined, and some modals are in bold.

>   The strangest job I have ever had was working in a fire tower. Sometimes, I would spend weeks at a time completely alone. <u>I had to alert the base camp if I saw smoke rising in the forest.</u> I brought along a guitar because I wanted to learn how to play it. Probably I **should have tried** harder. <u>Maybe if I had had a teacher with me, I would have learned some songs.</u> As it was, I spent the time playing with my dog, reading, writing, and just watching the birds.

In this chapter, you will identify and write modals, conditionals, gerunds, and infinitives.

Verb Consistency

A verb tense gives your readers an idea about the time that an event occurred. A **tense shift** occurs when you shift from one tense to another for no logical reason. When you write essays, ensure that your tenses are consistent.

Tense shift: Jean Roberts traveled to Santiago, Chile, where she interviews a salon owner.

Correct: Jean Roberts traveled to Santiago, Chile, where she **interviewed** a salon owner.

> **Hint** **Would and Could**
>
> When you tell a story about a past event, use *would* instead of *will* and *could* instead of *can*.
>
> $\qquad\qquad\qquad\qquad\qquad\qquad\qquad\qquad$ *couldn't*
> In 2001, Simon Brault wanted to be an actor. At that time, he <u>can't</u> find a good
> $\qquad\qquad\qquad\qquad\qquad\qquad$ *would*
> acting job. To earn extra cash, he <u>will</u> deliver telegrams wearing a costume.

PRACTICE 1 Underline and correct ten tense shifts in the next paragraphs.

$\qquad\qquad\qquad\qquad\qquad\qquad\qquad\qquad\qquad\qquad$ *decided*
EXAMPLE: In the 1990s, Gretta Zahn made a decision. She <u>decides</u> to work as a parts model.

1. Some people have very unusual jobs. In 1992, a modeling agent noticed seventeen-year-old Gretta Zahn's hands. He signed the young girl to a contract, and he said that he will make her famous as a "hand model." During Zahn's modeling years, her jobs were diverse. She soaked her fingers in dishwashing liquid, wear diamond rings, and demonstrated nail polish.

2. In the 1990s, Zahn's modeling career was lucrative. At the height of her career, she can earn up to $1500 a day. She will start her day at 5:00 a.m.,

and sometimes she will have to work for fourteen hours. To get a perfect shot, some photographers will take hundreds of pictures of her.

3. Zahn's agent told her that she will need to take special care of her hands. From 1992 to 2000, she cannot wear jewelry because it would leave tan lines. Also, during those years, she will not do the dishes, and she refused to pump her own gas.

4. In 2000, Zahn gave up modeling. Today, she enjoys gardening, and she likes to wear rings and bracelets. Her hands are no longer flawless, but she did not mind. "I have a life," she says. "I no longer worry about getting a cut or scrape."

Avoiding Double Negatives

A double negative occurs when a negative word such as *no* (*nothing, nobody, nowhere*) is combined with a negative adverb (*not, never, rarely, seldom,* and so on). The result is a sentence that has a double negative. Such sentences can be confusing because the negative words cancel each other.

Double negative: Mr. Lee doesn't want no problems.
(According to this sentence, Mr. Lee wants problems.)

He didn't know nothing about it.
(According to this sentence, he knew something about it.)

How to Correct Double Negatives

There are two ways to correct double negatives.

1. Completely remove *one* of the negative forms. Remember that you may need to adjust the verb to make it agree with the subject.

Mr. Lee **doesn't** want ~~no~~ problems.
Mr. Lee ~~doesn't~~ wants **no** problems.

2. Change "no" to *any* (*anybody, anything, anywhere*).

                  any
Mr. Lee doesn't want ~~no~~ problems.

PRACTICE 2   Correct five errors with double negatives. You can correct each error in more than one way.

             any   *have*
EXAMPLE: They don't have ~~no~~ openings. OR They ~~don't have~~ no openings.

Have you ever had a strange job? Jordan Woo has had his share of unusual occupations. In 2005, he couldn't find no summer job. Then he saw an ad for a sign holder. For three months, he stood beside a work crew and held up signs to direct traffic. Occasionally, for an hour or two, he didn't have nothing to do. The crew was working on a rural road, and sometimes there wasn't no traffic. He was bored, but he kept his job because he didn't have no better offers. Eventually, when he couldn't take it no more, he quit.

Nonstandard Forms—*Gonna, Gotta, Wanna*

Some people commonly say *I'm gonna, I gotta,* or *I wanna.* These are nonstandard forms, so avoid using them in written communication.

- Write "going to" instead of *gonna.*

             going to
The boss is ~~gonna~~ hire three new cashiers.

- Write "have to" instead of *gotta* or *got to.*

        have to
We ~~gotta~~ stay open until midnight.

- Write "want to" instead of *wanna.*

        want to
We ~~wanna~~ keep our jobs.

PRACTICE 3   Underline and correct eight nonstandard verbs.

have to find
EXAMPLE: You and I <u>gotta find</u> a better job.

1. If you wanna find work, there are many job-hunting sites on the Internet. One of the oldest and most established sites is Monster.com. The site was created in 1994. Jeff Taylor owned a job-recruitment agency, and he thought that an Internet site could help his business. He decided that his new site was gonna match job seekers with employers. That year, he created The Monster Board.

2. In 1995, Taylor sold his business because he didn't wanna pass up a great business offer. The new owners said that they were gonna change the name of the Web site. They didn't think that consumers would wanna associate "monster" and work. However, Taylor convinced them to keep the name.

3. In 1999, Monster Board joined with Online Career Center and became Monster.com. When you go on the site, you gotta find your region. Monster posts jobs in twenty-three countries. Then you gotta choose the job category that interests you. If you go on the site, you are probably gonna find interesting jobs in your city or area.

Problems in Conditional Forms

In **conditional sentences**, there is a condition and a result. There are three types of conditional sentences, and each type has two parts, or clauses. The main clause depends on the condition set in the *if* clause.

First Form: Possible Present or Future

The condition is true or very possible. Use the present tense in the *if* clause.

condition (*if* clause)   result
If you **ask** her, she **will hire** you.

Second Form: Unlikely Present

The condition is not likely, and probably will not happen. Use the past tense in the *if* clause.

condition (*if* clause)   result
If I **had** more money, I **would start** my own business

Note: In formal writing, when the condition contains the verb *be*, always use "were" in the *if* clause.

If Katrina **were** younger, she **would change** careers.

Third Form: Impossible Past

The condition cannot happen because the event is over. Use the past perfect tense in the *if* clause.

condition (*if* clause)   result
If the business **had closed** in 2002, many people **would have lost** their jobs.

Hint   **Be Careful with the Past Conditional**

In "impossible past" sentences, the writer expresses regret about a past event or expresses the wish that a past event had worked out differently. In the "if" part of the sentence, remember to use the past perfect tense.

if & past perfect tense ──────────▶ would have (past participle)

had stayed
If the factory ~~would have stayed~~ open, many workers would have kept their jobs.

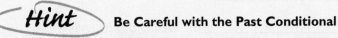

PRACTICE 4   Write the correct conditional forms of the verbs in parentheses.

EXAMPLE: If the miners (go, not) *had not gone* on strike, their working
                   conditions would have remained unsafe.

1. If you do research on the Internet, you (learn) _____

   that truck driving is one of the most dangerous professions. William Roach is a long-distance trucker, and he took a truck-driving course in 1992. If he

(fail) _____ the course, he would never have found his

passion.

2. Roach loves driving. "On a highway, with nothing but the road in front

    of me, I feel alive and free. Even if someone offered me a better job, I

    (remain) _____ a truck driver." Roach claims that the

    only drawback is the time he spends away from his family. He says, "If I

    (be) _____ able to, I would bring my wife and son

    with me."

3. In 2003, Roach was late for a delivery. To save time, he took an unfamiliar

    route. While driving, Roach fell asleep, and his truck rolled into a ditch. If

    he (have) _____ a nap earlier that day, perhaps he

    (not, have) _____ the accident. If he (stay)

    _____ on the main highway, perhaps the accident

    (involve) _____ more vehicles. According to medical

    professionals, if Roach had been awake during the accident, his injuries

    (be) _____ more severe. Because he was asleep, his

    body was relaxed and his injuries were minor.

4. Roach claims that even if he (know) _____ about the

    dangers in truck driving, he would still have chosen to be a long-distance

    driver. If you could, (you, become) _____ a long-

    distance driver?

Nonstandard Forms—*Would of, Could of, Should of*

Some people commonly say *would of, could of,* or *should of.* They may also say *woulda, coulda,* or *shoulda.* These are nonstandard forms and you should avoid using them in written communication. When you use the past forms of *should, would,* and *could,* always include *have* with the past participle.

> Dominique Brown is a nurse, but she really loves real estate. She
> *should have*
> ~~should of~~ become a real-estate agent. She ~~woulda~~ been very successful.
> *would have*

PRACTICE 5   Underline and correct nine errors in conditional forms or in the past forms of *could* and *should.*

have
EXAMPLE: The workers should of stayed home.

1. One of the world's most successful companies began in a small village

    in Sweden. In 1943, seventeen-year-old Ingvar Kamprad did well in his

    studies, and his father gave him a gift of money. Kamprad coulda

    bought anything he wanted. His mother thought that he shoulda

    continued his studies. The young man had other ideas. He decided

    to create a company called IKEA, and he sold small items through a

    mail-order catalogue.

2. In 1947, Kamprad decided to add furniture to his catalogue. One day, an

    employee from IKEA removed the legs from a table so that it would fit

    into his car trunk. Soon, the company created flat packaging designs. If the

    employee woulda owned a truck, perhaps IKEA would of continued to sell

    completely assembled furniture. If that had been the case, the company

    would not of been so successful.

3. Kamprad's extreme youth helped him in his quest to take chances. Maybe if he woulda been older, he woulda been more conservative. If IKEA would not have changed, perhaps it would of remained a small company.

Recognizing Gerunds and Infinitives

Sometimes a main verb is followed by another verb. The second verb can be a gerund or an infinitive. A **gerund** is a verb with an *–ing* ending. An **infinitive** consists of *to* and the base form of the verb.

verb + gerund
Edward <u>finished</u> **installing** the carpet.

verb + infinitive
He <u>wants</u> **to take** weekends off.

Some verbs in English are always followed by a gerund. Do not confuse gerunds with progressive verb forms.

Progressive verb: Julie is working now.
(Julie is in the process of doing something.)

Gerund: Julie <u>finished</u> **working**.
(*Working* is a gerund that follows *finished*.)

Some Common Verbs Followed by Gerunds

acknowledge	deny	keep	recall
adore	detest	loathe	recollect
appreciate	discuss	mention	recommend
avoid	dislike	mind	regret
can't help	enjoy	miss	resent
complete	finish	postpone	resist
consider	involve	practice	risk
delay	justify	quit	tolerate

Some Common Verbs Followed by Infinitives

afford	decide	manage	refuse
agree	demand	mean	seem
appear	deserve	need	swear
arrange	expect	offer	threaten
ask	fail	plan	volunteer
claim	hesitate	prepare	want
compete	hope	pretend	wish
consent	learn	promise	would like

CHAPTER 18

Some Common Verbs Followed by Gerunds or Infinitives

Some common verbs can be followed by gerunds or infinitives. Both forms have the same meaning.

>   begin   continue   like   love   start

>   Elaine <u>likes</u> **to read**. Elaine <u>likes</u> **reading**.
>   (Both sentences have the same meaning.)

Stop, Remember, and Used to

Some verbs can be followed by either a gerund or an infinitive, but there is a difference in meaning depending on the form you use.

Term	Form	Example	Meaning
Stop	+ infinitive	He often stops <u>to buy</u> gas every Sunday.	To stop an activity (driving) to do something else.
	+ gerund	I stopped <u>smoking</u> five years ago.	To permanently stop doing something.
Remember	+ infinitive	Please remember <u>to lock</u> the door.	To remember to perform a task.
	+ gerund	I remember <u>meeting</u> him in 2004.	To have a memory about a past event.
Used to	+ infinitive	Jane used <u>to smoke</u>.	To express a past habit.
	+ gerund	Jane is used <u>to living</u> alone.	To be accustomed to something.

Prepositions Plus Gerunds

Many sentences have the structure *verb + preposition + object*. If the object is another verb, the second verb is a gerund.

>   verb + preposition + gerund
>   I dream **about**   traveling to Greece.

> ## Some Common Words Followed by Prepositions plus Gerunds
>
> | | | | |
> |---|---|---|---|
> | accuse of | be enthusiastic about | be good at | prohibit from |
> | apologize for | feel like | insist on | succeed in |
> | discourage <u>him</u> from* | fond of | be interested in | think about |
> | dream of | forbid <u>him</u> from* | look forward to | (be) tired of |
> | be excited about | forgive <u>me</u> for* | prevent <u>him</u> from* | warn <u>him</u> about* |
>
> *Certain verbs can have a noun or pronoun before the preposition.

PRACTICE 6   Complete the sentence with the appropriate verb. Underline either the gerund or the infinitive form.

1. Do you remember (using / to use) a cell phone camera for the first time? When they first came out, I looked forward (owning / to own / to owning) one. When I first got my phone, I remember (to take / taking) pictures of myself when I accidentally hit the camera button.

2. A few weeks later, I insisted (to buy / buying / on buying) my grandfather a cell phone. I told him that he would need (using / to use) one during emergencies. My grandfather (is not used to speaking / didn't use to speak) on such tiny phones. Each time I visit him, I plan (to show / showing) him how to use it. However, my grandfather is not a technophobe. These days, he (used to work / is used to working) on a computer. He knows how to send e-mails, although he wishes that salespeople would stop (to send / sending) him spam. However, he just can't stand (to use / using / on using) a cell phone.

3. My grandfather is good (to think / thinking / at thinking) up solutions for problems. He wrote a letter to the cell phone manufacturer. He explained

that some older people dislike (to try / trying / of trying) to read the tiny

numbers, and they don't want (having / to have) all of the extra features

such as Internet links. He succeeded (to get / getting / in getting) a

response. In fact, the cell phone company offered my grandfather a job as

an advisor for the seniors market. Now, some cell phone companies are

excited (to promote / promoting / about promoting) a new larger-model

cell phone with large numbers and no extra features.

FINAL REVIEW

Underline and correct fifteen errors with verbs.

                  going to

EXAMPLE: Many jobs are <u>gonna</u> become obsolete.

1. Certain jobs disappear because of advances in technology or changing

   habits. For instance, if you would have

   been born one hundred years ago, you

   would of worn a hat every time you

   went outside. However, since the 1950s,

   hats have not been standard attire and,

   as a result, hatmaking is no longer a

   popular profession.

2. In 1949, Joseph Wade didn't know nothing about hats, yet he decided to

   open a hatmaking business in Boston. Wade created men's felt hats and

   sold them in his hat store. However, if he would have known what was

   coming, he woulda chosen another profession. By 1952, when the ducktail

   haircuts became popular, young men stopped wearing hats because they did not wanna ruin their hair styles. Wade's business eventually closed. He had no idea that hatmaking was gonna become obsolete.

3. In 1964, Theo Malizia enjoyed to deliver milk in his white van. The milk was bottled in glass containers, and it was deposited on the front steps of customers' homes. One day, he hit a pothole, a crate tipped over, and twelve bottles broke. If the bottles would have been made with a less breakable material, they would have been easier to transport. When supermarkets began carrying lighter milk containers, Malizia had to find another job. Home milk delivery wasn't popular no more.

4. In the 1990s, many people thought that any computer-related job would last for life. Carmen Morales took a nine-month course in Web site building in 1999. She thought that she was gonna earn a good living. Perhaps she shoulda seen what was coming. New software has become so user friendly that many businesses simply create their own Web sites. Perhaps if Morales would have taken a programming course, she would have found a job more easily. Since September, Morales has been taking some business courses because she wants to be an accountant. "People always gotta do their taxes, but very few people wanna do the math," she says. Morales hopes her accounting job will never become obsolete.

The Writer's Room **Topics for Writing**

Write about one of the following topics. Ensure that your verbs are correctly formed.

1. If you had lived one hundred years ago, what job would you have done? Describe the job using details that appeal to the senses.

2. Examine this photo. What terms come to mind? Define a term or expression that relates to the photo. Some ideas might be *mindless work, balancing act, glass ceiling, success, a go-getter,* or *a "suit."*

CHAPTER 18

CHECKLIST: OTHER VERB FORMS

When you edit your writing, ask yourself these questions.

Are my verb tenses consistent? Check for errors with the following:

- shifts from past to present or present to past
- *can/could* and *will/would*

$$\text{would}$$
When he drove trucks, he ~~will~~ drive when he was tired.

Do I use the correct conditional forms? Check for errors in the following:

- possible future forms (*If I meet . . . , I will go . . .*)
- unlikely present forms (*If I met . . . , I would go . . .*)
- impossible past forms (*If I had met . . . , I would have gone . . .*)

$$\text{had}$$
If he ~~would have~~ sold shoes, he would have been successful.

Do I use standard verbs? Do not write *gonna, wanna, gotta, shoulda,* etc.

want to
If you ~~wanna~~ know the truth about the Free Trade
have to
Agreement, you ~~gotta~~ do some research.

CHAPTER 19

Nouns, Determiners, and Prepositions

CONTENTS

- Count and Noncount Nouns
- Determiners
- Prepositions

Section Theme **FORCES OF NATURE**

In this chapter, you will read about some unusual weather events.

Grammar Snapshot

Looking at Nouns, Determiners, and Prepositions

In her article "Weird Weather: Sprites, Frogs, and Maggots," Pamela D. Jacobson describes unusual weather phenomena. The nouns, determiners, and prepositions are underlined.

Sprites are barely visible to the naked eye. They sometimes look bluish closest to the clouds, but extend red, wispy flashes upward. Some occur as high as sixty miles above the storm. On images from weather satellites and space shuttles, sprites appear as marvelously complex shapes.

In this chapter, you will identify and write nouns, determiners, and prepositions.

Count and Noncount Nouns

In English, nouns are grouped into two types: count nouns and noncount nouns.

Count nouns refer to people or things that you can count such as *tree*, *house*, or *dog*. Count nouns have both a singular and plural form.

> She wrote three <u>articles</u> about global warming.

Noncount nouns refer to people or things that you cannot count because you cannot divide them, such as *sugar* and *imagination*. Noncount nouns have only the singular form.

> The <u>weather</u> is going to turn cold.

Here are some examples of common noncount nouns.

Common Noncount Nouns

Categories of Objects		Food	Nature	Substances	
clothing	machinery	bread	air	chalk	paint
equipment	mail	fish	electricity	charcoal	paper
furniture	money	honey	energy	coal	
homework	music	meat	environment	fur	
jewelry	postage	milk	radiation	hair	
luggage	software	rice	water	ink	

Abstract Nouns

advice	effort	information	progress
attention	evidence	knowledge	proof
behavior	health	luck	research
education	help	peace	violence

Hint   **Latin Nouns**

Some nouns that are borrowed from Latin keep the plural form of the original language.

Singular	Plural	Singular	Plural
millennium	millennia	paparazzo	paparazzi
datum	data	phenomenon	phenomena

Determiners

Determiners are words that help to determine or figure out whether a noun is specific or general. Examples of determiners are articles (*a*), demonstratives (*this*), indefinite pronouns (*many*), numbers (*three*), possessive nouns (*Maria's*), and possessive adjectives (*my*).

> Gabriel Daniel Fahrenheit manufactured the first mercury thermometer in 1714. Fahrenheit's product was his claim to fame.

Commonly Confused Determiners

Some determiners can be confusing because you can only use them in specific circumstances. Review this list of some commonly confused determiners.

a, an, the

A and *an* are general determiners and *the* is a specific determiner.

> I need to buy a new winter coat. The winter coats in that store are on sale.

Use *a* and *an* before singular count nouns but not before plural or noncount nouns. Use *a* before nouns that begin with a consonant (*a storm*) and use *an* before nouns that begin with a vowel (*an institute*).

Use *the* before nouns that refer to a specific person, place, or thing. Do not use *the* before languages (*He speaks Italian*), sports (*They watch tennis*), or most city and country names (*Two of the coldest capital cities in the world are Ottawa and Moscow*). Two examples of exceptions are *the United States* and *the Netherlands*.

many, few, much, little

Use *many* and *few* with count nouns.

> Many satellites collect weather information, but few forecasts are completely accurate.

Use *much* and *little* with noncount nouns.

> Much attention is focused on solar power, but North Americans use very little solar energy.

this, that, these, those

This **and *these*** refer to things that are physically close to the speaker or at the present time. Use *this* before singular nouns and *these* before plural nouns. ***That*** **and *those*** refer to things that are physically distant from the speaker or in the past time. Use *that* before singular nouns and *those* before plural nouns.

Near the speaker:
this (singular)
these (plural)

Far from the speaker:
that (singular)
those (plural)

This **book** on my desk and those **books** on that **shelf** are about India. Did you know that in 1861, India had some very wet weather? In that **year**, Cherrapunji received 366 inches of rain. In those **days**, cities had trouble coping with so much rain, but these **days**, they are better equipped.

PRACTICE I   Underline the determiner in parentheses that best agrees with the noun before it. If the noun does not require a determiner, underline *X*.

EXAMPLE: (The / A / X) driest place on earth is (the / a / X) Arica, Chile.

1. (Much / Many) people all over (the / a / X) world talk constantly about

   (the / a / X) weather. (Few / Little) phenomena are as exciting as extreme

   weather. For example, (the / X) tornadoes are seasonal in (the / X) North

   America. (A / The) tornado lasts about fifteen minutes. In 1967, there

   were around 115 tornadoes in (a / the / X) Texas. In (this / that) year,

   meteorologists believed (a / the / X) hurricane caused the numerous

   tornadoes in the state.

2. (Many / Much) people are fascinated with thunderstorms. (A / An / X)

   interesting fact about (a / the / X) Empire State Building is that it is struck

   by lightning around five hundred times per year. During thunderstorms,

   (the / X) golfers should be very careful. They should spend as (few / little)

   time as possible outdoors if there is lightning. (A / The) thunderstorm can

   produce a few hundred megawatts of electrical power.

3. (The / X) United States launched its first weather satellite in 1961. In

(these / those) days, satellite pictures amazed weather researchers. Today,

(much / many) research is being done by meteorologists about weather

patterns. (These / Those) days, satellites gather (a / the / X) information

about global weather systems.

Prepositions

Prepositions are words that show concepts such as time, place, direction, and manner. They show connections or relationships between ideas.

<u>In</u> 1998, northern New York State experienced nearly a week of freezing rain.

Freezing rain fell <u>for</u> a few days.

Prepositions of Time and Place

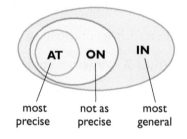

	Prepositions of Time	**Prepositions of Place**
in	in a year or month (in February)	in a city, country, or continent (in Phoenix)
on	on a day of the week (on Monday) on a specific date (on June 16) on a specific holiday (on Memorial Day)	on a specific street (on Lacombe Ave.) on technological devices (on TV, on the radio, on the phone, on the cell phone, on the computer)
at	at a specific time of day (at 9:15) at night at breakfast, lunch, dinner	at a specific address (at 18 Oriole Crescent) at a specific building (at the hospital)

(continued)

	Prepositions of Time	**Prepositions of Place**
from . . . to	from one time to another (from 10:00 AM to 1:00 PM)	from one place to another (from Fort Lauderdale to Orlando)
for	for a period of time (for five hours)	for a distance (for two miles)

Commonly Confused Prepositions

to versus *at*

Use *to* after verbs that indicate movement from one place to another. Use *at* after verbs that indicate being or remaining in one place (and not moving from one place to another). Exception: Do not put *to* directly before *home*.

> Each day, Suraya **runs** <u>to</u> the gym, and then she goes home and **sits** <u>at</u> the computer.

for, during, since

Use *during* to explain when something happens, *for* to explain how long it takes to happen, and *since* to indicate the start of an activity.

> <u>During</u> the summer, the restaurant closed <u>for</u> one week because of the heat.

> <u>Since</u> 2006, I have been taking skiing lessons <u>during</u> the winter.

PRACTICE 2   Write the correct preposition in the blanks.

EXAMPLE: _____*At*_____ 5:15 A.M. we heard the news.

1. _____ the beginning of human history, people have been trying

   to predict the weather. Many writers have created almanacs to record

   weather-related events.

2. _____ 1792, _____ George Washington's second

   term as president, *The Old Farmer's Almanac* was published. Robert B.

Thomas was its first editor. _____ 8:00 A.M. _____ 6:00 P.M., Thomas would work on his magazine. Sitting _____ his desk, he developed a successful formula to forecast weather. He had over an 80 percent accuracy rate. Thomas died _____ 1846, but people can go _____ Dublin, New Hampshire, and view his secret formula _____ the *Almanac*'s office.

3. *The Old Farmer's Almanac* has been published each year _____ it was first established. _____ World War II, the *Almanac* became notoriously associated with a German spy, whom the FBI captured _____ Long Island. The spy had the *Almanac* _____ his pocket. The U.S. government wanted to discontinue publishing the *Almanac* because it contained information that was useful _____ the Germans. After discussing the issue _____ the telephone, U.S. officials eventually allowed the *Almanac* to be published again.

Common Prepositional Expressions

Many common expressions contain prepositions. These types of expressions usually express a particular meaning. The meaning of a verb will change if it is used with a specific preposition. Examine the difference in meaning of the following expressions.

to turn on—to start a machine or switch on the lights
to turn off—to stop a machine or switch off the lights
to turn down—to decline something
to turn over—to rotate
to turn up—to arrive

The next list contains some of the most common prepositional expressions.

accuse (somebody) of	dream of	long for	satisfied with
acquainted with	escape from	look forward to	scared of
afraid of	excited about	participate in	search for
agree with	familiar with	patient with	similar to
apologize for	fond of	pay attention to	specialize in
apply for	forget about	pay for	stop (something) from
approve of	forgive (someone) for	prevent (someone) from	succeed in
associate with	friendly with	protect (someone) from	take advantage of
aware of	grateful for	proud of	take care of
believe in	happy about	provide (someone) with	thank (someone) for
capable of	hear about	qualify for	think about / of
comply with	hope for	realistic about	tired of
confronted with	hopeful about	rely on	willing to
consist of	innocent of	rescue from	wish for
count on	insist on	responsible for	worry about
deal with	insulted by		
depend on	interested in		

PRACTICE 3   Write the correct prepositions in the next paragraphs. Use the preceding list of prepositional expressions to help you.

EXAMPLE: Many people were upset ___*about*___ the damage from the storm.

1. In southern Asia, many people look forward _____ the monsoon. The word monsoon comes from the Arabic "mausin," which means "the season of the winds." During the wet season from June to September, India receives an average of 12 inches of rain each month. During the monsoon, people get tired _____ dealing with the rain.

2. Throughout the year, South Asians depend _____ the monsoon. Farmers hope _____ adequate rainfall for their crops. Children love the monsoon because it provides them _____ the opportunity to

play in the rain and the puddles. Although South Asians are often grateful

_____ a good rainy season, they are also realistic _____ nature's

forces and think _____ possible flooding, transportation delays, and

malaria.

FINAL REVIEW

Correct fifteen errors in singular nouns, plural nouns, determiners, and prepositions.

EXAMPLE: ~~Much~~ *Many* houses lost ~~electricities~~ *electricity* during the ice storm.

1. One of the most interesting weather phenomenon is an ice

    storm. Freezing rain coats all surfaces with a heavy layer of ice.

    On January 1998, Quebec and parts of the New England

    experienced the worst ice storm of the twentieth century.

    About 4 inches of freezing rain fell in the region since five days.

    There were much consequences because of the ice.

2. Over 900,000 households had no electricity for about a week.

    About 100,000 people had to leave their homes and go at

    refuge centers. Many people worried of the damage to their

    homes. Some people stayed at the home, but it was difficult

    without electricity. Others relied of their neighbors. Also, the

    authorities were concerned about some people getting

    hypothermia.

3. The environments looked like a disaster scene from a science fiction movie. Farmers lost pigs, sheep, and other livestock. Some business lost income at that period because they had no electricity to remain open. Citizens received few information from the authorities.

4. Although this time has passed, many friends and neighbors still talk about the ice storm. Those days, it is just a distant memory.

The Writer's Room **Topics for Writing**

Write about one of the following topics. Proofread your text to ensure that there are no errors in singular or plural forms, determiners, and prepositions.

1. What should people do to prepare for severe weather? List some steps.
2. What are some types of severe weather phenomena? Classify severe weather into three different types.

CHECKLIST: NOUNS, DETERMINERS, AND PREPOSITIONS

When you edit your writing, ask yourself these questions:

Do I use the correct singular or plural form of nouns? Check for errors with the spelling of regular and irregular plurals and count and noncount nouns.

> *Many children*   *in*   *snow*
> ~~Much~~ ~~childrens~~ love to play ~~on~~ the ~~snows~~.

Do I use the correct determiners? Check for errors with *a, an, the, much, many, few, little, this, that, these,* and *those.*

> *These*   *much*   *the*
> ~~This~~ days, there is too ~~many~~ information about ~~a~~ impact of global warming.

Do I use the correct prepositions? Check for errors with *in, on, at,* and *to,* with *for* and *during,* and with prepositional expressions.

>   *For*   *on*
> ~~During~~ three months each winter, the town depends ~~of~~
>   *at*
> tourists who stay ~~to~~ the ski resorts.

Pronouns

CONTENTS

- Pronoun and Antecedent Agreement
- Indefinite Pronouns
- Vague Pronouns
- Pronoun Shifts
- Pronoun Case
- Relative Pronouns

Section Theme **FORCES OF NATURE**

In this chapter, you will read about nature's power.

Grammar Snapshot

Looking at Pronouns

The following quote is from the article "The Weather: Friend and Tyrant," in which William Renaurd discusses the effects of weather on people's health. The pronouns are underlined.

"I can feel a cold weather front coming days ahead of its arrival," says Jane. "My teeth begin to hurt, and my entire lower jaw aches. I've been x-rayed, prodded by dentists, filled with pain-killing drugs, and examined by half a dozen neurologists. They can find no reason for my pain. I've decided that it's the weather and just try to bear it while waiting for the weather to change."

In this chapter, you will identify and write pronouns.

275

Pronoun and Antecedent Agreement

Pronouns are words that replace nouns (people, places, or things) and phrases. Use pronouns to avoid repeating nouns.

> *They*
> Hurricanes are large tropical storms. ~~Hurricanes~~ commonly form in the Caribbean.

GRAMMAR LINK

For a list of common collective nouns, see page 210 in Chapter 16.

A pronoun must agree with its **antecedent**, which is the word to which the pronoun refers. Antecedents are nouns and phrases that the pronouns have replaced, and they always come before the pronoun. Pronouns must agree in person and number with their antecedents.

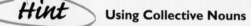
Sarah was late for **her** meeting because **she** drove slowly in the blinding rain.

CHAPTER 20

> ## *Hint* **Using Collective Nouns**
>
> Collective nouns refer to a group of people or things. The group acts as a unit; therefore, it is singular.
>
> The <u>organization</u> is very popular. Many people belong to **it**.
>
> The <u>company</u> was fined for polluting. **It** had to pay a large sum of money.

PRACTICE 1   Circle the pronoun and underline its antecedent.

EXAMPLE: Although hurricane <u>names</u> used to be only female, now (they) may also be male.

1. Anna Petrowski works for the World Meteorological Organization (WMO) where she helps to select hurricane names.

2. The WMO makes a list of distinctive names because they are easier to remember.

3. An Atlantic hurricane can have an English, a Spanish, or a French name because it mirrors the nationalities of people that may be affected.

4. In fact, when hurricanes become famous, the WMO retires their names.

5. The army usually sends its personnel to help with emergency relief during

a hurricane.

Indefinite Pronouns

Use **indefinite pronouns** when you refer to people or things whose identity is not known or is unimportant. This chart shows some common singular and plural indefinite pronouns.

Indefinite Pronouns				
Singular	another	each	nobody	other
	anybody	everybody	no one	somebody
	anyone	everyone	nothing	someone
	anything	everything	one	something
Plural	both, few, many, others, several			
Either singular or plural	all, any, half (and other fractions), none, more, most, some			

Singular

When you use a singular indefinite antecedent, also use a singular pronoun to refer to it.

Nobody remembered to bring **his** or **her** raincoat.

Plural

When you use a plural indefinite antecedent, also use a plural pronoun to refer to it.

Hurricanes and tornadoes arrive each year, and both have **their** own destructive power.

Either Singular or Plural

Some indefinite pronouns can be either singular or plural depending on the noun to which they refer.

Many meteorologists spoke at the conference. All gave important information about **their** research.

(*All* refers to meteorologists; therefore, the pronoun is plural.)

I read <u>all</u> of the newspaper and could not find **its** weather section.
(*All* refers to the newspaper; therefore, the pronoun is singular.)

> ## Hint   **Avoid Sexist Language**
>
> Terms like *anybody, somebody, nobody,* and *each* are singular antecedents, so the pronouns that follow must be singular. At one time, it was acceptable to use *he* as a general term meaning "all people." However, today it is more acceptable to use *he or she.*
>
> | | |
> |---|---|
> | **Sexist:** | <u>Everyone</u> should stay inside **his** house during a tornado. |
> | **Solution:** | <u>Everyone</u> should stay inside **his or her** house during a tornado. |
> | **Better Solution:** | <u>People</u> should stay inside **their** houses during a tornado. |
> | **Exception:** | In the men's prison, <u>everyone</u> has **his** own cell. (If you know for certain that the subject is male or female, then use only *he* or only *she*.) |

PRACTICE 2   Correct nine errors in pronoun–antecedent agreement by changing either the antecedent or the pronoun. If you change any antecedents, make sure that your subjects and verbs agree.

 their
EXAMPLE: Some of the workers had ~~his~~ own skis.

1. Everyone should know what to do if they are caught in extreme weather conditions. For example, people should be aware of lightning storms. All need to avoid open spaces, and he should get inside a building. No one should remain in the open because they could be struck by lightning. If lightning is nearby, each person who is outside should get into a crouching position but never lie down.

2. In the winter months, snowstorms can be dangerous. Somebody stranded in a blizzard should stay with their car. Nobody should wander outside on

their own during a blinding snowstorm. It is very dangerous if a car gets stuck in a snowbank. One of the most common problems is carbon monoxide poisoning, which happens when snow blocks the back of the car and carbon monoxide gas backs up in their exhaust pipe. To solve this problem, everyone should clear the snow from their exhaust pipe.

3. Many have heard his or her weather stations reporting on tornadoes. During a tornado warning, everybody should go into a basement or windowless room in their home. Knowing what to do during extreme weather can save people's lives.

Vague Pronouns

Avoid using pronouns that could refer to more than one antecedent.

> **Vague:** My father asked my brother where <u>his</u> umbrella was.
> (Whose umbrella? My father's or my brother's?)

> **Clearer:** My father asked my brother where **my brother's** umbrella was.

Avoid using confusing pronouns such as *it* and *they* that have no clear antecedent.

> **Vague:** <u>They</u> say that thousands of people lost their lives during the 1995 earthquake in Kobe, Japan.
> (Who are *they*?)

> **Clearer:** **Government officials** say that thousands of people lost their lives during the 1995 earthquake in Kobe, Japan.

> **Vague:** <u>It</u> stated in the newspaper that the scientific name for a thundercloud is cumulonimbus.
> (Who or what is *it*?)

> **Clearer:** **The journalist** stated that the scientific name for a thundercloud is cumulonimbus.

This, *that*, and *which* should refer to a specific antecedent.

Vague: My girlfriend said that the roads were icy. I was glad she told me <u>this</u>.
(What is *this?*)

Clearer: My girlfriend said that the roads were icy. I was glad she told me **this information.**

> ⟨ *Hint* ⟩   **Avoid Repeating the Subject**
>
> When you clearly mention a subject, do not repeat the subject in pronoun form.
>
> Thunder ~~it~~ occurs when cold air collides with hot air.

CHAPTER 20

PRACTICE 3   The next paragraphs contain vague pronouns or repeated subjects. Correct the nine errors in this selection. You may need to rewrite some sentences.

The journalist reported
EXAMPLE: ~~They said on television~~ that most tornadoes occur in agricultural areas around the world.

1. Meteorologist Patricia Bowles told her friend Sheila that her photo of the tornado would appear in the newspaper. They say that tornadoes are the most powerful storms on earth. Tornado winds they can often exceed 100 miles per hour. This can cause a lot of damage to property and sometimes kill people.

2. It says that tornadoes form during thunderstorms when cool air moves downward and hot air rises very quickly, creating a funnel effect. When this touches the ground, it becomes a tornado. The United States it has a "Tornado Alley." This consists of Texas, Oklahoma, Kansas, and Nebraska. These states they have more tornadoes than other parts of North America because cold air from Canada meets warm air from the Gulf of Mexico over the flat prairies.

Pronoun Shifts

If your essays contain unnecessary shifts in person or number, you may confuse your readers. They will not know exactly who or how many you are referring to. Carefully edit your writing to ensure that your pronouns are consistent.

Making Pronouns Consistent in Number

If the antecedent is singular, then the pronoun must be singular. If the antecedent is plural, then the pronoun must be plural.

> singular   his or her
> A **meteorologist** and ~~their~~ team spend years keeping meticulous records of weather patterns.

> plural   they
> When there are storm **warnings**, ~~it~~ should be taken seriously.

Making Pronouns Consistent in Person

Person is the writer's perspective. For some writing assignments, you might use the first person (*I, we*). For other assignments, especially most college essays and workplace writing, you might use the second person (*you*), or the third person (*he, she, it, they*).

Shifting the point of view for no reason confuses readers. If you begin writing from one point of view, do not shift unnecessarily to another point of view.

> They
> **Many** tourists like to travel, but **they** should be careful. ~~You~~ never
> They
> know when there will be bad weather. ~~You~~ should always be prepared for emergencies.

PRACTICE 4   Correct five pronoun shift errors.

EXAMPLE: Many people were saddened when they heard that thousands of
> They
people had died in the 2001 Indian earthquake. ~~One~~ donated money, clothes, and blankets to the victims.

In 2005, we were traveling in Pakistan. We had just finished our breakfast when you felt the ground moving. Everything in our tenth floor apartment started to shake and fall. We knew we should not panic, but one really didn't know what to do. We knew you had to get out of the high-rise and onto the ground because one could never be certain that the building would remain standing. There were no guarantees that you could make it out in time.

Pronoun Case

Pronouns are formed according to the role they play in a sentence. A pronoun can be the subject of the sentence or the object of the sentence. It can also show possession. This chart shows the three main pronoun cases: subjective, objective, and possessive.

Pronouns

Singular	Subjective	Objective	Possessive Adjective	Possessive Pronoun
1st person	I	me	my	mine
2nd person	you	you	your	yours
3rd person	he, she, it, who, whoever	him, her, it, whom, whomever	his, her, its, whose	his, hers
Plural				
1st person	we	us	our	ours
2nd person	you	you	your	yours
3rd person	they	them	their	theirs

Subjective Case and Objective Case

When a pronoun is the subject of the sentence, use the subjective form of the pronoun. When a pronoun is the object in the sentence, use the objective form of the pronoun.

subject   subject   object

He left the umbrella at work, and **I** asked **him** to bring it home.

Possessive Case

A possessive pronoun shows ownership.

- **Possessive adjectives** come before the noun that they modify.

    She finished **her** research on the polar ice caps, but we did not finish **our** research.

- **Possessive pronouns** replace the possessive adjective and the noun that follows it. In the next sentence, the possessive pronoun *ours* replaces both the possessive adjective *our* and the noun *research*.

    possessive adjective

    She finished **her** research on the polar ice caps, but we did not

    possessive pronoun

    finish **ours**.

Problems with Possessive Pronouns

Some possessive adjectives sound like certain contractions. When using the possessive adjectives *their*, *your*, and *its*, be careful that you do not confuse them with *they're* (they + are), *you're* (you + are), and *it's* (it + is).

GRAMMAR LINK

For more information about apostrophes, see Chapter 25.

hers   theirs
The book on clouds is ~~her's~~. The weather almanac is ~~their's~~.

> ## *Hint* ⟩ Choosing *His* or *Her*
>
> To choose the correct possessive adjective, think about the possessor (not the object that is possessed).
>
> If something belongs to a female, use **her** + noun.
>
> Malina and **her** dog like to walk in the snow.
>
> If something belongs to a male, use **his** + noun.
>
> Cliff used **his** new camera to photograph storm clouds.

PRACTICE 5   Underline the correct possessive adjectives or possessive pronouns in each set of parentheses.

EXAMPLE: Dr. Jane Woody wondered whether (his / <u>her</u>) theories would be accepted.

1. Scientists study volcanoes and (its / it's / their) effects on weather patterns. When a volcano erupts and throws (his / its / it's) ash particles into the surrounding air, the explosion causes a lot of lightning and thunderstorms in the region nearby.

2. I have just joined the International Society on Volcanic Studies. The members and (there / they're / their)

governments fund research into volcanic activity. A researcher and (their / his or her /its) assistants gather information about volcanic eruptions.

3. My assistant Judith, because of (her / hers) enthusiasm, painstakingly collects data from volcanic eruptions around the world. A lot of research is being done in this field. (Our / Ours) is just one small part of this study.

4. One day, we would like to present (our / ours) observations to climate scientists because we think it will be important to (they / them). Will you be in (you're / your / yours) office next Tuesday? Let's discuss (our / ours) work and (your / yours) when we meet.

Pronouns in Comparisons with *Than* or *As*

Avoid making errors in pronoun case when the pronoun follows *than* or *as*. If the pronoun is a subject, use the subjective case, and if the pronoun is an object, use the objective case.

If you use the incorrect case, your sentence may have a meaning that you do not intend it to have. Review the next examples. Notice that when the sentence ends with the subjective pronoun, it is advisable to add a verb after the pronoun.

objective case
a) I like rainy days as much as **him.**
   (I like rainy days as much as I like him.)

subjective case
b) I like rainy days as much as **he** (does).
   (I like rainy days as much as he likes rainy days.)

 **Complete the Thought**

To test which pronoun case to use, complete the thought.

> He likes winter more than **I** [like winter].
> (Do I want to say that he likes winter more than I like winter?)
>
> He likes winter more than [he likes] **me**.
> (Or, do I want to say he likes winter more than he likes me?)

Pronouns in Prepositional Phrases

In a prepositional phrase, the words that follow the preposition are the objects of the preposition. Therefore, always use the objective case of the pronoun after a preposition.

> To **him**, global warming is not a big deal. <u>Between</u> **you** and **me**, I think he's misinformed.

Pronouns with *and* or *or*

Use the correct case when nouns and pronouns are joined by ***and*** or ***or***. If the pronouns are the subject, use the subjective case. If the pronouns are the object, use the objective case.

> *She and I*
> ~~Her and me~~ had to read about the causes of desertification, and then
> *her and me*
> the instructor asked ~~she and I~~ to summarize the information.

 **Finding the Correct Case**

To determine that your case is correct, try saying the sentence with either the subjective case or the objective case.

Sentence:	The professor asked her and (**I or me**) to research the topic.
Possible answers:	The professor asked **I** to research the topic.
	(This would not make sense.)
	The professor asked **me** to research the topic.
	(This would make sense.)
Correct answer:	The professor asked **her** and **me** to research the topic.

PRACTICE 6 Correct any errors with pronoun case.

EXAMPLE: Last summer, my friend and ~~me~~ I visited Mexico.

1. Last year, my brother and me took a vacation together.

2. He likes exotic travel more than me but convinced me to accompany him to Antarctica.

3. The tour guide told my brother and I that at its thickest point, Antarctica has an ice cap three miles deep. If it were to melt, it would raise the oceans' water level by many feet.

4. Between you and I, it is frightening to think about melting ice caps.

5. My brother is a photographer. Him and me took a lot of photographs.

6. I will have good memories when my brother and me look at our photo album.

GRAMMAR
LINK

For more information about relative pronouns, see Chapter 11.

Relative Pronouns

Relative pronouns can join two short sentences. They include *who, whom, whoever, whomever, which, that,* and *whose.*

Choosing Who or Whom

To determine whether to use *who* or *whom,* replace *who* or *whom* with another pronoun. If the replacement is a subjective pronoun such as *he* or *she,* use **who.** If the replacement is an objective pronoun such as *her* or *him,* use **whom.**

I know a man **who** studies icebergs.
(He studies icebergs.)

The man to **whom** you gave your résumé is my boss.
(You gave your résumé to him.)

PRACTICE 7   Underline the correct relative pronoun in the parentheses.

EXAMPLE: People (<u>who</u> / which) live in the Arctic are used to harsh weather.

1. Ruth, (who / whom) I met in school, has been my best friend for twenty years.

2. Ruth, (who / whom) is a journalist, recently spent some time on Baffin Island.

3. The people on Baffin Island about (who / whom) Ruth is writing are mostly Inuit.

4. The Inuit (who / whom) are accustomed to extreme weather are active year round.

5. Ruth, (who / whom) loves the sun, sometimes feels depressed during the winter when there is very little daylight.

6. Many people (who / whom) Ruth has interviewed are worried about climate change.

FINAL REVIEW
Correct the fifteen pronoun errors in the next paragraphs.

EXAMPLE: Many people around the world have lost ~~one's~~ *their* relatives and property because of severe weather.

1. In 2004 and 2005, severe weather and natural disasters they caused havoc in the lives of people around the world. They say that forces of nature are

Katsushika Hokusai (1760–1849, Japanese)
"The Wave", 19th Century, Woodcut print.
© SuperStock, Inc.

uncontrollable and unpredictable. But with increasingly sophisticated technology, climatologists and there assistants should be able to improve natural disaster warnings around the world.

2. In December 2004, my friend and me were on holiday in Thailand. At that time, the strongest earthquake in forty years occurred in the Indian Ocean. It caused a tsunami that annihilated cities, villages, and holiday resorts. My friend, whom is from Indonesia, said that all members of his uncle's family lost his homes. Many people have suffered more than me.

3. Some months after the Asian tsunami, New Orleans experienced one of their worst hurricanes in history. Hurricane Katrina caused the levees to break and flood the city. This caused severe property damage and loss of life. Almost everybody in New Orleans had to leave their home.

4. Also in 2005, a severe earthquake in the mountainous regions of Pakistan caused death and destruction. They say that around 100,000 people died. I watched television reports of people living in tents and wanted to help them because you could see they had lost everything. So I collected donations from students at my college, and my brother, to who I sent our donations, passed them along to an aid organization in Pakistan.

5. The forces of nature are more powerful than us. We have no ability to control flooding, hurricanes, or earthquakes. With better warning systems and relief infrastructures, maybe one can reduce the misery caused by natural disasters.

 The Writer's Room   **Topics for Writing**

Write about one of the following topics. Proofread your text to ensure there are no pronoun errors.

1. Describe a severe weather event that you or someone you know experienced. What happened? Try to use descriptive imagery.

2. Argue that bicycles should be the only type of vehicle allowed in city centers. Support your argument with specific examples.

 CHECKLIST: PRONOUNS

When you edit your writing, ask yourself these questions.

Do I use the correct pronoun case? Check for errors with the following:

- subjective, objective, and possessive cases
- comparisons with *than* or *as*
- prepositional phrases
- pronouns following *and* or *or*

> *me*
> Between you and ~~I~~, my sister watches the weather reports
> *I (do)*
> more than ~~me~~ .

Do I use the correct relative pronouns? Check for errors with *who* or *whom.*

> *whom*
> My husband, ~~who~~ you have met, is a meteorologist.

Do my pronouns and antecedents agree in number and person? Check for errors with indefinite pronouns and collective nouns.

its
The bad weather and ~~their~~ aftermath were reported on the news.

Are my pronoun references clear? Check for vague pronouns and inconsistent points of view.

Scientists
~~They~~ say the weather will change rapidly. I read the report

I
and ~~you~~ could not believe what it said.

Adjectives and Adverbs

Section Theme **FORCES OF NATURE**

In this chapter, you will read about environmental issues and alternative energy sources.

Grammar Snapshot

Looking at Adjectives and Adverbs

In his article "Iceland's Ring Road: The Ultimate Road Trip," Mark Sundeen describes aspects of that country's landscape. The adjectives and adverbs are underlined.

> <u>Occasionally</u> an iceberg floated beneath the highway bridge, was carried to sea, then was dashed on the beach by the <u>windswept</u> waves. We walked along the <u>gray</u> strand where the blocks of glacier rocked <u>gently</u> in the tide, and we gathered in our hands the <u>cocktail-size</u> ice cubes that had washed up on shore and flung them back to the sea.

In this chapter, you will identify and write adjectives and adverbs.

Adjectives

Adjectives describe nouns (people, places, or things) and pronouns (words that replace nouns). They add information explaining how many, what kind, or which one. They also help you appeal to the senses by describing how things look, smell, feel, taste, and sound.

> The **young** <u>students</u> convinced their **imposing** <u>principal</u> to start an **important** <u>project</u> on air quality in the schools.

CHAPTER 21

Hint **Placement of Adjectives**

You can place adjectives either before a noun or after a linking verb such as *be*, *look, appear, smell,* or *become.*

Before the noun: The **nervous** <u>environmentalist</u> gave a suitable speech.

After the linking verb: The biologist <u>was</u> **disappointed**, and he <u>was</u> **angry**.

Problems with Adjectives

You can recognize many adjectives by their endings. Be particularly careful when you use the following adjective forms.

Adjectives Ending in *-ful* or *-less*

Some adjectives end in *-ful* or *-less*. Remember that *ful* ends in one *l* and *less* ends in double *s*.

> The Blue Oceans Club, a **peaceful** environmental organization, has promoted many **useful** projects. Protecting the environment is an **endless** activity.

Adjectives Ending in *-ed* and *-ing*

Some adjectives look like verbs because they end in *-ing* or *-ed*. When the adjective ends in *-ed*, it describes the person's or animal's expression or feeling. When the adjective ends in *-ing*, it describes the quality of the person or thing.

> The **frustrated** but **prepared** lobbyist confronted the politician, and his **challenging** and **convincing** arguments got her attention.

> ## Hint   **Keep Adjectives in the Singular Form**
>
> Always make an adjective singular, even if the noun following the adjective is plural.
>
> *year*
> Lucia was a forty-five-~~years~~-old woman when she sold her five-thousand-
> *dollar*
> ~~dollars~~ car and rode a bicycle to work.

Adverbs

Adverbs add information to adjectives, verbs, or other adverbs. They give more specific information about how, when, where, and to what extent an action or event occurred. Some adverbs look exactly like adjectives, such as *early*, *late*, *soon*, *often*, and *hard*. However, most adverbs end in *-ly*.

verb   adverb
Biologists <u>studied</u> the statistics on climate change **carefully**.

adverb adverb
They released the results **quite** <u>quickly</u>.

adverb adjective
The **very** <u>eloquent</u> speaker was Dr. Ying.

Forms of Adverbs

Adverbs often end in *-ly*. In fact, you can change many adjectives into adverbs by adding *-ly* endings.

- If you add *-ly* to a word that ends in *l*, then your new word will have a double *l*.

  professional + ly
  The journalist covered the story **professionally**.

- If you add *-ly* to a word that ends in *e*, keep the *e*. Exceptions to this rule are *true–truly* and *due–duly*.)

  close + ly
  Scientists monitor the polar ice caps **closely**.

> ## Hint: Placement of Frequency Adverbs
>
> **Frequency adverbs** are words that indicate how often someone performs an action or when an event occurs. Common frequency adverbs are *always, ever, never, often, sometimes,* and *usually.* They can appear at the beginning of sentences, or they can appear in the following locations.
>
> - Place frequency adverbs before regular present and past tense verbs.
>
>   Politicians **sometimes** <u>forget</u> the importance of the environment.
>
> - Place frequency adverbs after all forms of the verb *be.*
>
>   She <u>is</u> **often** an advisor for environmental agencies.
>
> - Place frequency adverbs after helping verbs.
>
>   They <u>have</u> **never** donated to an environmental group.

PRACTICE 1   Correct eight errors with adjectives or adverbs.

                                     quietly
EXAMPLE: I entered the room ~~quiet~~ because the lecture had started.

1. Many people frequent debate the issue of climate change. There are two

   clearly sources that cause global warming: natural and human. People

   forget often that natural forces have contributed to climate change

   throughout the history of the world. Scientists know that ice ages have

   developed and diminished rapid.

2. Global temperature increases naturaly for several reasons. For instance,

   explosions in the sun generate heat that causes the earth's temperature

   to rise abrupt. Another natural source for global warming is volcanic

   eruptions. A strong eruption gives off smoke and gases. These elements

   may act sometimes as a shield preventing sunlight from entering the

atmosphere. In addition, a minor change in the earth's orbit may

affect also the earth's temperature. So when debating climate change, keep

in mind the natural causes of temperature fluctuations.

Problems with Adverbs

Many times, people use an adjective instead of an adverb after a verb. Ensure that
you always modify your verbs using an adverb.

really quickly   *slowly*
The snowstorm developed ~~real quick~~. We had to drive very ~~slow~~.

PRACTICE 2 Underline and correct ten errors with adjective and
adverb forms.

really

EXAMPLE: Climate change is a <u>realy</u> controversial issue.

1. Human activity contributes great to global warming. With modernization,

   lifestyles are changing real quick. More people are driving cars, and more

   industries are consuming largely

   amounts of energy. When humans

   burn fossil fuels such as gasoline,

   coal, and oil, gases in the atmosphere

   that trap heat rise steady. This condition creates a dangerously greenhouse

   effect, which means that heat cannot escape the earth's atmosphere.

2. There is a general consensus by knowing scientists around the world that

   the earth is experiencing global warming. Rising temperatures could have

   extreme profound consequences for future generations. For instance, with

   melting ice caps, ocean levels could rise dramatical. Other areas in the

   world might experience harmfull desertification.

Good and Well / Bad and Badly

Good is an adjective, and **well** is an adverb. However, as an exception, you can use *well* to describe a person's health (for example, *I do not feel **well***).

> **Adjective:** We will have **good** weather tomorrow.
>
> **Adverb:** She slept **well** even though the storm was noisy.

Bad is an adjective, and **badly** is an adverb.

> **Adjective:** The **bad** weather remained during the past week.
>
> **Adverb:** The meteorologist spoke **badly** during the nightly forecast.

PRACTICE 3   Underline the correct adjectives or adverbs.

EXAMPLE: Generally, public servants who listen (good / <u>well</u>) make (<u>good</u> / well) policies.

1. My biology professor explains subjects (good / well). Yesterday, he spoke about the (bad / badly) effects of greenhouse gases. The sunlight heats the earth's surface really (good / well), but not all of the heat is absorbed. The extra heat is reflected back into the earth's atmosphere, and greenhouse gases prevent this heat from escaping into the atmosphere.

2. The students in my class reacted (good / well) to a personal challenge for reducing global warming. Nobody thought (bad / badly) of the need for taking personal responsibility. They came up with (good / well) ideas to change their lifestyles, including writing a newsletter about the public's need to change (bad / badly) habits. Two (good / well) ways to reduce greenhouse gases are to reduce driving times and to recycle. Most people have (good / well) intentions and know (good / well) that humans must reduce greenhouse gases.

Comparative and Superlative Forms

Use the **comparative form** to compare two items. Use the **superlative form** to compare three or more items. You can write comparative and superlative forms by remembering a few simple guidelines.

Using -er and -est endings

Add *-er* and *-est* endings to one-syllable adjectives and adverbs. Double the last letter when the adjective ends in *one vowel + one consonant.*

short	short**er** than	the short**est**
hot	hott**er** than	the hott**est**

When a two syllable adjective ends in *-y*, change the *-y* to *-i* and add *-er* or *-est.*

happy	happ**ier** than	the happ**iest**

Using *more* and *the most*

Add *more* and *the most* to adjectives and adverbs of two or more syllables.

beautiful	**more** beautiful than	the **most** beautiful

Using Irregular Comparative and Superlative Forms

Some adjectives and adverbs have unique comparative and superlative forms. Study this list to remember some of the most common ones.

good / well	better than	the best
bad / badly	worse than	the worst
some / much / many	more than	the most
little (a small amount)	less than	the least
far	farther / further	the farthest / the furthest

GRAMMAR LINK

Farther indicates a physical distance. *Further* means "additional." For more commonly confused words, see Chapter 23.

PRACTICE 4   Fill in the blanks with the correct comparative and superlative forms of the words in parentheses.

EXAMPLE: The problems of global warming are (serious) <u>*more serious*</u> than we previously believed.

1. The international community is trying to deal with one of the (urgent)

   _____ environmental problems the world is facing.

   Global warming is one of the (debated) _____ issues in

the scientific community. The Kyoto Protocol is an international agreement

made under the United Nations. Nations agreed to reduce their greenhouse

gas emissions and prevent the greenhouse effect from becoming (bad)

_____ than in previous years.

2. Dr. Anif Mohammed is a famous climatologist. His presentation was

(short) _____ than some of the others, but it was also

the (clear) _____. In fact, he seemed to be the (little)

_____ nervous speaker at the conference.

Problems with Comparative and Superlative Forms

Using *more* and *-er*

In the comparative form, never use *more* and *-er* to modify the same word. In the superlative form, never use *most* and *-est* to modify the same word.

> The photographs of the tornado were ~~more~~ better than the ones of the rainstorm, but the photos of the huge waves were the ~~most~~ best in the exhibition.

Using *fewer* and *less*

GRAMMAR LINK

For a list of common noncount nouns, refer to page 253 in Chapter 19.

In the comparative form, use *fewer* before count nouns (*fewer people, fewer houses*) and use *less* before noncount nouns (*less information, less evidence*).

> Diplomats have **less** <u>time</u> than they used to. **Fewer** <u>agreements</u> are being made.

> *Hint*   **Using *the* in the Comparative Form**
>
> Although you would usually use *the* in superlative forms, you can use it in some two-part comparatives. In these expressions, the second part is the result of the first part.
>
>   action   result
>
> <u>The more</u> you recycle, <u>the better</u> the environment will be.

PRACTICE 5 Correct the nine adjective and adverb errors in the next paragraphs.

fewer   *less*
EXAMPLE: If ~~less~~ people drove cars, we would have ~~fewer~~ air pollution.

1. The Amazon rainforest is the most largest in the world. It plays a vital role in regulating the global climate. Forests, such as the Amazon, create more better air quality for humans. Trees and plants remove carbon dioxide from the air and release oxygen into the air. The Amazon rainforest has been experiencing deforestation real rapidly.

2. There are several reasons for the Amazon deforestation. The most biggest causes of it are cattle ranching and road construction. Roads provide more greater access for logging and mining companies. Clearing the forest, farmers obtain more land for their cattle.

3. The depletion of the Amazon rainforest is one of the worse problems for our global climate. Less politicians than environmental activists are concerned with this issue. The more humanity waits to tackle this problem, the worst it will become. Perhaps over time, governments and the general public will try more harder to save the Amazon rainforest.

CHAPTER 2

FINAL REVIEW
Correct fifteen errors in adjectives and adverbs.

EXAMPLE: We need to find ~~more~~ better sources of renewable energy.

1. Our society has depended economic on oil for the past two hundred years.
   Oil is a nonrenewable energy source. Many politicians have reacted bad to
   the suggestion that we need to reduce our reliance on oil. They are
   concerned about economic progress, which is presently fueled by oil. Yet,
   worrying scientists and environmentalists believe that burning fossil fuels
   is causing temperatures around the world to become more warmer.
   Because of the threat of global warming, scientists are trying to develop
   alternative energy sources real quickly.

2. Wind energy is one powerfull alternative. Historically, countles efforts
   have been made to use wind to power millstones for grinding wheat and
   running pumps. Today, wind-powered turbines produce electricity
   25 percent of the time because winds might not blow strong or continual.
   Therefore, the wind is not a dependable source of energy.

3. Less people use geothermal energy to heat homes in North America
   than in some other parts of the world. Nevertheless, it is also one of the
   most best alternative energy sources. Steam and hot water from under
   the earth's surface are used to turn turbines quick enough to create
   electricity. Around the world, there are a few areas that have steam or
   hot water close to the earth's surface, making geothermal energy cost-

effective. Iceland uses geothermal energy to heat about

80 percent of its buildings.

4. The preceded energy sources are just a few of the alternative approaches

that researchers are working on perfecting. These alternatives do not

substitute completely for the versatility of oil. Scientists, government

officials, and concerned citizens know good that our society must reduce

its dependence on oil. The more money we spend on research, the best

the chances will be to develop and promote energy alternatives.

The Writer's Room Topics for Writing

Write about one of the following topics. Proofread your text to ensure that there
are no adjective and adverb mistakes.

1. Compare two types of transportation that you have owned. Explain which one
   you prefer.
2. Argue that our government should or should not address the issue of global
   warming.

✔ CHECKLIST: ADJECTIVES AND ADVERBS

When you edit your writing, ask yourself these questions:

Do I use adjectives and adverbs correctly? Check for errors in these cases:

- the placement, order, and spelling of adjectives
- the placement of frequency adverbs, and the spelling of adverbs
  ending in -*ly*

- the adjective and adverb form
- the use of *good/well* and *bad/badly*

                                    quietly   *interesting*
Magnus Forbes spoke very ~~quiet~~ about the ~~interested~~ article

                                                        often
on El Niño at the news conference. He was asked to speak
                                                          ^

~~often~~ on environmental topics. The environmental lobbyist

                          really well
hid his concern ~~real good~~.

Do I use the correct comparative and superlative forms? Check for errors in these cases:

- *more* versus *-er* comparisons
- *the most* versus *-est* comparisons
- *fewer* versus *less* forms

The ~~most~~ quickest tornado trackers take the first photographs.

                              fewer   *less*
The organization had ~~less~~ members, but it also has ~~fewer~~ bad publicity.

Exact Language

CONTENTS

- Using Specific and
  Detailed Vocabulary
- Avoiding Wordiness
  and Redundancy
- Avoiding Clichés
- Using Standard English

Section Theme **PLANTS AND INSECTS**

*In this chapter,
you will read
about plants.*

Grammar Snapshot

Looking at Exact Language

In his article "Deep in the Jungle of Suriname," Conger Beasley describes the beauty of a tropical jungle. The descriptive language is underlined.

> The view from the summit over the <u>rippling</u> tree canopy was impressive. The upper parts of the canopy <u>were drenched in sunlight</u>; it's here where the foliage is thickest that the majority of birds and animals range, not down on the floor where the sun rarely <u>penetrates</u> and <u>the air seems to hold its breath like a whale at the bottom of the sea.</u>

In this chapter, you will identify and write exact language.

Using Specific and Detailed Vocabulary

Effective writing evokes an emotional response from the reader. Great writers not only use correct grammatical structures, but they also infuse their writing with precise and vivid details that make their work come alive.

When you proofread your work, revise words that are too vague. **Vague words** lack precision and detail. For example, the words *nice* and *bad* are vague. Readers cannot get a clear picture from them.

Compare the following sets of sentences.

> **Vague:**   The flower smelled nice.
>
> **Precise:** The crimson rose smelled musky sweet.

> **Vague:**   The gardener planted some flowers.
>
> **Precise:** The gardener, Mr. Oliver, planted azaleas, hyacinths, and irises.

> *Hint*   **Some Common Vague Words**
>
> The following is a list of some frequently used vague words. Try to find substitutes for overly familiar and vague words: *good, bad, nice, pretty, big, small, great, happy, sad, thing.*

Creating Vivid Language

WRITING LINK

You can find more information about appealing to the five senses in Chapter 8, Description.

When you choose the precise word, you convey your meaning exactly. Moreover, you can make your writing clearer and more impressive by using specific and detailed vocabulary. To create vivid language, do the following:

- **Modify your nouns.**   If your noun is vague, make it more specific by adding one or more adjectives. You could also rename the noun with a more specific term.

> **Vague:**   the child
>
> **Vivid:**   the angry boy   the tearful and frightened orphan

- **Modify your verbs.**   Use more vivid, precise verbs. You could also use adverbs.

> **Vague:**   talk
>
> **More vivid:** bicker   debate passionately

- **Include more details.**   Add information to make the sentence more detailed and complete.

    Vague: Some herbs are good for the health.

    Precise: Garlic has antibiotic properties that can fight bacteria and viruses.

PRACTICE 1   Underline vague words in the following sentences. Then replace them with more precise and detailed vocabulary.

EXAMPLE: Our town's garden is <u>pretty</u>.

The pond in our town's garden is filled with pink and white water lilies and surrounded by ferns and wild poppies that attract green frogs, mallard ducks, and cardinals.

1. My neighbor likes to garden.

_____

_____

2. She has planted many flowers and plants.

_____

_____

3. There are also vegetables.

_____

_____

4. The herbs she has planted smell nice.

_____

_____

5. She has fun in her garden.

_____

_____

Avoiding Wordiness and Redundancy

Sometimes students fill their writing assignments with extra words to meet the length requirement. However, good ideas can get lost in work that is too wordy. Also, if the explanations are unnecessarily long, readers will become bored.

To improve your writing style, use only as many words or phrases as you need to fully explain your ideas.

The farm was big ~~in size~~.

(*Big* is a measure of size, so it is unnecessary to repeat it.)

Correcting Wordiness

You can cut the number of words needed to express an idea by substituting a wordy phrase with a single word. You could also remove the wordy phrase completely.

because
I don't like gardening ~~due to the fact that~~ I spend most of the time just pulling out weeds.

Some Common Wordy Expressions and Substitutions

Wordy	Substitution	Wordy	Substitution
at this point in time	now, currently	gave the appearance of being	looked like
at that point in time	then, at that time		
big / small in size	big / small	in order to	to
in close proximity	close *or* in proximity	in spite of the fact	in spite of
a difficult dilemma	a dilemma	in the final analysis	finally, lastly
due to the fact	because	past history	past *or* history
equally as good as	as good as	period of time	period
exactly the same	the same	still remain	remain
exceptions to the rule	exceptions	a true fact	a fact
final completion	end	the fact of the matter is	in fact
for the purpose of	for		

PRACTICE 2   Edit the following sentences by crossing out all unnecessary words or phrases. If necessary, find more concise substitutes for wordy expressions.

EXAMPLE: Medical researchers are conducting experiments with herbs ~~in order~~ to examine their medicinal value.

1. One true fact is that herbs have played an important part in the lives of human beings through the ages.

2. For example, in past history, the Romans put laurel in the crowns of the emperors.

3. The ancient Greeks ate parsley for the purpose of curing stomach aches.

4. During the Middle Ages, mint was popular due to the fact that people used it to purify drinking water.

5. The fact of the matter is that during the Middle Ages, people thought that herbs had magical powers.

6. The early settlers in North America grew herbs close in proximity to their houses.

7. At that point in time, the new immigrants also used herbs as medicine.

8. Today, some people believe that herbal medicines are equally as good as synthetic medicines.

Avoiding Clichés

Clichés are overused expressions. Avoid boring your readers with clichés, and use more direct and vivid language instead.

clichés	direct words
In this neck of the woods, she is considered an expert on orchids.	In this area

Other Common Clichés

a drop in the bucket	death trap
add insult to injury	easier said than done
as luck would have it	go with the flow
axe to grind	in the nick of time
better late than never	keep your eyes peeled
between a rock and a hard place	at a loss for words
break the ice	under the weather
calm, cool, and collected	time and time again
crystal clear	tried and true

CHAPTER 22

Hint ▸ Modifying Clichés

To modify a cliché, change it into a direct term. You might also try playing with language to come up with a more interesting description.

Cliché:	She was as happy as a lark.
Direct language:	She was thrilled.
Interesting description:	She was as happy as a teenager whose parents had gone away for the weekend.

PRACTICE 3   Cross out the clichéd expression in each sentence. If necessary, replace it with fresh or direct language.

greatly impressed
EXAMPLE: I was ~~blown away~~ by my neighbor's garden.

1. My neighbor threw caution to the wind and planted some strange plants.

2. She was playing with fire planting a ginkgo tree.

3. When I smelled something putrid, I was sure beyond a shadow of ~~a doubt~~ that it was the ginkgo tree.

Ginkgo leaves

4. To add insult to injury, she had also planted a corpse flower in her greenhouse.

5. I was at a loss for words when she asked me how I liked her new plants.

6. In the nick of time, my boyfriend arrived, so I could avoid answering her question.

Using Standard English

Most of your instructors will want you to write using **standard English**. The word "standard" does not imply better. Standard English is the common language generally used and expected in schools, businesses, and government institutions in the United States. **Slang** is nonstandard language. It is used in informal situations to communicate common cultural knowledge. In any academic or professional context, do not use slang.

Slang: Me an' some bros wanted to make some dough, so we worked on a farm picking apples. We made a bit of coin, and our grub was included. It was real cool. On the weekends, we mostly chilled.

Standard   My friends and I wanted to make some money, so we
American   worked on a farm picking apples. We were well paid,
English: and our food was included. We had a memorable time. On the weekends, we mostly relaxed.

Hint   **Reasons to Avoid Slang**

Slang changes depending on generational, regional, cultural, and historical influences. For example, one group might say "upset" whereas others might say "freaked out" or "having a fit." You should avoid using slang expressions in your writing because they can change very quickly—so quickly, in fact, that you might think that this textbook's examples of slang are "lame."

PRACTICE 4 Substitute the underlined slang expressions with the best possible choice of standard English.

EXAMPLE: Over five thousand years ago, the Chinese cultivated roses that
excellent
were <u>bad</u>.

1. The history of roses is <u>sweet</u>.

2. An <u>awesome</u> fact is that the rose is about 35 million years old.

3. I was <u>blown away</u> when I learned that there are 150 species of roses.

4. Throughout history, famous <u>chicks</u>, such as Napoleon's wife Josephine, cultivated roses.

5. From the eighteenth century onwards, Europeans thought it was <u>tight</u> to grow roses in their gardens.

6. Cultivating a successful rose garden is <u>no cakewalk</u>.

7. Roses need a lot of <u>TLC</u> to blossom.

8. The roses in my garden are <u>fly</u>.

FINAL REVIEW

Edit the following paragraphs for twenty errors in wordiness, slang, clichés, and vague language to make the text more effective.

1. At this point in time, many people are freaking out about genetically modified foods. Genetic modification (GM) is a technology that lets scientists fool around with the genetic composition of plants.

Historically, people have always tried to change the characteristics of
plants for the purpose of making them more disease-resistant.
That process has traditionally been done through hybridization,
a tried and true method. That is, two parent plants from the same genus
are bred to create an improved hybrid plant. One true fact is that hybrid
wheat is hardier than traditional wheat.

2. Today, in North America, hundreds of foods that we use daily are
genetically modified. In the final analysis, there is great controversy
about genetically modified foods. Proponents of this technology say
time and time again that food will contain higher levels of nutrition, be
resistant to disease, and produce higher yields. In spite of the fact of such
arguments, opponents are all fired up about genetically modified foods
because they say that there is not enough knowledge about how such
foods will affect human health. They believe such foods might become
a death trap. For example, will humans who are allergic to peanuts have a
reaction if they are eating tomatoes that have been genetically modified
with a peanut gene? Furthermore, opponents also believe that the loss
of diversity in crops and plants really bites. Another worry is that
food production will go into the hands of super-sized agricultural
companies who will control growth and distribution of food. Moreover,
the bigwigs in this debate stress out about the ethics of mixing genes
from species to species.

3. The genetically modified food industry is growing rapidly in size. But it is important to have a healthy and open debate over this issue. Presently, consumers are faced with a difficult dilemma. Most people are in a fog and are unknowingly buying genetically modified foods because such foods lack complete labeling. For example, most cooking oil comes from genetically modified grains. The public should be in the know about this technology. Consumers need to be clued in so that they make the right choices.

CHAPTER 22

 The Writer's Room **Topics for Writing**

Write about one of the following topics. Proofread your text to ensure that you have used detailed vocabulary and avoided wordiness, clichés, and slang.

1. Examine this photo. What are some terms that come to mind? Some ideas might be *family farm, agribusiness, healthy living, back to basics, farm aid,* or *green thumb.*

2. Why are fast foods and other unhealthy foods so popular? Think of some reasons.

CHECKLIST: EXACT LANGUAGE

When you edit your writing, ask yourself these questions.

Have I used specific and detailed vocabulary? Check for errors with vague words.

Vague: My son likes to garden.

Detailed: My fifteen-year-old son, Kiran, is an enthusiastic gardener.

Have I used exact language? Check for errors with wordiness, clichés, and slang.

now
Julian works in the garden center ~~at this point in time~~.

evident
It is ~~as plain as black and white~~ that many people like organic food.

easy
The biology exam was ~~a no-brainer.~~

23 Spelling and Commonly Confused Words

CHAPTER

CONTENTS

- Spelling Rules
- 120 Commonly Misspelled Words
- Look-Alike and Sound-Alike Words

Section Theme **PLANTS AND INSECTS**

In this chapter, you will read about insects.

Grammar Snapshot

Looking at Spelling

In this excerpt from the article "Songs of Insects," writer Sy Montgomery discusses how insects communicate. Writers often misspell the underlined words.

If you share this poet's <u>sensibilities</u>, now is the time to <u>fulfill</u> your longing. Though <u>widely</u> loved for <u>its</u> changing <u>leaves</u> and migrating birds, early fall is, in some circles anyway, yet more <u>renowned</u> for the sweetness of <u>its</u> insect voices.

In this chapter, you will identify and correct misspelled words.

Spelling Rules

It is important to spell correctly because spelling mistakes can detract from important ideas in your work. Here are some strategies for improving your spelling skills.

How to Become a Better Speller

- **Look up words** using the most current dictionary because it will contain new or updated words. For tips on dictionary usage.
- **Keep a record of words that you commonly misspell.** For example, write the words and definitions in a spelling log, which could be in a journal or binder. See Appendix 5 for more information about your spelling log.
- **Use memory cards or flash cards** to help you memorize the spelling of difficult words. With a friend or a classmate, take turns asking each other to spell difficult words.
- **Write out the spelling of difficult words at least ten times** to help you remember how to spell them. After you have written these words, try writing them in a complete sentence.

Six Common Spelling Rules

Memorize the following common rules of spelling. If you follow these rules, your spelling will become more accurate. Also try to remember the exceptions to these rules.

1. **Writing *ie* or *ei*** Write *i* before *e*, except after *c* or when *ei* is pronounced as *ay*, as in *neighbor* and *weigh*.

i before *e*:	chief	field	grief
ei after *c*:	receipt	deceit	receive
ei pronounced as *ay*:	weigh	beige	vein

Here are some exceptions:

ancient	either	neither	foreigner	leisure	height
science	species	society	seize	their	weird

2. **Adding *-s* or *-es*** Add *-s* to form plural nouns and to create present-tense verbs that are third-person singular. However, add *-es* to words in the following situations.

   - When words end in *-s*, *-sh*, *-ss*, *-ch*, or *-x*, add *-es*.

noun	box–boxes	**verb**	miss–misses

- When words end in consonant *-y*, change the *-y* to *-i* and add *-es*.

    noun   baby–babies   **verb**   marry–marries

- When words end in *-o*, add *-es*. Exceptions are *pianos, radios, logos, stereos, autos, typos,* and *casinos*.

    noun   tomato–tomatoes   **verb**   go–goes

- When words end in *-f* or *-fe*, change the *-f* to a *-v* and add *-es*. Exceptions are *beliefs* and *roofs*.

    life–lives   wolf–wolves

3. **Adding Prefixes and Suffixes** A **prefix** is added to the beginning of a word, and it changes the word's meaning. For example, *con-, dis-, pre-, un-,* and *il-* are prefixes. When you add a prefix to a word, keep the last letter of the prefix and the first letter of the main word.

    im + mature = immature   mis + spell = misspell

A **suffix** is added to the ending of a word, and it changes the word's tense or meaning. For example, *-ly, -ment, -ed,* and *-ing* are suffixes. When you add the suffix *-ly* to words that end in *-l*, keep the *-l* of the root word. The new word will have two *-l*s.

    casual + ly = casually   factual + ly = factually

4. **Adding Suffixes to Words Ending in *-e*** If the suffix begins with a vowel, drop the *-e* on the main word. Some common suffixes beginning with vowels are *-ed, -er, -est, -ing, -able, -ent,* and *-ist*.

    bake–baking   create–created

Some exceptions are words that end in *-ge*, which keep the *-e* and add the suffix.

    outrage–outrageous   manage–manageable

If the suffix begins with a consonant, keep the *-e*. Some common suffixes beginning with consonants are *-ly, -ment, -less,* and *-ful*. Some exceptions are *acknowledgment, argument,* and *truly*.

    sure–surely   aware–awareness

5. **Adding Suffixes to Words Ending in -y**   If the word has a consonant before the final -y, change the -y to an -i before adding the suffix. Some exceptions are *ladybug*, *dryness*, and *shyness*.

> pretty–prett**i**est   happy–happ**i**ness

If the word has a vowel before the final -y, if it is a proper name, or if the suffix is -ing, do not change the y to an i. Some exceptions are *daily*, *laid*, and *said*.

> employ–employed   apply–applying   Levinsky–Levinskys

6. **Doubling the Final Consonant**   Double the final consonant of one-syllable words ending in a consonant-vowel-consonant pattern.

> ship–shi**pp**ing   swim–swi**mm**er   hop–ho**pp**ed

Double the final consonant of words ending in a stressed consonant-vowel-consonant pattern. If the final syllable is not stressed, then do not double the last letter.

> re<u>fer</u>–refe**rr**ed   oc<u>cur</u>–occu**rr**ed   <u>hap</u>pen–happened

120 Commonly Misspelled Words

The next list contains some of the most commonly misspelled words in English.

absence	careful	especially	loneliness
absorption	ceiling	exaggerate	maintenance
accommodate	cemetery	exercise	mathematics
acquaintance	clientele	extraordinarily	medicine
address	committee	familiar	millennium
aggressive	comparison	February	minuscule
already	competent	finally	mischievous
aluminum	conscience	foreign	mortgage
analyze	conscientious	government	necessary
appointment	convenient	grammar	ninety
approximate	curriculum	harassment	noticeable
argument	definite	height	occasion
athlete	definitely	immediately	occurrence
bargain	desperate	independent	opposite
beginning	developed	jewelry	outrageous
behavior	dilemma	judgment	parallel
believable	disappoint	laboratory	performance
business	embarrass	ledge	perseverance
calendar	encouragement	leisure	personality
campaign	environment	license	physically

possess	reference	surprise	vacuum
precious	responsible	technique	Wednesday
prejudice	rhythm	thorough	weird
privilege	schedule	tomato	woman
probably	scientific	tomatoes	women
professor	separate	tomorrow	wreckage
psychology	sincerely	truly	writer
questionnaire	spaghetti	Tuesday	writing
receive	strength	until	written
recommend	success	usually	zealous

PRACTICE 1 Edit the next paragraphs for twenty misspelled words.

strength
EXAMPLE: Some insects have an incredible amount of ~~strenght~~.

CHAPTER 23

1. Throughout history, humans have either been fascinated or repulsed by insects. In fact, humans have developped a close connection to insects and recognize the power and importance of insects for sustaining life. For example, insects pollinate plants and aerate soil. Without such help, the enviroment would suffer. Thus, human cultures have acknowleged insects through art, literature, and religion.

2. First, the ancient Egyptians honored different insects. The dung beetle or scarab was definatly an important religious symbol. The Egyptians called it Khepera, the god of virility and rebirth. They beleived that he was responsable for pushing the sun along the horizon. To honor Khepera, the Egyptians wore scarab amulets as precious jewlry and buried them in pots and boxs with the dead. The ancients thought that the scarabs helped the dead who were

enterring the afterlife. Furthermore, ancient Egyptian kings took the name of Khepera when they became rulers. For example, Tutankhamen's royal name was Neb Kheperu Ra.

3. Another insect, the cricket, was valued in Chinese culture. The Chinese kept both singing and fighting varieties. Singing crickets were expecialy crucial to farmers. They knew it was time to plow when crickets and other insects began to wake and sing. Wealthy ladyes and palace concubines kept crickets as pets in cages. People surmised that the crickets represented the women themselfs, who had very little status in the community. Fighting crickets were also very popular, and many people lost much of their savings beting on cricket fights.

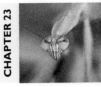

4. Western artists are also fascinated with insects. There are many fables that feature different speceis as the main characters. In modern literature, insects play a noticable role. For example, in Franz Kafka's *Metamorphosis*, the main character turns into a giant cockroach. Insects are common symbols in modern film. Jiminy Cricket is Pinocchio's consceince. In the movie *The Fly*, a scientist is unaturaly transformed into a six-foot human fly. Flys and other insects can also symbolize human fear and repugnance.

5. Humans and insects have had a truely unique relationship for many millennia. Different cultures have integrated insects into the fields of art, music, religion, and history. Indeed, some people say that the teeny creepy crawlers are survivors and will surly outlive humans.

Look-Alike and Sound-Alike Words

Sometimes two English words can sound the same but have different spellings and meanings. These words are called **homonyms**. Here are a few commonly confused words and basic meanings. (For more specific definitions for these and other words, consult a dictionary.)

accept	to receive; to admit	We must accept the vital role that insects play in our culture.
except	excluding; other than	I like all insects except ants.
allowed	permitted	We were not allowed to view the exhibit.
aloud	spoken audibly	We could not speak aloud, so we whispered.
affect	to influence	Pesticides affect the environment.
effect	the result of something	Scientists are examining the effects of pesticides on our health.
been	past participle of the verb *to be*	He has been to the Imax film about caterpillars.
being	present progressive form (the *-ing* form) of the verb *to be*	She was being kind when she donated to the butterfly museum.
by	preposition meaning *next to, on,* or *before*	A bee flew by the flowers. By evening, the crickets were making a lot of noise.
buy	to purchase	Will you buy me that scarab necklace?
complement	to add to; to complete	The film about the monarch butterfly was a nice complement to the exhibit.
compliment	to say something nice about someone	The film was informative and the director received many compliments.
conscience	a personal sense of right or wrong	After spraying pesticides, the gardener had a guilty conscience.
conscious	to be aware; to be awake	He made us conscious of the important role insects play in our society.

PRACTICE 2   Underline the correct word in the parentheses.

EXAMPLE: Many people (by / buy) clothes made out of silk.

1. Silk has (been / being) produced (by / buy) the Chinese for at least four

    thousand years. The silkworm is actually a caterpillar that eats nothing

    (accept / except) mulberry leaves, grows quickly, and then encircles itself into a cocoon of raw silk. The cocoon contains a single thread around 300 to 900 yards in length, so it's not surprising that it takes about 2,000 cocoons to make one pound of silk. (Been / Being) very (conscious / conscience) of the long and intense silk-making process, most people (accept / except) the high cost of the material.

2. The Chinese valued silk and guarded the secret of its making carefully. In ancient China, only the emperor and his family were (allowed / aloud) to wear silk garments. Sometimes, members of royalty wore the fabric as a (complement / compliment) to their regular clothes. Of course, less fortunate people admired the emperor's beautiful clothes and always (complimented / complemented) him.

3. By the fifth century, the secret of silk-making had been revealed to Korea, Japan, and India. How did the secret get out? Legend says that a princess with no (conscious / conscience) smuggled out silkworm larvae to Korea by hiding them in her hair. The emperor was outraged (by / buy) the actions of the princess, and there was great debate about her treachery.

CHAPTER 23

everyday	ordinary or common	Swatting mosquitoes is an <u>everyday</u> ritual of camping.
every day	each day	<u>Every day</u>, I check my roses for aphids.
imminent	soon to happen	The journalist reported that the arrival of locusts in parts of Africa was <u>imminent</u>.
eminent	distinguished; superior	Professor Maurice Kanyogo is an <u>eminent</u> entomologist.
imply	to suggest	The entomologist <u>implied</u> that he received a large grant.
infer	to conclude	His students <u>inferred</u> that they would have summer jobs because of the grant.
its	possessive case of the pronoun *it*	The worker bee went into <u>its</u> hive.
it's	contraction for *it is*	<u>It's</u> well known that the queen bee is the largest in the colony.

knew	past tense of *to know*	I <u>knew</u> that I should study for my test on worms.
new	recent or unused	But my <u>new</u> book on honey making was more interesting.
know	to have knowledge of	The beekeepers <u>know</u> that there has been a decline of bees in recent years.
no	a negative	There were <u>no</u> books on beekeeping in the library.
lose	to misplace or forfeit something	Do not <u>lose</u> the mosquito repellent.
loose	too baggy; not fixed	You should wear <u>loose</u> clothes when camping.
loss	a decrease in an amount; a serious blow	Farmers would experience a <u>loss</u> if there were no bees to pollinate crops.
peace	calmness; an end to violence	The <u>peace</u> in the woods was wonderful.
piece	a part of something else; one item in a group of items	The two <u>pieces</u> of amber had insects in them.
principal	director of a school; the most important item in a group; main	The <u>principal</u> of our school is an expert on beetles. They are his <u>principal</u> hobby.
principle	rules or standards	Julius Corrant wrote a book about environmental <u>principles</u>.
quiet	silent	The crickets remained <u>quiet</u> this evening.
quite	very	They usually make <u>quite</u> a noise.
quit	stop	I would like them to <u>quit</u> making so much noise.

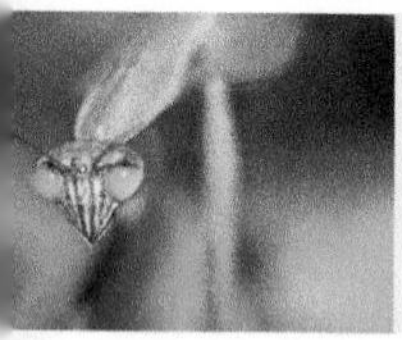

(Side margin: CHAPTER 23)

PRACTICE 3   Identify and correct ten word choice errors.

EXAMPLE: I need some ~~piece~~ *peace* and quiet.

1. I am reading a book on pollination by professor Zoe Truger, an imminent entomologist who specializes in butterfly behavior. Its very interesting. On it's cover, there is a beautiful photograph of a butterfly. Everyday, during the summer, thousands of monarch butterflies are found in southern Canada, their summer home. As autumn arrives, these butterflies know that migration to warmer climates is eminent.

2. The principle of Jake's school took the students on a nature walk to look for earthworms. The students were very quite when the guide told them there are 2,700 species of earthworms.

3. Did you no that beekeeping is one of the world's oldest professions? Some beekeepers may loose their businesses because bees are dying due to pesticide overuse. Citizens need to quite spraying their fields, parks, and gardens with pesticides.

taught	past tense of *to teach*	I taught a class on pollination.
thought	past tense of *to think*	I thought the students enjoyed it.
than	word used to compare items	There are more mosquitoes at the lake than in the city.
then	at a particular time; after a specific time	He found the termite nest. Then he called the exterminators.
that	word used to introduce a clause	They told him that they would come immediately.
their	possessive form of *they*	They wore scarab amulets to show their respect for the god Khepera.
there	a place	The ant colony is over there.
they're	contraction of *they are*	The ants work hard. They're very industrious.
to	part of an infinitive; indicates direction or movement	I want to hunt for bugs. I will go to the hiking path and look under some rocks.
too	also or very	My friend is too scared of bugs. My brother is, too.
two	the number after *one*	There were two types of butterflies in the garden today.
where	question word indicating location	Where did you buy the book on ladybugs?
were	past tense of *be*	There were hundreds of ladybugs on the bush.
we're	contraction of *we are*	We're wondering why we have this infestation.

who's	contraction of *who is*	Isabelle, <u>who's</u> a horticulturist, also keeps a butterfly garden.
whose	pronoun showing ownership	
write	to draw symbols that represent words	I will <u>write</u> an essay about the common earthworm.
right	correct; the opposite of the direction left	In the <u>right</u> corner of the garden, there is the compost bin with many worms in it. You are <u>right</u> when you say that earthworms are necessary for composting.

PRACTICE 4   Identify and correct sixteen word choice errors.

There
EXAMPLE: ~~Their~~ are many different types of hobbies.

1. Their are both professional and amateur beekeepers. Beekeepers wear special clothes, but even with protective gear, there usually stung at least once while practicing there profession. Some beekeepers have a greater resistance to stings then others have. All of them know than there is a small danger of death from anaphylactic shock because of a bee sting. A person whose interested in beekeeping should know the risks. Than he or she can make the write choice about beekeeping as a hobby.

2. We recently read to books on ladybugs. We went to the library

were an expert thought us about ladybugs. The expert, who's bug collection was on display, said each ladybug controls pests because it eats around 5,000 aphids in its lifetime. Ladybugs eat other pests, to. We where extremely surprised when we heard that information. Were going to do more research on ladybugs. I will right an e-mail to the expert asking for more information.

FINAL REVIEW

Correct the twenty spelling errors and mistakes with commonly confused words in the essay.

carries
EXAMPLE: The bee ~~carrys~~ pollen grains from one plant to another.

1. Around the world, unatural causes such as climate change, pollution, and human activities are threatening the enviroment. Forests are expecialy vulnerable to these pressures because of loging, increasing pests, and global warming. Conserving biodiversity is important to protect forests.

2. Biodiversity, a contraction of the words *biological diversity*, means that a variety of plants, animals, and microorganisms coexist in an ecosystem. Today, imminent scientists concerned with species' extinction refer to the necesity of maintaining biodiversity on our planet. Scientists are conscience of the value of each species. Argueing for conserving biodiversity, scientists believe that if species become extinct, than their ecosystem will become unstable.

3. Insects are crucial to sustain the biodiversity of an ecosystem and are the most diverse life form on earth. Currently, there are approximately 800,000 identified species of insects, all of which are usefull in balancing the ecosystem. For example, they pollinate plants, and they eat other insects and plants. Their also important to the global economy. For

instance, insects are used for honey production, silk making, and agricultural pest control. If an insect species becomes extinct, they're will be a variety of consequences on the remaining species in the ecosystem, such as an increase in predatory insects or a lost of another species higher on the food chain. Such a change in the ecosystem would have an eminent effect on all life forms.

4. Most people think that insects are troublesome and should be eradicated. Of course, insects such as mosquitos carry diseases, including malaria and West Nile virus, which are harmfull to human health. But its important to keep in mind that most insects provide important services for the natural world, to. Were there are insects, there is a thriving ecosystem. Extinction of an insect species will have a serious affect on nature, so the next time you are tempted to swat a fly or step on an ant, you might think twice.

 *The Writer's Room* **Topics for Writing**

Write about one of the following topics. Proofread your text to ensure there are no spelling and commonly confused word errors.

1. Discuss types of insects that are particularly annoying, repulsive, or frightening.
2. Are laws banning the use of pesticides on lawns a good idea? Explain your ideas.

✓ **CHECKLIST: SPELLING RULES**

When you edit your writing, ask yourself these questions.

Do I have any spelling errors? Check for errors in words that contain these elements:

- *ie* or *ei* combinations
- prefixes and suffixes

> *Dragonflies*   *lovely*   *Their*
> ~~Dragonflys~~ are ~~lovly~~. ~~There~~ wings are transparent, but
>
> *their*
> ~~they're~~ bodies are a variety of colors. They eat other
>
>   *mosquitoes*
> insects such as ~~mosquitos~~.

Do I repeat spelling errors that I have made in previous assignments? I should check my previous assignments for errors or consult my spelling log.

24 Commas

CHAPTER

Section Theme
HUMAN DEVELOPMENT

In this chapter, you will read about life stages.

Grammar Snapshot

Looking at Commas

On an episode of the *ABC News* program *Primetime*, Connie Chung interviewed citizens from Yuzuri Hara, Japan, a small mountainous village two hours outside of Tokyo. In the excerpt that follows the commas are highlighted.

> Mr. Takahashi attributes his smooth skin, even after working fifty years in the sun, to sticking to the local traditional diet. The skin on his arms felt like a baby's, and the skin on his legs barely had a wrinkle. Some of what Mr. Takahashi eats is on the menu every day at a hotel in Yuzuri Hara. The innkeeper, Mrs. Ishi, is eighty and looks pretty good herself.

In this chapter, you will learn to use commas correctly.

What Is a Comma?

A **comma (,)** is a punctuation mark that helps identify distinct ideas. There are many ways to use a comma. In this chapter, you will learn some helpful rules about comma usage.

Notice how comma placement changes the meanings of the following sentences.

> The baby hits, her mother cries, and then they hug each other.
>
> The baby hits her mother, cries, and then they hug each other.

Commas in a Series

Use a comma to separate items in a series of three or more items. Remember to put a comma before the final "and."

Unit 1	,	unit 2	,	and	unit 3
			,	or	

> Canada, the United States, and Mexico have psychology conferences.
>
> The experiment required patience, perseverance, and energy.
>
> Some teens may work part time, volunteer in the community, and maintain high grades at school.

> ### Hint Comma Before *and*
>
> There is a trend, especially in the media, to omit the comma before the final *and* in a series. However, in academic writing, it is preferable to include the comma because it clarifies your meaning and makes the items more distinct.

PRACTICE 1 Underline series of items. Then add fifteen missing commas.

EXAMPLE: Some psychological studies are simple, obvious, and extremely important.

1. Mary Ainsworth was born in Ohio attended the University of Toronto and worked in Uganda. She became an expert in the childhood development

field. Ainsworth's most significant research examined the attachment of infants to their caretakers.

2. Ainsworth designed an experiment called The Strange Situation. She measured how infants reacted when the primary caretaker left the room a stranger entered and the primary caretaker returned. She determined that children have four attachment styles. They may be secure avoidant ambivalent or disoriented.

3. Secure children may leave their mother's lap explore happily and return to the mother. Avoidant babies are not upset when the mother leaves do not look at the stranger and show little reaction when the mother returns. Ambivalent babies are clinging unwilling to explore and upset by strangers. Disoriented infants react oddly to their mother's return. They look fearful avoid eye contact and slowly approach the returning mother.

CHAPTER 24

Commas After Introductory Words and Phrases

Place a comma after an **introductory word** or **phrase**. Introductory words include interjections (*well*), adverbs (*usually*), or transitional words (*therefore*). Introductory phrases can be transitional expressions (*of course*), prepositional phrases (*in the winter*), or modifiers (*born in Egypt*).

Introductory word(s)	,	sentence.

Introductory word: Yes, the last stage of life is very important.

Introductory phrase: After the experiment, the children returned home.

Feeling bored, he volunteered at a nearby clinic.

PRACTICE 2   Underline each introductory word or phrase. Then add twelve missing commas.

EXAMPLE: <u>Before leaving home</u>, adolescents assert their independence.

1. In *Childhood and Society* Erik Erikson explained his views about the stages of life. According to Erikson there are eight life stages. In his opinion each stage is characterized by a developmental crisis.

2. In the infancy stage babies must learn to trust others. Wanting others to fulfill their needs babies expect life to be pleasant. Neglected babies may end up mistrusting the world.

3. During adolescence a young man or woman may have an identity crisis. Confronted with physical and emotional changes teenagers must develop a sense of self. According to Erikson some adolescents are unable to solve their identity crisis. Lacking self-awareness they cannot commit to certain goals and values.

4. In Erikson's view each crisis must be solved before a person develops in the next life stage. For example a person may become an adult chronologically. However that person may not be an adult emotionally.

Commas Around Interrupting Words and Phrases

Interrupting words or phrases appear in the middle of sentences, and while they interrupt the sentence's flow, they do not affect its overall meaning. Some interrupters are *as a matter of fact, as you know,* and *for example.* Prepositional phrases can also interrupt sentences.

Sentence,	interrupter,	sentence.

The doctor, <u>for example</u>, has never studied child psychology.

Adolescence, <u>as you know</u>, is a difficult life stage.

The child, <u>with no prompting</u>, started to laugh.

Hint Using Commas with Appositives

An appositive gives further information about a noun or pronoun. It can appear at the beginning, in the middle, or at the end of the sentence. Set off an appositive with commas.

beginning
A <u>large hospital</u>, the Mayo Clinic has some of the world's best researchers.

middle
Gail Sheehy, <u>a journalist</u>, has written about life passages.

end
The doctor's office is next to Sims Wholesale, <u>a local grocery store</u>.

PRACTICE 3   The following sentences contain introductory words and phrases, interrupters, and series of items. Add the missing commas. If the sentence is correct, write C in the space provided.

EXAMPLE: Erik Erikson﹐a child development expert, wrote about his identity crisis. _____ ^

1. Erik Erikson during his youth, had an identity crisis. _____

2. At age sixteen he learned about his past. _____

3. His mother admitted that Erik was the result of an extramarital affair. _____

4. He felt surprised, confused and angry. _____

5. At that time, he did not know his birth father. _____

6. Erikson's mother a Danish woman had moved to Germany. _____

7. His adopted father a pediatrician named Theodore Homburger was
   Jewish. _____

8. Erikson felt confused about his nationality his religion, and his
   genealogy. _____

9. In the early 1920s, Erikson went to Vienna. _____

10. Erikson, at a conference met Anna Freud._____

11. Anna Freud Sigmund Freud's daughter, analyzed Erikson._____

12. Using psychoanalysis she helped him resolve his identity crisis._____

Commas in Compound Sentences

In compound sentences, place a comma before the coordinating conjunction
(*for, and, nor, but, or, yet, so*).

| Sentence | , and | sentence. |

Adulthood has three stages, **and** each stage has its particular challenge.

Carolina lives with her mother, **but** her sister lives on her own.

She goes to school, **yet** she also works forty hours a week.

 **Commas and Coordinators**

To ensure that a sentence is compound, cover the conjunction with your finger
and read the two parts of the sentence. If one part of the sentence is incomplete,
then no comma is necessary. If each part of the sentence contains a complete idea,
then you need to add a comma.

No comma: Ben still lives with his parents **but** is very self-sufficient.

Comma: Ben still lives with his parents, **but** he is very self-sufficient.

PRACTICE 4 Edit the next paragraphs and add ten missing commas.

EXAMPLE: She is not an adult‸yet she is not a child.

1. Adulthood is another stage in life but the exact age of adulthood is unclear. Some cultures celebrate adulthood with high school graduation ceremonies and others celebrate with marriage. Some people define adulthood as the moment a person has full-time work and is self-sufficient yet many people only become independent in their thirties.

2. Various cultures treat early adulthood differently. Irene Berridge has a culturally mixed background. Her mother is German and her father is British. She was encouraged to leave home and get an apartment at age nineteen. Today, twenty-one-year-old Irene washes her clothing at a laundromat and she does her own cooking. She has a part-time job and she splits the bills with her roommate. Irene, an independent woman, admits that she often misses her family.

3. Alexis Khoury's parents are recent immigrants from Greece and they want their daughter to stay home until she marries. Alexis is thirty-one years old and she sometimes feels embarrassed to be living at home. She does not feel like an adult and her parents encourage her dependence. However, Alexis will respect her parents' wishes and she will not leave home until she has found a life partner.

Commas in Complex Sentences

A **complex sentence** contains one or more dependent clauses (or incomplete ideas). When you add a **subordinating conjunction**—a word such as *because*, *although*, or *unless*—to a clause, you make the clause dependent.

dependent clause   independent clause
<u>**After** Jason graduated from college</u>, he moved out of the family home.

Using Commas After Dependent Clauses

If a sentence begins with a dependent clause, place a comma after the clause. Remember that a dependent clause has a subject and a verb, but it cannot stand alone. When the subordinating conjunction comes in the middle of the sentence, it is generally not necessary to use a comma.

Dependent clause,	main clause.

Comma: <u>When I find a better job</u>, I will move into an apartment.

Main clause	dependent clause.

No comma: I will move into an apartment <u>when I find a better job</u>.

PRACTICE 5   Edit the following sentences by adding or deleting commas.

EXAMPLE: Although thirty-year-old Samuel Chong lives at home he is not
ashamed.

1. When he examined the 2001 census Mark Noble noticed a clear trend.

2. Although most people in their twenties lived on their own about 40 percent of young adults still lived with their parents.

3. In 1981, the results were different, because only 25 percent of young adults lived at home.

4. After examining the statistics Noble determined several causes for the shift.

5. Because the marriage rate is declining fewer people buy their own homes.

6. When the cost of education increases people cannot afford to study and

    pay rent.

7. Other young adults stay with their parents, because the rents are so

    high.

8. Because these conditions are not changing many young adults will likely

    continue to live with their parents.

GRAMMAR LINK

For more information about choosing *which* or *that*, see Chapter 11, Sentence Variety.

Using Commas to Set Off Nonrestrictive Clauses

Clauses beginning with *who*, *that*, and *which* can be restrictive or nonrestrictive. A **restrictive clause** contains essential information about the subject. Do not place commas around restrictive clauses. In the following example, the underlined clause is necessary to understand the meaning of the sentence.

> **No commas:** The local company <u>that creates computer graphics</u> has no job openings.

A **nonrestrictive clause** gives nonessential or additional information about the noun but does not restrict or define the noun. Place commas around nonrestrictive clauses. In the following sentence, the underlined clause contains extra information, but if you removed that clause, the sentence would still have a clear meaning.

> **Commas:** Her book, <u>which is in bookstores</u>, is about successful entrepreneurs.

Hint   *Which, That, and Who*

Which   Use commas to set off clauses that begin with *which*.
   The brain, **which is a complex organ**, develops rapidly.
That   Do not use commas to set off clauses that begin with *that*.
   The house **that** I grew up in was demolished last year.
Who   If the *who* clause contains nonessential information, put commas around it. If the *who* clause is essential to the meaning of the sentence, then it does not require commas.

> **Essential:**   Many people **who** have brain injuries undergo subtle personality changes.
>
> **Not essential:** Dr. Jay Giedd, **who** lives in Maryland, made an important discovery.

PRACTICE 6   Edit the following sentences by adding twelve missing commas.

EXAMPLE: The neurologist, whom I have never met, made an exciting
discovery.

1. Twenty years ago, scientists thought that the brain stopped changing in late
   childhood. They believed that after children reached twelve years of age
   their brains would stop growing. In 1997, a team of doctors who specialized
   in brain research made an exciting discovery. Neuroscientist Dr. Jay
   Giedd who works at the National Institute of Mental Health realized that
   brain cells have a growth spurt just before puberty and continue growing
   well into adulthood. Scientists discovered that myelin which connects brain
   cells increases during adolescence. However, not all parts of the brain receive
   myelin at once, and the last region to receive it is the frontal lobe.

2. The frontal lobe, which is responsible for rational decision making stops an
   individual from making impulsive choices. For example imagine that you are
   driving your car. When another car cuts you off the primitive part of your
   brain wants to hurt the other driver. The frontal lobe helps you to think about
   alternatives. Thus, you may simply accept that all drivers make mistakes.

3. According to specialists the delay in receiving myelin to the frontal lobe
   affects many teens, and they may have trouble curbing their impulses.
   They may react quickly violently or irrationally, and they are more likely
   than people in other age groups to engage in risky behavior. When the
   frontal lobe has fully developed people generally become less impulsive.

Final Review

Edit this essay by adding seventeen missing commas and removing three unnecessary commas.

EXAMPLE: If people want to have longer lives, they can exercise, eat well, and avoid risky behavior.

1. In 350 BC, Aristotle wrote an essay about life spans. Everybody has a maximum life span and nothing can be done to prolong that span. Until recently scientists agreed with Aristotle. They would argue that today's life expectancies are about as high as they can possibly get. However a group of researchers believes that human life expectancy will increase significantly in the future.

2. Dr. James Vaupel a researcher at Duke University, believes that our life spans can be extended significantly. He gives a concrete example. In 1840, Swedish women had the world's longest life expectancy and the average Swedish woman lived to age forty-five. Today, Japanese women, who live to an average age of eighty-five have the world's longest life expectancy. This huge increase in life expectancy was partly due to the decrease in infant mortality. In 1800, about 25 percent of babies died in the first year of life. Surgery vaccines and antibiotics have helped to lower the childhood death rates. Also,

because they have access to new medical interventions people over age sixty-five are living longer. Still, only about 2 percent of the population lives to one hundred years of age.

3. According to Dr. Vaupel, today's babies will have much longer life expectancies than their parents had and half of all newborns could live to one hundred years of age. Dr. Aubrey De Grey, a professor at Cambridge University believes that human life expectancy will increase to five hundred years or more. Certainly, there are very promising discoveries on the horizon. Cures for cancer, and heart disease will help increase life expectancy. Also, because so many women delay childbirth the period of human fertility may lengthen which could have an eventual impact on life expectancy.

4. Some experts disagree with Vaupel and De Grey. Leonard Hayflick, discovered that human cells divide and reproduce about fifty times before slowing down and stopping. The longest average life span humans can attain in Hayflick's view is 120 years of age. However, some research labs are experimenting with ways of increasing the life spans of cells. For example scientists have isolated a part of the chromosome that shrinks with age. If scientists find a way to slow down cell aging the results could significantly increase life expectancies of all humans.

CHAPTER 24

5. A very long life expectancy, would force humans to rethink life stages. When would childhood end? Would you want to live to 150 years of age or more?

The Writer's Room **Topics for Writing**

Write about one of the following topics. After you finish writing, make sure that you have used commas correctly.

1. What problems could occur if the human life expectancy gets a lot longer? Think about the effects of an increased life expectancy.

2. Which life stage is the most interesting? Give anecdotes to back up your views.

✔ CHECKLIST: COMMAS

When you edit your writing, ask yourself these questions.

Do I use commas correctly? Remember to use commas in the following situations:

- between words in a series of items
- after an introductory word or phrase
- around an interrupting word or phrase

> The conference will be in Santa Fe, San Francisco, or Phoenix.
>
> Beyond a doubt, many psychologists will attend.
>
> The key speaker, in my opinion, is extremely interesting.

Do I use commas correctly in compound and complex sentences? Remember to use commas in the following situations:

- before the coordinator in a compound sentence
- after a dependent clause in a complex sentence
- around nonrestrictive clauses

> She will discuss brain development, and she will present case studies.
>
> When her presentation ends, participants can ask questions.
>
> The questions, which must be short, are about the brain.

Apostrophes

CHAPTER

CONTENTS

- What Is an Apostrophe?
- Apostrophes in Contractions
- Apostrophes to Show Ownership
- Apostrophes in Expressions of Time

Section Theme **HUMAN DEVELOPMENT**

In this chapter, you will read about artistic ability and creativity.

Man Reclining, 1978, Fernando Botero, Private Collection.

Grammar Snapshot

Looking at Apostrophes

In an interview with Diane Sawyer for *ABC News*, musician Paul McCartney discusses his art show and his initial feelings about painting. Review the highlighted words.

The way I was brought up, in the working class, only people who went to art school painted. It **wasn't** for us to paint. We **didn't** ride horses. They did. You know, **we'd** we ride bikes if we were lucky. I **would've** felt like I was a bit uppity to paint, you know. "Oh, **you're** painting now, are you?"

In this chapter, you will learn to use apostrophes correctly.

What Is an Apostrophe?

An **apostrophe** is a punctuation mark showing a contraction or ownership.

Emma **Chong's** art gallery is very successful, and **it's** still growing.

Apostrophes in Contractions

To form a **contraction**, join two words into one and add an apostrophe to replace the omitted letter(s). The following are examples of common contractions.

1. **Join a verb with *not*.** The apostrophe replaces the letter "o" in *not*.

   is + not = isn't   has + not = hasn't
   are + not = aren't   have + not = haven't
   could + not = couldn't   should + not = shouldn't
   do + not = don't   would + not = wouldn't
   does + not = doesn't

   Exception: will + not = <u>won't</u>, can + not = <u>can't</u>

2. **Join a subject and a verb.** Sometimes you must remove several letters to form the contraction.

   I + will = I'll   she + will = she'll
   I + would = I'd   Tina + is = Tina's
   he + is = he's   they + are = they're
   he + will = he'll   we + will = we'll
   Joe + is = Joe's   who + is = who's
   she + has = she's   who + would = who'd

   Exception: Do not contract a subject with the past tense of *be*. For example, do not contract *he + was* or *they + were*.

> ## *Hint*   **Common Apostrophe Errors**
>
> Do not use apostrophes before the final -*s* of a verb or a plural noun.
>
>   *wants*   *galleries*
> Mr. Garcia ~~want's~~ to open several ~~gallery's~~.
>
> In contractions with *not*, remember that the apostrophe replaces the missing *o*.
>
>   *doesn't*
> He ~~does'nt~~ understand the problem.

PRACTICE 1   Edit the next sentences for fifteen apostrophe errors. Each word counts as one error.

EXAMPLE: Making a great work of art is̲n̲t̲' a simple process.

1. Whos a great artist? Why do some people have amazing artistic abilities whereas others do'nt? Researchers in biology, sociology, and psychology haven't unlocked the keys to human creativity. However, expert's in each field have proposed theories about creativity.

2. Sigmund Freud proposed that creativity is an occurrence of the subconscious. If someones in pain, he or she may create an artwork to relieve the suffering. Near the end of his life, Freud changed his mind. He said that he didnt believe that suffering was a prerequisite to creativity.

3. Neurologists look inside the brain to answer questions about creativity. Theyve said that the left portion of the brains responsible for logical processing and verbal skills. The right sides responsible for artistic, abstract thinking. In the past, neurologists did'nt believe that the left side of the brain had an impact on creative impulses, but recent brain scan's have shown that both sides of the brain are used in creative thinking.

4. Whats the source of creativity? Maybe its never going to be understood. What everybody know's for certain is that artistic talent isnt evenly distributed. Some people are'nt as talented as others.

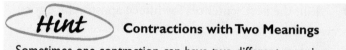

> **Hint**   **Contractions with Two Meanings**
>
> Sometimes one contraction can have two different meanings.
>
> **I'd** = I had *or* I would   **He's** = he is *or* he has
>
> When you read, you should be able to figure out the meaning of the contraction by looking at the words in context.
>
> **Joe's** working on a painting. **Joe's** been working on it for a month.
> (Joe is)   (Joe has)

PRACTICE 2   Look at each underlined contraction, and then write out the complete words.

EXAMPLE: They <u>weren't</u> ready to start a business.   *were not*

1. Rachel <u>Wood's</u> very happy with her sculpture.   _____

2. <u>She's</u> been a professional artist since 2002.   _____

3. <u>She's</u> an extremely creative woman.   _____

4. I wish <u>I'd</u> gone to art school.   _____

5. <u>I'd</u> like to be an artist, too.   _____

Apostrophes to Show Ownership

You can also use apostrophes to show ownership. Review the following rules.

Possessive Form of Singular Nouns

Add -'s to the end of a singular noun to indicate ownership. If the singular noun ends in s, you must still add -'s. Add 's to singular nouns ending in s if you pronounce the s (*boss's*). If you would not pronounce the final s, add only an apostrophe (*Moses'*).

Lautrec's artwork was very revolutionary.

Morris's wife is a professional dancer.

Possessive Form of Plural Nouns

When a plural noun ends in -s, just add an apostrophe to indicate ownership. Add -'s to irregular plural nouns.

Many **galleries'** Web sites contain images from their exhibits.

The **men's** and **women's** paintings are in separate rooms.

Possessive Form of Compound Nouns

When two people have joint ownership, add the apostrophe to the second name. When two people have separate ownership, add apostrophes to both names.

Joint ownership: Marian and **Jake's** gallery is successful.

Separate ownership: **Marian's** and **Jake's** studios are in different buildings.

PRACTICE 3   Write the possessive forms of the following phrases.

EXAMPLE: the sister of the doctor   *the doctor's sister* _____

1. the brush of the artist   _____

2. the brushes of the artists   _____

3. the lights in the studio   _____

4. the room of the child   _____

5. the rooms of the children   _____

6. the entrances of the galleries   _____

7. the photo of Ross and Anna   _____

8. the photo of Ross and the
   photo of Anna   _____

> ## Hint   Possessive Pronouns Do Not Have Apostrophes
>
> Some contractions sound like possessive pronouns. For example, *you're* sounds like *your*, and *it's* sounds like *its*. Remember that the possessive pronouns *yours, hers, its,* and *ours* never have apostrophes.
>
> $\qquad\qquad$ *its*
> The conference is on ~~it's~~ last day.
>
> $\qquad\qquad$ *yours* $\qquad\qquad$ *hers*
> The document is ~~your's~~ and not ~~her's~~.

PRACTICE 4   Correct nine errors. You may need to add, move, or remove apostrophes.

CHAPTER 25

1. Many artist's paintings are unique. Have you ever heard of Fernando Botero? The Colombian painters work has been exhibited in the Museum of Modern Art in Washington. Several of his painting's have also appeared in New York galleries. His painting "Man Reclining" appears at the beginning of this chapter.

2. Botero's paintings usually contain images of people. What makes his work unique is it's humor. He makes generals, religious figures, and dictators look like children. Theyre small and bloated, and the images are filled with color.

3. Another great artist is Georgia O'Keeffe. Its not difficult to recognize an artwork that is her's. Shes known for her paintings of white bones, bull skulls, and flowers. In many art galleries, youll find her artwork.

Apostrophes in Expressions of Time

If an expression of time (*year, week, month, day*) appears to possess something, you can add -'*s*.

Alice Ray gave two **weeks**' notice before she left the dance company.

When you write out a year in numerals, an apostrophe can replace the missing numbers.

The graduates of the class of '**99** hoped to find good jobs.

However, if you are writing the numeral of a decade or century, do not put an apostrophe before the final -*s*.

In the **1900s**, many innovations in art occurred.

PRACTICE 5   Correct ten errors. You may need to add, move, or remove apostrophes.

EXAMPLE: Octavio Cruz ~~doesnt~~ *doesn't* have a studio.

1. In the summer of 2000, Octavio Cruz did a years worth of painting. He felt incredibly inspired. In the early 1990's, hed sold some artworks, but his paintings were uninspired, and he had trouble becoming motivated. Then, in 1999, he was in a car accident. He spent three week's in a hospital. Since then, hes been extremely creative. His wife's astonishment is evident. "Hes a different man," she says. "His paintings are so much more vivid and colorful."

2. Cruz has been studied by a neurologist, Dr. Wade. The doctors theory is that Cruzs injury "disinhibited" his right brain, thus allowing him to become more creative. Many other peoples stories are similar to Cruz's. In fact, since the 1970's, scientists have recognized that certain brain injuries can stimulate creativity.

Donald Martin, after Van der
Weyden (20th Century
American), "Portrait", Airbrush
on wood. © Donald C. Martin/
SuperStock.

FINAL REVIEW

Edit the next paragraphs and correct fifteen apostrophe errors. You
may need to add, remove, or move apostrophes.

artist's
EXAMPLE: What is an ~~artists~~ motivation to create?

1. In 1982, Dr. Teresa Amabile made an interesting study in
    creativity. For Amabiles study, she divided schoolgirl's into two
    groups. Both groups rooms were filled with collage material, includ-
    ing colored paper, paste, and construction paper. The doctor chose
    collage-making because it doesnt require drawing skills.

2. Both groups were invited to an "art party" in separate rooms. The
    first groups goal was to create art to win a prize, such as a toy. The doctor
    offered toys to the three best artists. Thus, the childrens motivation to create
    was to win the exciting prize. The girls in the second group didnt have to
    compete for a prize. They were simply told that three name's would be
    randomly drawn for prizes.

3. The doctors hypothesis was that a persons creativity would lessen if he or
    she were motivated by a reward. Amabile asked local artists and art critics
    to judge the collages when the children werent in the room. The judges
    scores for the first group were consistently lower than those for the second
    group. Thus, the doctors hypothesis was correct. A reward, such as money
    or a prize, isnt helpful to the creative process. When people create art for
    arts sake, they tend to be more imaginative.

The Writer's Room **Topics for Writing**

Write about one of the following topics. After you finish writing, make sure that you have used apostrophes correctly.

1. Describe the work of a painter, illustrator, photographer, or sculptor that you like. Explain what is most interesting about that artist's work.

2. Define a term or expression that relates to this photo. Some ideas might be *creativity*, *graffiti*, *art*, *vandalism*, or *beauty*.

CHAPTER 25

CHECKLIST: APOSTROPHES

When you edit your writing, ask yourself these questions.

Do I use apostrophes correctly? Check for errors in these cases:

- contractions of verbs + *not* or subjects and verbs
- possessives of singular and plural nouns (*the student's* versus *the students'*)
- possessives of irregular plural nouns (*the women's*)
- possessives of compound nouns (*Joe's and Mike's cars*)

    shouldn't   *Wong's*
You ~~should'nt~~ be surprised that Chris ~~Wong'~~ going to exhibit his paintings.

    Chris's
~~Chris'~~ artwork will be on display next week.

Do I place apostrophes where they do not belong? Check for errors in possessive pronouns and present tense verbs.

    looks   *its*
It ~~look's~~ like the gallery is moving ~~it's~~ collection to Houston.

26 CHAPTER

Quotation Marks, Capitalization, and Titles

Section Theme **HUMAN DEVELOPMENT**

In this chapter, you will read about artists and musicians.

Grammar Snapshot

Looking at Quotation Marks

This excerpt is translated from Paul Gauguin's book, *Avant et Apres*. It recounts when Vincent Van Gogh cut off part of his own ear. Notice that the quotation marks and some capital letters are highlighted.

> The man in the bowler hat harshly questioned me: "Well, sir, what have you done to your friend?"
> "I don't know," I replied.
> "But you know that he is dead," he said.
> I would not wish such a moment on anyone, and it took me a while before I could think. My heart pounded, and I was choking with anger and pain. I felt everyone's eyes staring at me. I stammered, "Sir, let's go upstairs and discuss it there."

In this chapter, you will learn how to use direct quotations correctly. You will also learn about capitalization and title punctuation.

Quotation Marks (" ")

Use **quotation marks** to set off the exact words of a speaker or writer. When you include the exact words of more than one person in a text, then you must make a new paragraph each time the speaker changes. If the quotation is a complete sentence, punctuate it in the following ways.

- Capitalize the first word of the quotation.
- Place quotation marks around the complete quotation.
- Place the end punctuation inside the closing quotation marks.

> Oscar Wilde declared, "All art is useless."

Generally, attach the name of the speaker or writer to the quotation in some way. Review the following rules.

1. **Introductory Phrase**   When the quotation is introduced by a phrase, place a comma after the introductory phrase.

   > Pablo Picasso said, "Art is a lie that makes us realize the truth."

2. **Interrupting Phrase**   When the quotation is interrupted, place a comma before and after the interrupting phrase.

   > "In the end," says dancer Martha Graham, "it all comes down to breathing."

3. **End Phrase**   When you place a phrase at the end of a quotation, end the quotation with a comma instead of a period.

   > "Great art picks up where nature ends," said Marc Chagall.

   If your quotation ends with other punctuation, put it inside the quotation mark.

   > "Who is the greatest painter?" the student asked.

   > "That question cannot be answered!" the curator replied.

4. **Introductory Sentence**   When you introduce a quotation with a complete sentence, place a colon (:) after the introductory sentence.

   > George Balanchine explains his philosophy about dance: "Dance is music made visible."

5. **Inside Quotations**   If one quotation is inside another quotation, then use single quotation marks (' ') around the inside quotation.

   > To her mother, Veronica Corelli explained, "I am not sure if I will succeed, but you've always said, 'Your work should be your passion.'"

CHAPTER 26

> Hint   **Integrated Quotations**
>
> If the quotation is not a complete sentence, and you simply integrate it into your sentence, do not capitalize the first word of the quotation.
>
> Composer Ludwig Van Beethoven called music "the mediator between the spiritual and the sensual life."

Suzanne Valadon (1867–1938 French) "Portrait of Madam Coquiot," 1915. Oil on canvas. Musée du Palais Carnoles, Menton, France. © Artists Rights Society (ARS), New York.

CHAPTER 26

PRACTICE I In each sentence, the quotation is set off in bold. Add quotation marks and periods, commas, or colons. Also, capitalize the first word of the quotation, if necessary.

EXAMPLE: Professor Wayne Johnson asks ,"W ~~w~~here are the great female artists?"

1. Art student Alex Beale says **the lack of great female artists throughout history is puzzling**

2. Professor Aline Melnor states **one must consider the conditions for producing art**

3. **Art schools did not accept women** she points out.

4. **Until a hundred years ago, the only alternative to family life for women was the convent** proclaimed writer and feminist Germaine Greer.

5. **Suzanne Valadon** says historian Maria Sage **went from being an artist's model to being an artist**

6. Historian Andre Villeneuve writes that sculptor Camille Claudel was **the mistress of Auguste Rodin**

7. Germaine Greer shows the connection between female and male artists **the painter Rosa Bonheur learned about art from her father, who was also an artist**

8. **In the twentieth century, the numbers of female artists exploded**

   declared gallery owner Jon Sidell.

9. Angel Trang told her mother **I know that I shouldn't have drawn on the**

   walls, but you always say Express yourself

10. Louise Otto-Peters has a strong opinion about women in the arts **women**

   will be forgotten if they forget to think about themselves

PRACTICE 2   Correct ten punctuation errors in the next dialogue.

EXAMPLE: She told me**,** "Your future is in your hands **."**

Jamilla was concerned about her son, "I don't understand why you are
leaving college".

Omar looked at her and replied: "I need to try and make it as a musician."

"How will you make a living in the arts"she asked?

He replied, "I do not need to earn a lot of money to be happy."

"You're being very naïve." Jamilla retorted.

Shocked, Omar said, "I'm simply following your advice. You always say, "Find
work that you love. " "

"Perhaps you have to take some chances" his mother responded, "and learn
from your own mistakes."

Omar stated firmly, "my decision will not be a mistake!"

Using Quotations in Research Essays

Use quotations to reveal the opinions of an expert or to highlight ideas that are
particularly memorable and important. When quoting sources, remember to limit
how many you use in a single paper and to vary your quotations by using both
direct and indirect quotations.

Direct and Indirect Quotations

A **direct quotation** contains the exact words of an author, and the quotation is set off with quotation marks.

> A shopping tip from Consumer 4 Kids Reports states, "The name brands are always displayed up front when you first walk into the department."

An **indirect quotation** keeps the author's meaning but is not set off by quotation marks.

> A shopping tip by the Consumer 4 Kids Reports states that name-brand clothes are always put on view at the front of the clothing department.

Integrating Quotations

Short Quotations

Introduce short quotations with a phrase or sentence. (Short quotations should not stand alone.) Read the following original selection, and then view how the quotation has been introduced using three common methods.

> The selection, written by Mary Lou Stribling, appeared on page 6 of her book Art from Found Materials.

Original Selection
Picasso is generally acknowledged as being the first major artist to use found objects in his paintings. About the same time, however, a number of other artists who were active in the Cubist movement began to make similar experiments. The collages of Braque and Gris, which were made of printed letters, newspapers, wallpaper scraps, bottle labels, corrugated cardboard, and other bits of trivia, are especially notable.

Phrase Introduction
In Art from Found Materials, Mary Lou Stribling writes, "Picasso is generally acknowledged as being the first major artist to use found objects in his paintings" (6).

Sentence Introduction
In her book Art from Found Materials, Mary Lou Stribling suggests that Picasso was not the only artist to use found objects in his work: "About the same time, however, a number of other artists who were active in the Cubist movement began to make similar experiments" (6).

Integrated Quotation

In *Art from Found Materials*, Mary Lou Stribling reveals that artists incorporated everyday objects into their paintings, including "wallpaper scraps, bottle labels, corrugated cardboard, and other bits of trivia" (6).

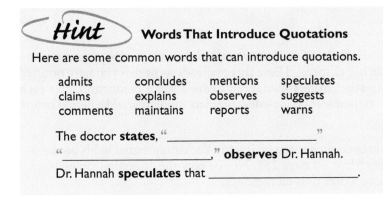

Hint   **Words That Introduce Quotations**

Here are some common words that can introduce quotations.

admits	concludes	mentions	speculates
claims	explains	observes	suggests
comments	maintains	reports	warns

The doctor **states**, "_____"

"_____," **observes** Dr. Hannah.

Dr. Hannah **speculates** that _____.

Long Quotations

If you use a quotation in MLA style that has four or more lines (or in APA style, more than forty words), insert the quotation in your research paper in the following way.

- Introduce the quotation with a sentence ending with a colon.
- Indent the entire quotation about ten spaces from the left margin of your document.
- Use double spacing.
- Do not use quotation marks.
- Cite the author and page number in parentheses after the punctuation mark in the last sentence of the quotation.

Review the next example from a student essay about art history that uses MLA style. The quotation is from page 132 of Germaine Greer's *The Obstacle Race*. The explanatory paragraph introduces the quotation and is part of an essay.

Much great art has been lost due to a variety of factors:

> Panels decay as wood decays. Canvas rots, tears, and sags. The stretchers spring and warp. As color dries out it loses its flexibility and begins to separate from its unstable ground; dry color flakes off shrinking or swelling wood and drooping canvas. (Greer 132)

CHAPTER 26

> ### Hint   Using Long Quotations
>
> If your research paper is short (two or three pages), avoid using many long quotations. Long quotations will only overwhelm your own ideas. Instead, try summarizing a long passage or using shorter quotations.

Using Ellipses (. . .)

If you want to quote key ideas from an author, but do not want to quote the entire paragraph, you can use **ellipses**. These three periods show that you have omitted unnecessary information from a quotation. Leave a space before and after each period, and if the omitted section includes complete sentences, add a period before the ellipses.

The original selection, written by Jeremy Yudkin, appeared in his book *Understanding Music* on page 253. Notice how the quotation changes when the essay writer uses ellipses.

Original Selection
In his early years, Elvis Presley symbolized something very important for American youth. He was the symbol of freedom and rebellion. His unconventional clothes, the messages of his music, and especially his raw sexuality appealed to the new and numerous groups of American teenagers. The spirit of rebellion was in the air.

Quotation with Omissions
In his book *Understanding Music*, Jeremy Yudkin describes the impact of Elvis: "In his early years, Elvis Presley symbolized something very important for American youth. . . . The spirit of rebellion was in the air" (253).

PRACTICE 3   Read the following selection and then use information from it to write direct and indirect quotations. The selection, written by David G. Martin, appeared on page 567 of his book *Psychology*.

Until fairly recently, up to the early or mid-nineteenth century, events that could not be explained were often attributed to supernatural causes. Human behavior that was bizarre was thought to be the work of demons. Demonology is the study of the ancient belief that mental disorders are caused by possession by demons. Autonomous evil beings were thought to enter a person and control his or her mind and body.

1. Make a direct quotation.

_____

_____

_____

2. Make an indirect quotation.

_____

_____

_____

Capitalization

Remember to capitalize the following:

- the pronoun *I*
- the first word of every sentence

> **M**y brothers and **I** share an apartment.

There are many other instances in which you must use capital letters. Always capitalize in the following cases.

- **days of the week, months, and holidays**

> Thursday June 22 Labor Day

Do not capitalize the seasons: summer, fall, winter, spring.

- **titles of specific institutions, departments, companies, and schools**

> Microsoft Department of Finance Elmwood High School

Do not capitalize general references.

> the company the department the school

- **names of specific places such as buildings, streets, parks, cities, states, and bodies of water**

> Eiffel Tower Times Square Los Angeles, California
> Sunset Boulevard Florida Lake Erie

Do not capitalize general references.

> the street the state the lake

- **specific languages, nationalities, tribes, races, and religions**

> Greek Mohawk Buddhist a French restaurant

- **titles of specific individuals**

| General Franklin | the President | Doctor Blain |
| Professor Sayf | Prime Minister Blair | Mrs. Robinson |

If you are referring to the profession in general, or if the title follows the name, do not use capital letters.

| my doctor | the professors | Ted Kennedy, a senator |

- **specific course and program titles**

| Physics 201 | Marketing 101 | Advanced German |

If you refer to a course, but do not mention the course title, then it is not necessary to use capitals.

| He is in his math class. | I study engineering. |

- **the major words in titles of literary or artistic works**

| *The Miami Herald* | *Prison Break* | *The Lord of the Rings* |

- **historical events, eras, and movements**

| World War II | Post-Impressionism | Baby Boomers |

> *Hint* **Capitalizing Computer Terms**

Always capitalize the following computer terms.

| Internet | Netscape | World Wide Web | Microsoft Office |

PRACTICE 4   Add twenty missing capital letters to this selection.

EXAMPLE: Mozart was born in ~~s~~alzburg, Austria.
(S above the s)

1. Erich Schenk describes the life of Wolfgang Amadeus Mozart in his book

   Mozart and his times. Mozart, born on january 27, 1756, was a gifted

   musician who composed his first pieces at age five. By the age of thirteen,

   he had written a german and an italian opera. In Salzburg, his employer was prince-archbishop Colloredo. Then, in Vienna, he wrote

compositions for emperor joseph II. At that time, Austria was a part of the

holy roman empire.

2. Mozart's best-known works include *the marriage of figaro* and

the magic flute. Mozart, a catholic, died mysteriously at the age of thirty-

five, and his body was put into a communal grave, which was the common

practice for the poor in Vienna at that time. His final resting place is near a

river called the danube.

Titles

Place the title of a short work in quotation marks. Italicize the title of a longer
document.

Short Works		**Long Works**	
short story:	"The Lottery"	novel:	*The Grapes of Wrath*
chapter:	"Early Accomplishments"	book:	*The Art of Emily Carr*
newspaper article:	"The City's Hottest Ticket"	newspaper:	*The New York Times*
magazine article:	"New Artists"	magazine:	*Rolling Stone*
Web article:	"Music Artists Lose Out"	Web site:	*CNET News.com*
essay:	"Hip-Hop Nation"	textbook:	*Common Culture*
TV episode:	"The Search Party"	TV series:	*Lost*
song:	"Mouths to Feed"	CD:	*Release Therapy*
poem:	"Howl"	anthology:	*Collected Poems of Beat Writers*

Capitalizing Titles

When you write a title, capitalize the first letter of the first word and all the major
words.

    To Kill a Mockingbird   "Stairway to Heaven"

Do not capitalize the word ".com" in a Web address. Also, do not capitalize
the following words, unless they are the first word in the title.

articles	a, an, the
coordinators	for, and, nor, but, or, yet, so
prepositions	of, to, in, off, out, up, by, . . .

> ⌒ *Hint* ⌒   **Your Own Essay Titles**
>
> In essays that you write for your courses, do not underline your title or put quotation marks around it. Simply capitalize the first word and the main words.
>
> Why Music Is Important

PRACTICE 5   Add twelve capital letters to the following selection. Also, identify five titles. Add quotation marks or underline any titles that should normally be italicized.

EXAMPLE: The magazine ~~f~~orbes featured successful female entrepreneurs.
(F above the f)

1. The singer known as Pink was born Alecia Moore on september 8, 1979. During her teen years, she regularly performed at Club fever near girard street in Philadelphia. One saturday night, after her five-minute slot, a representative from MCA records spotted her and asked her to audition for the band Basic instinct.

2. After some time playing in bands, Pink decided to become a solo artist. Her first CD, called Can't take me home, was released in 2000. It was a double-platinum hit, and spun off three singles. Pink then went on to record Patti LaBelle's hit song Lady Marmalade with three other artists. In the april 2006 issue of Rolling Stone, Barry Walter reviewed Pink's fourth CD I'm Not Dead. He had particular praise for her song Stupid girls.

FINAL REVIEW

Identify and correct twenty-five errors. Look for capitalization errors. Also ensure that titles and quotations have the necessary capital letters, quotation marks, and punctuation. Underline any titles that should normally be italicized.

EXAMPLE: The marketing manager said ,"Each generation is distinct."

1. People who belong to a generation may have wildly different life experiences. Nonetheless, as Ted Rall points out in his book Marketing Madness, "you are more likely to share certain formative experiences and attitudes about life with your age cohorts".

2. In the last century, each generation was anointed with a title. F. Scott Fitzgerald named his cohorts when he wrote the book The Jazz Age, which described 1920s flappers who frequented jazz clubs. Tom Brokaw, in his book *The greatest generation*, discussed people who came of age in the 1930s. Born between 1911 and 1924, they grew up during the Great depression. However, perhaps the best-known spokesperson for a generation is Douglas Coupland.

3. Douglas Coupland was born in 1961 and raised in Vancouver, british Columbia. Even as a young student at Sentinel secondary school, Coupland knew that he would be an artist. When he got older, he took Sculpture classes at Vancouver's Emily Carr institute of Art and design. He also studied at the European Design Institute in italy. As a sculptor,

Coupland had some success and, in november 1987, he had a solo show called "The floating world" at an art gallery in Vancouver.

4. Most know Coupland from his second career. While writing a comic strip for the magazine Vista, Coupland was approached by St. Martin's press and asked to write a guidebook about his generation. Instead, he wrote a complete novel called *generation X*.

5. Coupland's novel, which describes the generation that came of age in the 1970s and 1980s, is filled with original terminology. For instance, Coupland writes: "Clique maintenance is the need of one generation to see the generation following it as deficient so as to bolster its own collective ego". One chapter in his book is called, "Our Parents had more." On page 27, a character has a mid-twenties breakdown that occurs because of "An inability to function outside of school or structured environments coupled with a realization of one's essential aloneness in the world."

6. Every current generation has unique characteristics. Music, clothing, and slang words help define a generation. What name will define the youths who are growing up today?

The Writer's Room **Topics for Writing**

Write about one of the following topics. Include some direct quotations. Proofread to ensure that your punctuation and capitalization are correct.

1. List some characteristics of your generation. What political events, social issues, music, and fashion bind your generation?

2. List three categories of art. Describe some details about each category.

3. Examine the photograph. What do you think the people are saying to each other? Write a brief dialogue from their conversation.

✔ CHECKLIST: QUOTATION MARKS

When you edit your writing, ask yourself these questions.

Are there any direct quotations in my writing? Check for errors with these elements:

- punctuation before or after quotations
- capital letters
- placement of quotation marks

"Art is making something out of nothing and selling it," said musician Frank Zappa.

Do my sentences have all the necessary capital letters?

War
Munch's greatest works were painted before World ~~war~~ II.

Are the titles of small and large artistic works properly punctuated?

The Scream.
Edvard Munch's painting was called ~~The scream.~~

Numbers and Additional Punctuation

Section Theme **HUMAN DEVELOPMENT**

*In this chapter,
you will
read about
photography and
photographers.*

Grammar Snapshot

Looking at Numbers and Hyphens

This excerpt is taken from *History of Photography and the Camera* by Mary Bellis.
Abbreviations, numbers, and hyphenated words are in boldface type.

> Nitrate film is historically important because it allowed for the development of roll films.
> The first flexible movie films measured **35-mm** wide and came in long rolls on a spool. In the
> **mid-1920s**, using this technology, **35-mm** roll film was developed for the camera. By the late
> **1920s, medium-format** roll film was created. It measured **six** centimeters wide and had
> a paper backing making it easy to handle in daylight. This led to the development of the
> **twin-lens-reflex** camera in **1929**.

In this chapter, you will learn about using numbers and punctuation such as hyphens.

Numbers

When using numbers in academic writing, follow these rules:

- Spell out numbers that can be expressed in one or two words.

  We spent **eighteen** days in Mexico City.

  There were **forty-seven** people waiting for another flight.

  The airline had room for **four hundred**.

  That day, **thousands** of people cleared customs.

- Use numerals with numbers of more than two words.

  The manager booked rooms for **358** guests.

- Spell out fractions.

  Only **one-third** of the residents have their own homes.

- When the sentence begins with a number, spell out the number. If the number has more than two words, do not place it at the beginning of the sentence.

  Three hundred people were invited to the gallery.

  There were **158** guests.

- Spell out *million* or *billion* if the word appears in a sentence.

  There were about four **million** residents in the surrounding suburbs.

- Use numerals when writing addresses, dates, times, degrees, pages, or divisions of a book. Also use numerals with prices and percentages. However, write out the word "dollar" or "percent."

  A yearly subscription costs **29** dollars, which is about **15** percent less than the cover price.

 **Several Numbers in a Sentence**

When writing two consecutive numbers, write out the shorter number.

  We used **two 35-mm** rolls of film.

Be consistent when writing a series of numbers. If some numbers require numerals, then use numerals for all of the numbers.

  The gallery guests consumed **300** appetizers, **8** pounds of cheese, and **120** glasses of wine.

PRACTICE I   Correct any errors with numbers in the next sentences.

nine
EXAMPLE: She was just ~~9~~ years old when she picked up a camera.

1. Photographer Moyra Davey has ~~six~~ cameras, 184 rolls of film, and

    thirty-three different lenses.

2. She has worked professionally as a photographer for 10 years.

GRAMMAR LINK

For practice using semicolons, see Chapters 10 and 13.

3. A small art gallery exhibited 25 of Davey's photos.

4. 40 people came to the opening.

5. Davey would like to publish her photos and sell each book for

    one hundred and twenty nine dollars.

6. She wants to self-publish 20 168-page books.

Additional Punctuation

Semicolon (;)

Use a semicolon

- between two complete and related ideas.
    The photograph was stunning; Sherman was very pleased.
- between items in a series of ideas, if the items have internal punctuation or are very long.
    Sherman's works were exhibited in Birmingham, Alabama; Fort Worth, Texas; Toronto, Ontario; and London, England.

Colon (:)

Use a colon

- after a complete sentence that introduces a quotation.
    The photographer Henri Cartier Bresson stated his view: "Photographers are dealing with things that are continually vanishing."
- to introduce a series or a list after a complete sentence.
    The new museum includes the work of some great photographers: Ansel Adams, Cindy Sherman, Edward Weston, Alfred Stieglitz, Dorothea Lange, and Annie Leibowitz.

- to introduce an explanation or example.

    The tiny sculpture is outrageously expensive: it costs $2.5 million.

- after the expression "the following."

    Please do the following: read, review, and respond.

- to separate the hour and minutes in expressions of time.

    The exhibit will open at 12:30 P.M.

Hyphen (-)

Use a hyphen

- with some compound nouns. (Note that *compound* means "more than one part.") The following nouns always require a hyphen.

    sister-in-law   mother-in-law   show-off

- when you write the complete words for compound numbers between twenty-one and ninety-nine.

    twenty-five   ninety-two   seventy-seven

- after some prefixes such as *ex-*, *mid-*, or *self-*.

    self-assured   mid-December   ex-husband

- when you use a compound adjective before a noun. The compound adjective must express a single thought.

    one-way street   well-known actor   thirty-year-old woman

    There is no hyphen if the compound adjective appears after the noun.

    The street is one way.   The actor was well   The woman is thirty years
                             known.   old.

Hint   **Nonhyphenated Compound Adjectives**

Some compound adjectives never take a hyphen, even when they appear before a noun. Here are some common examples.

World Wide Web   high school senior   real estate agent

Dash (—)

You can use a dash to set off information that you want to emphasize. Use dashes sparingly.

    Marge Stranton raised her camera to take the picture, but it was too late—the moment had passed.

Parentheses ( )

You can use parentheses to set off incidental information such as a date or abbreviation. Use parentheses sparingly.

> Lange's photo of the migrant mother, which was taken during the height of the Depression era (1936), has become an enduring image.

> The United Press Photographer's Association (UPPA) was founded in 1946.

 **Hint** Using Abbreviations

Sometimes you will not want to repeat the name of an organization over and over in an essay. To use abbreviations correctly, mention the complete name of an organization the first time you mention it, put the abbreviation in parentheses immediately after the full name, and then use only the abbreviation throughout the rest of the essay.

> The North Atlantic Treaty Organization (NATO) supports an international security agreement that was signed in 1949 in Washington, DC. Today, NATO's headquarters are in Brussels, Belgium.

There are two types of abbreviations: **initialisms** and **acronyms**. When saying an initialism, pronounce each of the first letters of an organization's title individually. Examples are IBM, FBI, and CIA. When saying an acronym, pronounce it as a full word. Examples of acronyms are NATO (pronounced "nay-toh") and WHO (pronounced "hoo").

PRACTICE 2   Add either a colon, hyphen, dash, or a set of parentheses to each sentence.

EXAMPLE: Dorothea Lange rushed home and printed the photos—a decision that would change her life.

1. Florence Thompson and her husband, Cleo, were living in Merced Falls, California, when there was a tragedy the Crash of 1929.

2. A couple of years later, the Merced Falls Mill MFM lost business and let go many of the employees.

3. Many laid off workers, including the Thompson family, left Merced Falls and went from town to town looking for work.

4. Cleo's short life 1899 to 1931 ended in a tiny cabin near Feather River.

5. Cleo was a thirty two year old man when he died.

6. Florence decided to keep her children with her "I made a promise to Cleo to see his six kids raised, and by God I'm going to keep that promise!"

7. In the back of her truck were Florence's possessions a small stove, a few pieces of clothing, some blankets, and a canvas tent.

8. Florence and her children took many low-wage jobs they struggled and rarely had enough to eat.

9. Florence and the other migrant workers stooped over in fields to pick the following items strawberries, peas, corn, and asparagus.

10. One day, Florence was in a tent by the highway waiting for her son to return a day that would make her famous.

FINAL REVIEW

Identify and correct any errors in numbers, semicolons, colons, hyphens, dashes, or parentheses. Write C next to correct sentences. (Note: You can see the photograph <u>Migrant Mother</u> on the first page of this chapter.)

ten-year-old
EXAMPLE: The ~~ten-year-old~~ truck broke down. _____

1. In 1936, Dorothea Lange had joined the Farm Security Administration FSA and was traveling around Nipomo Valley in California. _____

2. On a warm day in March, Lange was driving home when she saw a sign for a migrant camp. _____

3. Lange described what happened that day "I saw and

     approached the hungry and desperate mother, as if drawn by a magnet."

     _____

4. Sitting in her dust covered canvas tent, Florence Thompson

     was holding her baby, and her children were crowded around

     her. _____

5. Florence Thompson described their encounter "She just took my picture.

     She did not ask me my name." _____

6. The next day, Lange delivered the photos to a popular San Francisco news-

     paper. _____

7. The front page story described the migrant workers and their suffering.

     _____

8. Immediately, concerned citizens sent 184 tins of food, forty tents, and

     3 boxes of tools to the migrant camp. _____

9. Some doctors came to the camp to care for the sick, and some local

     employers offered jobs. _____

10. However, Florence Thompson was not there to see the outpouring

      of generosity because her brother in law had brought her to his

      home. _____

11. Her 12 year old son, who was staying in town with his uncle, had seen his

      mother's face on the front page of the newspaper. _____

12. He ran to his uncle in a panic "My mother has been shot!" _____

13. An ink stain appeared on the photo, the boy thought it was a bullet hole in his mother's head. _____

14. The photo—an iconic image of the Depression—has been reproduced in 1000s of books and magazines. _____

15. The compassionate photographs of Dorothea Lange 1895–1965 have influenced modern documentary photography. _____

The Writer's Room   **Topics for Writing**

Write about one of the following topics. Proofread for errors in numbers or punctuation.

1. Describe a personal photograph that you cherish. When was the photo taken? What is in the photo? Why is it so compelling?
2. Compare two art forms. For example, you could compare a photograph and a painting.

CHAPTER 27

✔ CHECKLIST: NUMBERS AND PUNCTUATION

When you edit your writing, ask yourself these questions.

Are there any numbers in my writing? Check that your numbers are consistently written, and verify that you have used words rather than numerals when necessary.

thousands
Lange took ~~1000s~~ of photographs.

Are my semicolons, colons, hyphens, dashes, and parentheses used in a correct and appropriate manner?

:   *well-used*
She brought the following supplies,̶ a camera, a ~~well used~~ chair, and a camera stand.

CHAPTER 27

To conquer Mount Everest, climbers meet the physical and mental challenges through practice and training. To write good essays, students perfect their skills by revising and editing.

Why Bother Editing?

After you finish writing the first draft of an essay, always make time to edit it. Editing for errors in grammar, punctuation, sentence structure, and capitalization can make the difference between a failing paper and a passing one or a good essay and a great one. Editing is not always easy; it takes time and attention to detail. But, it gets easier the more you do it. Also, the more you edit your essays (and your peers' essays, too), the better your writing will be, and the less time you will need to spend editing!

PRACTICE I   EDIT AN ESSAY

Correct fifteen errors in this student essay. An editing symbol appears above each error. To understand the meaning of each symbol, refer to the revising and editing symbols on the inside back cover of this book.

Climbing Everest

//

1   The Nepalese and Indians name it Sagarmatha, and people from Tibet call

cap

it Qomolangma. The rest of the world knows it as mount Everest. In 1852, a

geological survey of the Himalayan mountain range identified the highest peak as

"Peak XV." By 1865, the British named the peak "Everest" after a surveyor named

Sir George Everest. For mountain climbers, Everest became a challenge as soon

shift

as it is named the highest peak in the world.

sp

2   By 1921, Tibet opened it's borders to the outside and gave climbers easy access

to Everest. The first Europeans to attempt to climb Everest were George Mallory

ro

and Andrew Irvine in 1924, unfortunately, they both perished in the attempt.

Many other unsuccessful endeavours were made to reach the Everest summit.

Then in 1953, Edmund Hillary, a New Zealander, and Tenzing Norgay, a Nepalese

Sherpa, became the first climbers to reach the top of the world at 29,028 feet

sp

above sea level. Both men became world-famous heros. In addition, in 1978, two

Austrian climbers, Reinhold Messner and Peter Habeler, reached the Everest summit without the aid of supplemental oxygen. Two years later, Messner again attained the summit without extra oxygen. A solo climb.

3   Since 1921, around 2,200 mountaineers reached the summit; others have paid a great price. About 185 climbers have died in the attemt. There is a graveyard on the ascent to the summit. Mountaineers see the remains of corpses, tents, and bottles that were filled with oxygen. The dead remain on Everest. Even if climbers wanted to carry the corpses down, you could not because of the altitude.

4   The popularity of climbing the world's most highest peak has become so great that critics call Everest just another tourist trap. Many climbers set up businesses as guides. A Nepalese businessmen is planning to develop a cyber café at the base camp, and some snowboarders want to surf down from the summit. There are also a lot of trash on the summit trail. Nonetheless, Everest still catches the imagination of persons all over the world.

PRACTICE 2   EDIT AN ESSAY

Correct fifteen errors in this student essay. An editing symbol appears above each error. To understand the meaning of each symbol, refer to the revising and editing symbols on the inside back cover of this book.

The Man Who Discovered King Tutankhamen

1   Howard Carter's persistence helped him make a great contribution to the history of human civilization. Carter was born in 1874 near London, England. He became interested in Egyptology at the age of 17, when he was working in Egypt *[sp]* on an archaeological sight. His job was to trace drawings and inscriptions. Howard *[wc]* Carter discovered one of the greatest archaeological finds in history: the tomb of King Tutankhamen.

2   At the age of twenty-five Carter became the first inspector general for *[p]* monuments in Upper Egypt. He was responsible for supervising digs around the area of the Valley of the Kings. Which had a great number of tombs. He became *[frag]* very fascinating by the story of the young pharaoh, King Tutankhamen, and he *[ad]* was absolutly certain that the tomb was located in the general area of the *[sp]* Valley of the Kings.

3   For excavations, Carter received funding from Lord Carnarvon, a wealthy

patron of many digs. From 1914–1922, Carnarvon funded Carters [sp] search for the

legendary tomb of King Tut. By 1922, Lord Carnarvon became frustrated at the

lack of success and decided that he would only support the search for one more

year. Carter got real [ad] lucky when, one morning, one of his workers tripped over a

flat rock, [ro] when Carter went to see what it was, he realized that it was the top of a

staircase.

4   Carter was elated by the discovery [p] but his workers had a completely different

reaction. They were convinced that the tomb had a curse on it. Whoever broke

the door seal was doomed for death. Carter ignored the superstition. And went [frag]

inside the tomb. Inside he found everything intact and spent the next ten years

cataloguing his find. Some people continued to believe at [wc] the curse and blamed

it for the death of six workers. Eventually an urban legend formed called the

Mummy's Curse, which exagerated [sp] the power of the curse. Carter never believed

in no curse, [wc] and he dies [shift] of natural causes at the age of sixty-six.

PRACTICE 3   EDIT A FORMAL LETTER

Correct twelve errors in this formal business letter.

George Bates

5672 Manet street west

Lazerville, TX 76202

August 15, 2008

Customer Service

The Furniture store

1395 Division Street

Denton, TX 76205

Subject: Desk

Attention: Sales manager

I bought a desk from your store on august 13 2008, and the store delivered it thursday morning. After the delivery people had left, I discovered a large scratch on the surface of the desk. Its also lopsided. Since I have always found your products to be of excellent quality I would like to have a replacement desk delivered to my home and the damaged desk taken away. If you do not have replacement desk of the same model, then I would like to have a full reimbursement.

Thank you very much for your cooperation in this matter, I look forward to receiving my new desk.

Yours sincerly,

George Bates

George Bates

PRACTICE 4   EDIT AN ESSAY

Correct twenty errors in the following essay.

Discovering Venice

1   My brother and me are spending this summer in one of the most beautiful city in the world. Venice, Italy. It is unique because it is composed of a number of small islands in the Adriatic sea. It has over one hundred canals and over four hundred bridges. One of Italy's must-see places, Venice has an intriguing history.

2   Venice was founded in the fifth century by Romans escaping the ferocious Gothic tribes. According to legend. In the tenth century, Venice became a city of wealthy merchants who profited from the Crusades. By the twelfth century, after its successful war against Genoa, Venice had become a powerful city-state, trading with the Byzantines, the Arabs, and many others.

3   One of it's most famous citizens was the explorer Marco Polo (1254–1324), a businessman who was one of the first europeans to reach China. Him and his father spent about twenty-four years in China and was reputedly friends and confidants of Kublai Khan, the emperor of China. Polo may have brought back noodles from China. Which have become the basis for italian pasta.

4   When the Polos returned from China, they recounted the adventures they had had. The citizens of Venice did not believe them. Even today, scholars differ about weather Marco Polo actually reached China. Some say it was highly unlikly because he did not mention things such as chopsticks tea, or Chinese script. Others think that Polo reached China because he talked about paper money and the Chinese postal system.

5   Venice been written about in many works of fiction. For example, Shakespeare's *Merchant of Venice* is set in this city. Shakespeare also set the first part of his tragedy *Othello* in Venice. In fact, the first scenes of the Shakespearean tragedy takes place in the Duke's palace. Another famous book, Thomas Mann's Death in Venice, takes place on a Venetian island that is popular among tourists.

6   My brother has traveled more than me, and he says that of all the cities he's seen, Venice is his absolute favorite. If I would have known how fascinating the city is, I would have visited it a long time ago.

PRACTICE 5   EDIT A WORKPLACE MEMO

Correct ten errors in the following excerpt from a memo.

To: Career development faculty members

From: Maddison Healey

Re: Internships

I'm gonna take this opportunity to remind you that their are financial resources to hiring two new interns for the Career development Program. If anyone wishes to participate in this collaboration, please let Danielle or I know. The current deadline for applying to the internship program is the beginning of april. The internship program, provides valuable mentoring to college students. Treating an intern with respect, it is very important. If you hire an intern, you are responsible for training them. Also, you must provide constructive feedback to the intern and to the college administrator. For those who are interested, please let me know as quick as possible.

PRACTICE 6   EDIT A SHORT ARTICLE

Correct fifteen errors in the next selection.

Forget What Your Fifth Grade Teacher Taught You

1   The solar system no longer has nine planets, on August 24, 2006, the International Astronomical union, which has a voting membership of about 2,500 scientists, met in Prague. It decided to demote Pluto from a planet to a dwarf planet. The astronomers said that Pluto does not exhibit the same characteristics as the other major planets. According to scientists, a planet must orbit the sun, it must be having a spherical shape, and it must have a clear orbit. Unfortunatly, Pluto's orbit overlaps Neptune's orbit, so it does not meet the third criterion for a planet.

2   At the begining of the twentieth century, much astronomers suspected the possibility of another planet in the solar system. In 1930, while working for the Lowell Conservatory in Flagstaff, Arizona, astronomer Clyde Tombaugh took photographs of a sphere that was composed mainly of ices and rocks. It also had a satellite, Charon, orbiting it. Evenutaly, this sphere was named the nineth planet in the solar system.

3   Scientists were very exciting about the discovery. People from all over the world suggested names for the new planet. The scientists from the observatory received so many suggestions that they had difficulty choosing one. An eleven-years-old girl from Oxford, England, suggested the name Pluto. Venetia Burney was interested in Greek and Roman mythology, and Pluto is the Roman name

for Hades, the Greek God of the Dead. She was giving her suggestion to her grandfather, who then wired it to the Lowell Observatory.

4   The scientific community and the public have had a mixed reaction to the declassification of Pluto. As a planet. Some refuse to accept it. But I wonder why are they resistant. Perhaps teachers don't wanna change astronomy textbooks. Maybe humans feel particularly wary when the scientific community "revises" what it once asked them to accept as fact.

The Basic Parts of a Sentence

Parts of Speech	Definition	Some Examples
Noun	Names a person, place, or thing.	singular: woman, horse, person plural: women, horses, people
Verb	Expresses an action or state of being.	action: look, make, touch, smile linking: is, was, are, become
Adjective	Adds information about the noun.	small, pretty, red, soft
Adverb	Adds information about the verb, adjective, or other adverb; expresses time, place, and frequency.	quickly, sweetly, sometimes, far, usually, never
Pronoun	Replaces one or more nouns.	he, she, it, us, ours, themselves
Preposition	Shows a relationship between words (source, direction, location, etc.).	at, to, for, from, behind, above
Determiner	Identifies or determines if a noun is specific or general.	a, an, the, this, that, these, those, any, all, each, every, many, some
Conjunction	Coordinating conjunction: Connects two ideas of equal importance. Subordinating conjunction: Connects two ideas when one idea is subordinate (or inferior) to the other idea.	but, or, yet, so, for, and, nor although, because, even though, unless, until, when
Conjunctive adverb	Shows a relationship between two ideas. It may appear at the beginning of a sentence, or it may join two sentences.	also, consequently, finally, however, furthermore, moreover, therefore, thus
Interjection	Is added to a sentence to convey emotion.	hey, yikes, ouch, wow

Appendix 2
Irregular Verbs

Irregular Verb List

Base Form	Simple Past	Past Participle	Base Form	Simple Past	Past Participle
arise	arose	arisen	eat	ate	eaten
be	was, were	been	fall	fell	fallen
bear	bore	borne / born	feed	fed	fed
beat	beat	beat / beaten	feel	felt	felt
become	became	become	fight	fought	fought
begin	began	begun	find	found	found
bend	bent	bent	flee	fled	fled
bet	bet	bet	fly	flew	flown
bind	bound	bound	forbid	forbade	forbidden
bite	bit	bitten	forget	forgot	forgotten
bleed	bled	bled	forgive	forgave	forgiven
blow	blew	blown	forsake	forsook	forsaken
break	broke	broken	freeze	froze	frozen
breed	bred	bred	get	got	got, gotten
bring	brought	brought	give	gave	given
build	built	built	go	went	gone
burst	burst	burst	grind	ground	ground
buy	bought	bought	grow	grew	grown
catch	caught	caught	hang	hung	hung
choose	chose	chosen	have	had	had
cling	clung	clung	hear	heard	heard
come	came	come	hide	hid	hidden
cost	cost	cost	hit	hit	hit
creep	crept	crept	hold	held	held
cut	cut	cut	hurt	hurt	hurt
deal	dealt	dealt	keep	kept	kept
dig	dug	dug	kneel	knelt	knelt
do	did	done	know	knew	known
draw	drew	drawn	lay	laid	laid
drink	drank	drunk	lead	led	led
drive	drove	driven	leave	left	left

Base Form	Simple Past	Past Participle	Base Form	Simple Past	Past Participle
lend	lent	lent	slit	slit	slit
let	let	let	speak	spoke	spoken
lie[1]	lay	lain	speed	sped	sped
light	lit	lit	spend	spent	spent
lose	lost	lost	spin	spun	spun
make	made	made	split	split	split
mean	meant	meant	spread	spread	spread
meet	met	met	spring	sprang	sprung
mistake	mistook	mistaken	stand	stood	stood
pay	paid	paid	steal	stole	stolen
put	put	put	stick	stuck	stuck
prove	proved	proved / proven	sting	stung	stung
quit	quit	quit	stink	stank	stunk
read	read	read	strike	struck	struck
rid	rid	rid	swear	swore	sworn
ride	rode	ridden	sweep	swept	swept
ring	rang	rung	swell	swelled	swollen
rise	rose	risen	swim	swam	swum
run	ran	run	swing	swung	swung
say	said	said	take	took	taken
see	saw	seen	teach	taught	taught
sell	sold	sold	tear	tore	torn
send	sent	sent	tell	told	told
set	set	set	think	thought	thought
shake	shook	shaken	throw	threw	thrown
shine	shone	shone	thrust	thrust	thrust
shoot	shot	shot	understand	understood	understood
show	showed	shown	upset	upset	upset
shrink	shrank	shrunk	wake	woke	woken
shut	shut	shut	wear	wore	worn
sing	sang	sung	weep	wept	wept
sink	sank	sunk	win	won	won
sit	sat	sat	wind	wound	wound
sleep	slept	slept	withdraw	withdrew	withdrawn
slide	slid	slid	write	wrote	written

[1]*Lie* can mean "to rest in a flat position." When *lie* means "tell a false statement," then it is a regular verb: *lie, lied, lied.*

Appendix 3
Verb Tenses

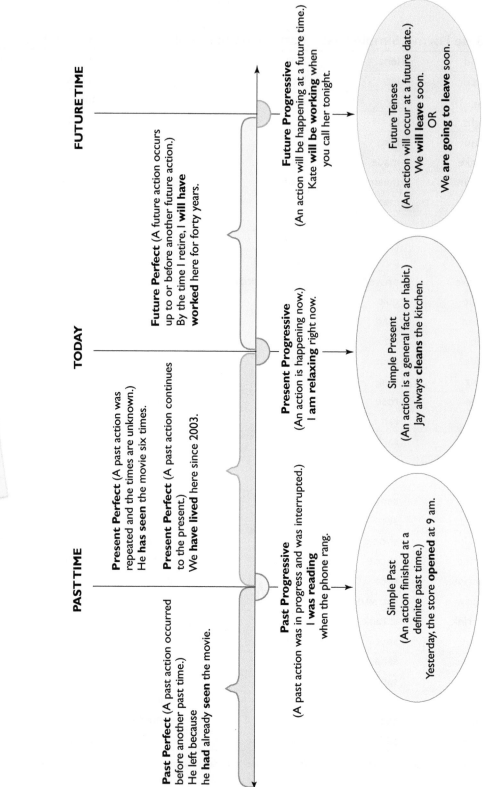

PAST TIME

TODAY

FUTURE TIME

Present Perfect (A past action was repeated and the times are unknown.)
He **has seen** the movie six times.

Present Perfect (A past action continues to the present.)
We **have lived** here since 2003.

Future Perfect (A future action occurs up to or before another future action.)
By the time I retire, I **will have worked** here for forty years.

Past Perfect (A past action occurred before another past time.)
He left because he **had** already **seen** the movie.

Past Progressive
(A past action was in progress and was interrupted.)
I **was reading** when the phone rang.

Present Progressive
(An action is happening now.)
I **am relaxing** right now.

Future Progressive
(An action will be happening at a future time.)
Kate **will be working** when you call her tonight.

Simple Past
(An action finished at a definite past time.)
Yesterday, the store **opened** at 9 am.

Simple Present
(An action is a general fact or habit.)
Jay always **cleans** the kitchen.

Future Tenses
(An action will occur at a future date.)
We **will leave** soon.
OR
We **are going to leave** soon.

Making Compound Sentences

A.

Complete idea

, coordinator
, for
, and
, nor
, but
, or
, yet
, so

complete idea.

B.

Complete idea

;

complete idea.

C.

Complete idea

; transitional expression,
; however,
; in fact,
; moreover,
; therefore,
; furthermore,

complete idea.

Making Complex Sentences

D.

Complete idea

subordinator
although
because
before
even though
unless
when

incomplete idea.

E.

Subordinator
Although
Because
Before
Even though
Unless
When

incomplete idea

,

complete idea.

In the first few pages of your writing portfolio or copybook, try keeping three "logs" to help you avoid repeating errors and improve your writing.

Spelling Log

The goal of keeping a spelling log is to stop repeating errors. Every time you misspell a word, record both the mistake and the correction in your spelling log. Then, before you hand in a writing assignment, consult the list of misspelled words.

EXAMPLE:

Incorrect	*Correct*
finaly	*finally*
responsable	*responsible*

Grammar Log

The goal of keeping a grammar log is to stop repeating errors in sentence structure, mechanics, and punctuation. Each time a writing assignment is returned to you, identify one or two repeated errors and add them to your grammar log. Next, consult the grammar log before you hand in new writing assignments in order to avoid making the same errors. For each type of grammar error, you could do the following:

1. Identify the assignment and write down the type of error.
2. In your own words, write a rule about the error.
3. Include an example from your writing assignment.

EXAMPLE: <u>*Cause and Effect Essay*</u> *(Mar. 10)*   *Fragment*

Sentences must have a subject and verb and express a complete thought.

> *Also, an overbearing parent.~~That~~ can cause a child to become controlling.*

Vocabulary Log

The vocabulary log can provide you with interesting new terms to incorporate in your writing. As you use this book, you will learn new vocabulary. Keep a record of the most interesting and useful words and expressions. Write a synonym or definition next to each new word.

EXAMPLE: <u>*ubiquitous*</u> *means widespread*

Spelling Log

Grammar Log

Vocabulary Log

Credits

TEXT:

Page 24: *Meatless Days*, Sara Suleri, University of Chicago Press. Copyright © 1989 by The University of Chicago Press. Reprinted with permission; **pp. 24–25:** Reprinted by permission of the European Food Information Council; **p. 25:** *Sociology*, 11e, John J. Macionis, Prentice Hall © 2007, p. 95; **p. 65:** From *Newsweek*, January 30, 2006 © 2006 Newsweek, Inc. All rights reserved. Used by permission and protected by the copyright Laws of the United States. The printing, copying, redistribution or retransmission of the material without express written permission is prohibited. The credit shall accompany the first or last page of the article and if the article and if the article is reprinted in digital format on a website. User shall provide a link to (www.newsweek.com); **pp. 66–67:** *The New World of International Relations*, 6e, Michael G. Roskin and Nicholas O. Berry, Pearson Education © 2005; **p. 67:** *The Twenty-First-Century Campus: Where Are The Men?*, John J. Macionis, *Sociology*, Pearson Education; **p. 77:** "Phishing," Mike Musgrove, *The Washington Post*, Oct. 22, 2005; **p. 77:** Reprinted with permission of Dorothy Nixon; **p. 187:** http://www.rbgkew.org.uk/sihort/tropamerica/peru/index.htm, Royal Botanic Kew; **p. 342:** *Art from Found Materials*, Mary Lou Stribling, p. 6; **p. 343:** *The Obstacle Race*, Germaine Greer, 2001, p. 132; **p. 344:** *Understanding Music*, Jeremy Yudkin, 2002, Pearson, p. 446; **p. 344:** *Psychology*, David G. Martin, p. 567; **p. 352:** 2007 by Mary Bellis http://inventors.about.com/library/inventors/blphotographytwo.htm). Used with permission of About, Inc., which can be found online at www.about.com. All rights reserved; **pp. 372–374:** "CSI Effect Has Juries Wanting More Evidence", Richard Will-

ing, *USA Today*, August 5, 2004. Reprinted with permission of the Copyright Clearance Center; **pp. 375–579:** "Types of Rioters," David A. Locher, *Collective Behaviors*, pp. 121–128; **pp. 380–383:** *Essence* © 1997; **pp. 385–390:** From *Me Talk Pretty One Day* by David Sedaris. Copyright © 2000 by David Sedaris. By permssion of Little Brown & Company; **pp. 392–393:** Reprinted with permission of Avi Frideman; **pp. 396–398:** Reprinted with permission of Eugene Henry; **pp. 399–401:** © 2004, The Washington Post, reprinted with permission; **pp. 403–404:** "Google's China Web," Frida Ghitis, *Boston Globe*, January 26, 2006. Reprinted with permission of the Copyright Clearance Center; **pp. 407–409:** Reprinted by permission of Pamela D. Jacobsen; **pp. 410–412:** Copyright © 2007 Laurence Gonzales; **pp. 414–416:** From *Into Thin Air* by Jon Krakauer, copyright © 1997 by Jon Kraukauer. Used by permission of Villard Books, a divison of Random House, Inc.; **pp. 417–418:** Reprinted with permission of Rahul Goswami; **pp. 421–428:** Reprinted with the permission of The Massachusetts Society for the Prevention of Cruelty to Animals. www.mspca.org; **pp. 424–426:** Reprinted with permission of The National Geographic Society; **pp. 429–431:** Reprinted with permission of Ariel Levy; **pp. 432–433:** Reprinted with permission of the Scripps Howard News Service; **pp. 435–436:** "The Untranslatable Word 'Macho'", Rose Del Castillo Guibaullt, *San Francisco Chronicle*, 2005, Reprinted by permission of the Copyright Clearance Center; **pp. 438–440:** Reprinted with permission of Robyn Sarah.

PHOTOS:

p. 32: Courtesy of www.istock.photo.com; p. 51: Courtesy of www.istockphoto.com; p. 63: Courtesy of www.istockphoto.com; p. 82: Courtesy of www.istockphoto.com; p. 83: Courtesy of www.istockphoto.com; p. 84: Courtesy of www.istockphoto.com; p. 86, top: Courtesy of www.istockphoto.com; p. 86, mid: Pixtal/Superstock Royalty Free; p. 89: Courtesy of www.istockphoto.com; p. 133: Photos.com; p. 140: Courtesy of www.istockphoto.com; p. 141: Comestock/Superstock Royalty Free; p. 152: Courtesy of www.istockphoto.com; p. 153: Photos.com; p. 156: Underwood Photo Archives/SuperStock, Inc.; p. 162: Courtesy of www.istockphoto.com; p. 163: Courtesy of www.istockphoto.com; p. 164: Photos.com; p. 168: Courtesy of www.istockphoto.com; p. 173: Steve Vidler/SuperStock, Inc.; p. 174: Patricia Schwimmer (Canadian, b. 1953) "My San Francisco", 1994, Tempera, Private Collection. © Patricia Schwimmer/SuperStock; p. 176: Courtesy of www.istockphoto.com; p. 181: Richard Cummins/SuperStock, Inc.; p. 184: Michele Burgess/SuperStock, Inc.; p. 185: Michele Burgess/SuperStock, Inc.; p. 186: Richard Cummins/SuperStock, Inc.; p. 187: Courtesy of www.istockphoto.com; p. 189: Yoshio Tomii/SuperStock, Inc.; p. 192: Hidekazu Nishibata/SuperStock, Inc.; p. 195: Photos.com; p. 203: Courtesy of www.istockphoto.com; p. 205: Courtesy of www.istockphoto.com; p. 215: Mario Carreno (b. 1913/Cuban) *La Siesta* 1946. Oil on canvas.

© Christie's Images/SuperStock; p. 217: Photos.com; p. 218: Photos.com; p. 236: Ritu Manoj Jethani/Shutterstock; p. 238: Courtesy of www.istockphoto.com; p. 240: Robert Llewellyn/SuperStock, Inc.; p. 249: SuperStock, Inc.; p. 251: Courtesy of www.istockphoto.com; p. 252: Courtesy of www.istockphoto.com; p. 260: Photos.com; p. 261: Superstock Royalty Free; p. 263: Photos.com; p. 271: Donna and Steve O'Meara/Superstock Royalty Free; p. 276: Katsushika Hokusai (1760–1849, Japanese) "The Wave", 19th Century, Woodcut print. © SuperStock, Inc.; p. 279: Courtesy of www.istockphoto.com; p. 283: Pixtal/Superstock Royalty Free; p. 287: Tony Linck/SuperStock, Inc.; p. 291: Courtesy of www.istockphoto.com; p. 296: Shutterstock; p. 300: Courtesy of www.istockphoto.com; p. 302: Courtesy of www.istockphoto.com; p. 306: SuperStock, Inc.; p. 312: Charles Marden Fitch/SuperStock, Inc.; p. 316: Courtesy of www.istockphoto.com; p. 326: Photos.com; p. 329: The Bridgeman Art Library International; p. 336: Donald Martin, after Van der Weyden (20th Century American), "Portrait", Airbursh on wood. © Donald C. Martin/SuperStock; p. 337: Photos.com; p. 338: Courtesy of www.istockphoto.com; p. 340: © 2007 Artists Rights Society (ARS), New York; p. 351: Photos.com; p. 352: Courtesy of the Library of Congress; p. 361: Photos.com; p. 384: Courtesy of www.istockphoto.com; p. 395: Courtesy of www.istockphoto.com; p. 395: Courtesy of www.istockphoto.com; p. 420: Courtesy of www.istockphoto .com; p. 428: Courtesy of www.istockphoto.com; p. 442: Courtesy of www.istockphoto.com.